David Laing, Andrew of Wyntoun

The Orygynale Cronykil of Scotland

Vol. 1

David Laing, Andrew of Wyntoun

The Orygynale Cronykil of Scotland
Vol. 1

ISBN/EAN: 9783337325688

Printed in Europe, USA, Canada, Australia, Japan

Cover: Foto ©ninafisch / pixelio.de

More available books at **www.hansebooks.com**

The Orygynale Cronykil of Scotland.

BY ANDROW OF WYNTOUN.

EDITED BY

DAVID LAING.

IN THREE VOLUMES.

VOL. I.

EDINBURGH
EDMONSTON AND DOUGLAS
1872.

TABLE OF CONTENTS.

	PAGE
INTRODUCTORY NOTICE,	ix
MACPHERSON'S PREFACE TO THE EDITION OF THE CRONYKIL, 1795,	xvii
FACSIMILE OF MSS.,	*to face* xl

THE ORYGYNALE CRONYKIL OF SCOTLAND :—

THE FYRST BUKE,	1
THE SECUND BUKE,	67
THE THYRDE BUKE,	129
THE FERD BUKE, .	171
THE FYFT BUKE,	269

INTRODUCTORY NOTICE.

IN the proposed series of the Early Historians of Scotland, the Metrical Chronicle by the Prior of St. Serf's Inch in Lochleven could not be overlooked. It belongs to the reign of King James the First, having been completed about the year 1426 ; but how long the author had been employed in compiling it can only be conjectured. We do not find the Prior's Chronicle mentioned by Walter Bowar, Abbot of Inchcolm, the continuator of Fordun in his *Scotichronicon*, yet it must, for at least a century, have been esteemed a work of historical importance, as may be inferred from the numerous transcripts of which we find traces, or which are still extant.

In modern times Wyntoun's Chronicle was first introduced to notice by Dr. William Nicolson, Bishop of Carlisle, in his *Scottish Historical Library*, 1702. It was also described by Dr. George Mackenzie in Volume First of his *Lives and Characters*, 1708. But Father Thomas Innes, in his *Critical Essay* in 1729, having carefully examined a number of MSS., was the first to point out some of the chief variations, and to express the opinion that the Royal MS. was "the most entire and most valuable of them all;" he further adds, "that it appears to be the last review and edition (if I may speak so) that Winton made of his Chronicle, containing several corrections, additions, and alterations made in it upon better information." A zealous antiquary of that time, Captain Robert Seton, in the meanwhile, had set himself most diligently to prepare the entire work for the press.

Public attention had already been awakened to our older historians and poets by such publications as the *Chronica de Mailros*, by Bishop Fell, in his collection *Rerum Anglicarum Scriptorum Veterum*, tom. i., 1684; of *Johannis de Fordun Scotorum Historia*, by Dr. Thomas Gale, 1691; and again in a separate and more perfect form by Thomas Hearne, 1722; Douglas's *Virgil's Æneis* by Thomas Ruddiman, 1710; and, I may add, of Knox's *Historie of the Reformatioun*, in a genuine form, by Matthew Crawford, 1732. The preface to Captain Seton's transcript of Wyntoun's Chronicle is dated at Edinburgh, December 21, 1724. Having copied the text of the Edinburgh (Denmylne) MS., he afterwards, by a careful and minute collation of one or two other MSS., added on the margins numerous various readings. But want of encouragement or some other cause prevented his scheme from being realized; and on his death, in 1731, his transcript was sold, when his library was dispersed by auction.[1] At a later period

[1] A short notice of Captain Seton will be added in Vol. III. to the description of his Manuscript.

INTRODUCTORY NOTICE. xi

this volume was acquired by Pinkerton the historian,[1] who announced in 1786 his intention of publishing the chief portion of the Chronicle: but some time was still to elapse before the work became accessible in a printed form.

At length, in the year 1795, THE ORYGYNALE CRONYKIL OF SCOTLAND, by Wyntoun, appeared in two large and handsome volumes, edited by Mr. DAVID MACPHERSON. It was fortunate that the work was undertaken by a person so thoroughly competent as an Editor. In preparing his edition for the press, Macpherson had chiefly recourse to Manuscripts preserved in the British Museum. The text of the Royal MS., which by general consent was reckoned as the earliest and most perfect copy of the work, he accordingly adopted, and adhered to it, on the whole, most faithfully, using only some small liberties by changing the *ff*'s and *ll*'s to a single *f* and *l*. It might perhaps have been well had he extended such emendations to other peculiarities of that MS., more especially by rejecting the use of the letters *w* and *ẅ*, also of *v*, for the usual forms of *u*, *v*, and *w*; as, according to his orthography, such words as *swn* (a son), *swnnys* (sons), *lywyng* (living), *ẅertu* (virtue), *wywe* (wife), *vaknyd* (wakened), and *vod* (wood), in their ordinary meaning, are not at once apparent. His volumes were welcomed at the time as a valuable accession to Scottish literature,

[1] Captain Seton's MS. now belongs to myself.

and the Editor was justly commended for the diligence and learning he had displayed in such a satisfactory manner.

The copies of these volumes in late years had become scarce and high priced, and although the earlier portions of the Chronicle (beginning with the Creation of the World), omitted by Macpherson, have no claims to historical importance, an edition of the entire work had long been an object of desire. There were also early manuscripts unknown to him which required examination and collation. To what extent the Author actually revised and enlarged his Chronicle will afterwards have to be considered. At present it may be noticed that the chief alterations, made by the Author, are contained in Book IV., Chap. viii. p. 212—

> In this Chapiter yhe sall here,
> Qwhen the Scottis beset be Peychtis were;

and Chap. xix. p. 237—

> Now quhen the Peychtis in Scotlande
> Come, and in it wes regnande.

Instead, however, of pointing out these alterations, as Macpherson has done, among the Various Readings in his last volume, I have given both texts on the same page, as the most distinct mode of exhibiting some important variations in regard to the history and succession of the Pictish rule in Scotland.

In undertaking this task, as I had long been satisfied by occasional examination and comparison with other early MSS., that the Royal MS. still retained its pre-eminence, it appeared to be the easiest and safest mode to follow Macpherson's text. Neither could I discover any good reason for attempting to supersede his Introduction, Notes, and Glossary, by altering the form for the sake of apparent novelty. I therefore prefer to let these volumes appear as a republication of Macpherson's edition, revised and enlarged, wherever it seemed to be required. To have done otherwise would have, I think, been an act of injustice to his memory.

Although thus professing to be a New Edition, it is by no means to be regarded as a mere verbal reprint. All the suppressed or omitted portions, forming nearly one-third of the entire work, are now published for the first time, from the Royal MS.; and the text throughout has been carefully revised, without adhering too slavishly, like Macpherson, to the peculiarities of the original transcriber in retaining unnecessary contractions, for instance "Ðe" "þe," or "þat" for *The, thé* (thee), or *that*. Such a mode of editing can serve no useful purpose, but is rather calculated to render the pages unreadable. I ought perhaps to express regret in not having also changed the letters *w, v, u,* to the usual form of *v, u,* and *w*. Obvious errors have been corrected, but no liberties taken in altering the text; and words supplied from other copies are enclosed with brackets. Had I been forming a new text, I might have preferred the orthography of some other MSS.; but there prevails at present a kind of pedantic conceit in a literal adherence to the peculiar orthography or ignorance of unknown transcribers.

In order that no unnecessary delay should occur in completing the successive volumes for Subscribers to this series of the Early Scottish Historians, some matters have for the present been reserved. The Third and concluding Volume of Wyntoun's Chronicle will therefore contain, along with the Ninth and last Book of the Chronicle, such additional notices of the Author as may be discovered, along with a detailed description of all the known MSS. of his work. The Various Readings furnished by a diligent collation, and Macpherson's Notes, and Glossary, will likewise be considerably enlarged.

As all this was a task of no ordinary labour, I could not personally have undertaken it within any limited period. It was fortunate therefore that the publishers were able to secure the services of Mr. ANDREW GILLMAN, of London, for the more tedious work of transcription and collation; and I think I cannot pay him a greater compliment than to say that his application and accuracy are not unworthy of David Macpherson himself.

DAVID LAING.

EDINBURGH, *November* 1872.

An exact facsimile of the Title-page of Macpherson's Edition is given on the page opposite.

DE

ORYGYNALE CRONYKIL

OF

SCOTLAND,

BE

ANDROW OF WYNTOWN,

PRIOWR OF SANCT SERFIS YNCHE IN LOCH LEVYN.

NOW FIRST PUBLISHED,
WITH
NOTES, A GLOSSARY, &c.
BY
DAVID MACPHERSON.

THE FIRST VOLUME.

LONDON:

PRINTED BY T. BENSLEY;

AND SOLD BY THOMAS EGERTON, WHITEHALL;
AND WILLIAM LAING, EDINBURGH.

M.DCC.XCV.

PREFACE

BY

DAVID MACPHERSON. 1795.

THE earliest historians of a country are undoubtedly the most valuable, if, upon a fair critical trial of their agreement with the writers of the neighbouring countries, but more especially with the sure testimony of public records and charters still remaining, they appear to have made a faithful use of the works of preceding writers and of other vouchers extant in their times, most of which being now lost, they, as the earliest faithful copiers of them, are entitled to our respect and gratitude for furnishing us with the only means of obtaining the knowledge of many of the transactions of past ages. Hence it evidently follows, that the truest and most essential service that can be done to the history of any nation, is to lay before the public genuine editions of its most antient and authentic historical monuments, and of the works of those who first attempted its general history.

Of the few general historians of Scotland, JOHN OF FORDUN has generally been esteemed the best, as well as the original one. He certainly deserves much praise for his industry;[1] and we must ever regret that he did not live to finish his work.

[1] Some notices, or conjectures, concerning his labours in acquiring materials for his work, are dispersed in the Preface to Hearne's edition of it.

ANDROW OF WYNTOWN, not inferior to Fordun in historic merit, has also an equal claim to the title of an *original historian of Scotland*; for, though he survived Fordun, it is certain that he never saw his work; and his Chronicle has the advantage not only of being completed to the period which he proposed, but even of being revised and greatly improved by himself in a second copy. It has also the further advantage, for such it surely ought to be esteemed, of being written in the language of the country

"Tyl ilkè mannys wndyrstandyng;"

whereas the information contained in all the other histories of Scotland preceding the middle of the seventeenth century, if we except the brief chronicle subjoined to some manuscripts of Wyntown, and the translations of Ballenden and Read, was effectually concealed from the unlearned part of mankind under the veil of a dead or a foreign language.[1]

In Wyntown's Chronicle the historian may find what for want of more antient records, which have long ago perished, we must now consider as the original accounts of many transactions, and also many events related from his own knowledge or the reports of eye-witnesses. His faithful adherence to his

[1] Boyse and Buchanan are the only historians of Scotland, if they may be so called, whose works have been translated; and they are the very two who ought to have been consigned to the deepest obscurity. Hence in a great measure proceed the corrupt ideas of Scottish history, which are so deeply rooted in the minds of many people. The evil is greatly increased by some teachers of Latin putting Buchanan's history into the hands of their pupils, because, forsooth, his Latin style is very fine, which is but a wretched excuse for perverting the youthful mind, though they could prove his latinity superior to Cicero's.

So firmly established was the custom of writing in Latin, that Sir David Lindsay, about a century after Wyntown, thought it necessary to apologise in the beginning of his *Monarchy* for writing in his native language by producing the examples of Moses, Aristotle, Plato, Virgil, Cicero, &c., who all wrote in their own languages.

authorities appears from comparing his accounts with unquestionable vouchers, such as the *Fœdera Angliæ*, and the existing remains of the *Register of the Priory of St. Andrews*, that venerable monument of antient Scottish history and antiquities, generally coeval with the facts recorded in it, whence he has given large extracts, almost literally translated. All these we have hitherto been obliged to take at second or third hand in copies by Bower and others, with such additions and embellishments as they were pleased to make to Wyntown's simple and genuine narrative.[1]

An ecclesiastical historian of Scotland can nowhere find so good an account of the Bishops of St. Andrews, with occasional notices concerning the other sees, as from Wyntown, who in describing the churches, their buildings, and paraphernalia, shows himself quite at home.

The compiler of a Scottish Peerage may obtain from Wyntown more true information concerning the antient noble families of Scotland than is to be found in any work extant, except the accurate and elaborate research made by the late Lord Hailes in the celebrated Sutherland case, wherein he has repeatedly had recourse to our author for proofs of the laws and customs of succession.

In this view the lawyer will also find the Chronicle of Wyntown an useful addition to his library, and may consult it with advantage when called upon to adjust a disputed inheritance in an antient family.

As a specimen of the language of Scotland, a faithful and correct edition of Wyntown must be an acquisition to the philologists of every country whose language is of Gothic origin, seeing that no manuscript of any Scottish work known

---

[1] Ruddiman, in his elaborate notes on Buchanan's history, has had frequent occasion to show that his author, when departing from Wyntown's authority, generally departed from the truth.

to exist comes into any degree of comparison in point of antiquity and purity with the royal manuscript of Wyntown, nor even with the Cotton one. In Wyntown's work we have near three hundred lines of Barber, the only Scottish writer prior to himself now extant, in a more genuine state than in any manuscript or edition of Barber's own work [*see Index, vo. Barber*]; and, what is infinitely more valuable, he has fortunately preserved to us a little elegiac song on the death of King Alexander III., which must be near ninety years older than Barber's work. This is alone sufficient with every reader of taste to stamp a very high value on Wyntown.

Valuable and curious as Wyntown's work thus appears in so many points of view, how can it be accounted for that he has been allowed to remain in manuscript for so many centuries, eclipsed and superseded by writers of far inferior merit, almost forgotten and even unknown to many, whose business it was to have consulted him?

For above two centuries after the art of printing was introduced in Scotland,[1] the Scottish press produced scarcely any historic works, indeed not one deserving the name of *history*. The fury of religious controversy and the rage of civil wars deprived the generality of the people of inclination as well as opportunity to cultivate letters or the sciences, so that during the long continuance of this intellectual darkness, while England was making great additions to the public stock of historic knowledge, the interests of Scottish literature, history, and science were abandoned to perish, or consigned to the care of strangers.[2] After the accession of King James VI. to the Crown

---

[1] From a patent of King James IV. it appears that a printing-press was first established at Edinburgh in 1507. [*Life of Thomas Ruddiman by Mr. Chalmers*, p. 80.]

[2] While scarcely any books but those of religious controversy were produced in Scotland, and the few Scottish historic or scientific works were

PREFACE. xxi

of England, the language in which Wyntown wrote was almost completely proscribed by Scottish writers, and carefully avoided by every person who wished to be thought above the vulgar. In such circumstances a work, of which the language was even then partly obsolete in Scotland, which cherished no religious prejudices, nor sacrificed truth on the altars of national vanity, was sure to be neglected; and during this time it is very probable that many valuable manuscripts of it have perished.

But in the present age, when the study of history is in general estimation, and when the history of Scotland in particular begins by the abilities and exertions of some of her literary sons to be cleared of the thick mist of fable under which Hector Boyse had buried it, to be studied in a rational manner, and to engage the attention of the learned in general; when even the language of Scotland attracts the attention of philologists in various countries as illustrative of their own, it is truly surprising that one of the earliest and most authentic histories, and the very earliest and purest specimen of the language of that country, has not ere now been drawn forth

published at Paris, Amsterdam, &c., where the uncorrected errors of printers and engravers were superadded to the errors of the authors ; while most of the learned natives of Scotland chose to reside abroad, as if their own country were the only one which ought not to be enlightened by their genius and learning, several learned men in England were with the most laudable industry and patriotism employing their time and their talents in publishing those historic treasures which had for ages lain dormant in churches and libraries. Nor was their attention entirely confined to English history : to these friends of the republic of letters Scotland stands indebted for the only editions of the *Chronicles of Melros* and *of Holyroodhouse*, for the first edition of the *Chronicle of Mann*, and for the first and second editions of *Fordun*. These, being all historical works and written in Latin, may be considered as the common concern of the literary world ; but even *Douglas's Virgil* and *King James's Christ-Kirk on the green*, though written in the dialect of Scotland and not historical, were published in England long before a Scottish edition of either of them was thought of.

from the obscurity or invisibility which has so long concealed it even from the researches of men of literature.

Seeing the labour of publishing this most valuable antient Scottish historian declined by all others, I thought I could not employ my leisure more usefully to my country, or more agreeably to myself, than by laying before the public a genuine edition of Wyntown. As however unequal I may be to the task in respect of talents and learning, an edition by me, with the care and attention which I intended to bestow upon it, must surely be much better than no edition at all.

With this intention I applied to the Trustees of the British Museum for permission to transcribe the royal manuscript of Wyntown, which was immediately granted with a politeness and attention to the interests of literature worthy of the guardians of the greatest literary treasure in Britain.

Wyntown, like most other historians of his own and the preceding ages, begins his work at the creation; and he gives a general history of the world in the first five books, with very little of Scottish or British history till the commencement of the sixth; after which he gradually drops foreign affairs, and comes home to the proper business of his undertaking. Exactly the same was the plan of Fordun, whose numerous pages, as further stuffed with superfluous matter by his continuator, I have often turned over with great labour and disgust in search of some minute particle of early Scottish history, which was lost in the mass of trifling and extraneous matter. On these occasions I could not help wishing that the editor had taken the trouble of selecting the few sentences, which are useful, and suppressing the vast quantity of lumber, which loads the work and distresses the reader.

In order to save the readers of Wyntown the labour of wandering through a wilderness of Asiatic, Greek and Roman history, in search of minute notices concerning Scotland or

Britain, I have carefully selected all that in any respect concerns the British islands, whether true or fabulous, and have suppressed all the foreign matter in the first five books,[1] only preserving the metrical contents of the chapters, whereby the reader will know the nature of what is withheld, and will, I trust, be pleased to find that the book is not swelled by printing what would never be read. This separation of the useful from the useless has had the approbation of some of the best judges of Scottish history.

From the beginning of the sixth book the work is published entire *verbatim et literatim* to the conclusion.

Of the several manuscripts of Wyntown, it is sufficiently known from Innes, who had examined many, [*see his excellent Critical Essay*, pp. 624, 683, 823,] that the one, which belongs to the Royal library now in the Museum, is greatly superior to all others. It not only has the author's improvements, but is also much purer in the language than any other copy that I have been able to get any knowledge of: it is moreover the only one which is not mutilated by accident or curtailed by design; and the few omissions in it are fully supplied from another manuscript belonging to the Cotton library.

From this most valuable manuscript I have made my transcript, which, from careful and repeated collation, I may venture to say, is exact, notwithstanding the inconveniencies inseparable from writing it at a considerable distance from my own house, and at limited hours. But when I say that my transcript is exactly copied from the Royal manuscript, I do not wish to be understood, as if I had rigidly adhered to errors, which are evidently slips of the pen. While transcribing, as well as

---

[1] In this I have the examples of the great editors Gale and Hearne, the former of whom has suppressed the extraneous part of Higden's Polychronicon, and the latter has passed over the fabulous part of the British history in Robert of Brunne's work.

while collating, I had constantly the Cotton and Harleian manuscripts before me, and carefully compared the whole; and, as it is my earnest desire that the edition may be more perfect than any one manuscript taken singly, I have corrected all obvious errors from these two, but chiefly from the Cotton, and, where neither of them were satisfactory, by extracts from the manuscripts in the Advocates' Library at Edinburgh. There are moreover a few instances of obvious defects, which I have been obliged to supply, and such insertions, however minute, are constantly distinguished by being inclosed in crochets. This liberty, however, I have very seldom taken, as I have, during the progress of this work, as well as on other occasions, frequently felt the bad consequences of the very common liberty taken by transcribers and editors in new-modelling the works of their authors. I have accordingly let many a line go to the press with defective or redundant measure, which a very slight alteration might have rectified, had I not determined to abstain from all corrections not absolutely necessary for restoring the sense of my author where evidently vitiated by transcribers, and to let him appear with his own imperfections on his head, rather than to give the reader the smallest reason to doubt, that what he sees before him is the genuine work of Wyntown.[1]

Wyntown has divided his work into nine books of very

[1] I have in several instances corrected the Elegiac Chronicle, which Wyntown has incorporated with his work from a collation of other manuscripts wherein it is found. I thought it the more incumbent on me to do this, as the reading is monstrously corrupted by the transcriber, who, if not entirely ignorant of the Latin language, was at least utterly unacquainted with Latin prosody. Being moreover not the work of my author, I thought myself more at liberty in it; and I trust that I have only restored his reading, and in so doing given a more correct copy of the whole of the original part of this antient elegiac poem than has ever yet been published. In doing this I am supported by the example of that correct editor Ruddiman, who restored the true readings of antient authors, which Buchanan had transcribed in the third book of his history from erroneous editions.

unequal length, the eighth alone containing more pages of the manuscript than the first four; and these books are divided into chapters, which being also very unequal, the long ones are subdivided into sections or portions, which the rubricators and transcribers, because they begin with illuminated letters, have generally converted to chapters. It seemed to me the best rule to call only those chapters, which I found ushered in by metrical titles,[1] which often run in such words as these—

"This Chapiter sall yhow tell," &c.

Now we cannot pretend to make four or five chapters out of what the author expressly calls only one. I have, however, as nearly as possible, preserved the distinction by beginning every section with an open capital answering to the illuminated letter in the Royal manuscript, and setting a space between it and the preceding one, as was usually done in the antient magnificent manuscripts.

The faults, which may be found in the punctuation, are wholly my own, as the manuscript is entirely destitute of any such distinctions. The irregular grammar (as it appears to us) and frequent inverted order, common in antient composition, have in some instances left me uncertain, if I have divided the sentences according to the author's meaning; but I hope that there are not many instances of gross blunders.

The author's text is followed by the *Various Readings*, to which is prefixed a short notice explaining the method used in quoting them.

The *Notes* are placed together at the end of the work in

[1] I was obliged to make an exception to this rule, and it is the only one, in the very first chapter of the work, which the rubricator had neglected. As to the propriety or impropriety of giving the name of chapters to divisions sometimes longer than what are called books in other works, I leave it to the critics.

order to avoid breaking the uniformity of the page.[1] They are chiefly employed in endeavouring to illustrate such portions of Scottish history as seem to be casually involved in obscurity, or intentionally perverted by fiction: not that I pretend to discover the truth on all occasions: we can often perceive the existence of error without being able absolutely to disprove it; and even when we think our proofs are undeniable, we are sometimes far from the truth. So fully convinced am I of this, that, instead of presuming dictatorially to assert facts, I only lay before the reader for his consideration such evidence as has occurred to me in the course of my reading;[2] and I may justly say with a late learned and worthy labourer in the thorny field of Scottish antiquities, " *Utinam tam facile vera invenire possem, quam falsa convincere.*"[3]

Some may perhaps think me too rigorous in giving no quarter to certain stories, which from their early youth they have taken pleasure in believing. If these stories are true, their truth will be the more firmly established by investigation; but if they are false, history ought by all means to be cleared of them, more particularly of those which appear to

---

[1] Except a few very short ones in the five first books, which it was necessary to have immediately under the eye for supplying the want of connection occasioned by the suppression of the context.

[2] In adducing authorities I have been careful to quote the earliest authors without encumbering the pages with the names of their followers: only when quoting *Fordun* I have generally added the parallel place in *Goodal's* edition of the *Scotichronicon*, because *Hearne's* edition of Fordun's own work is a scarce book.

[3] Lord Hailes, in p. 1 of his *Remarks on the history of Scotland*, published in 1773, to which this wish of Cicero is prefixed as a motto, could " hardly venture to express [his] doubts as to the historical evidence" of the antient alliance with France. But during the few years which have elapsed since he published that work, the mental illumination of Scotland has been great and rapid; and the study of history in particular has made such advances, that no one need now fear to give offence by clearing away the rubbish of fable, and restoring the truth of history as far as is practicable. " *Ne quid falsi dicere audeat, ne quid veri non audeat historicus.*"

have originated in malitious or interested calumny, such as the wickedness and tyranny of King Macbeth, the treachery of Menteth and Cumin, with others of the like stamp, my abhorrence of which may perhaps be in some degree heightened by the recollection of my own sufferings from malitious and interested falsehoods. But surely even scepticism, if such a name is to be given to a withholding of our assent where we see no grounds of belief, or to the detection of error, is preferable to a supine, lazy, and unmanly acquiescence in the belief of unfounded fiction, as a total privation of history is unquestionably preferable to the masses of fable and gross absurdity formerly called histories of Britain, Scotland, and Ireland, preceding the Christian æra. The deposition of the usurper *Falsehood*, who has for near three centuries reigned triumphant in Scottish history, at least makes room for the restoration of the lawful sovereign *Truth;* and even the starting of doubts may stimulate some who have better opportunities to researches, which may at length bring about that desirable event. If my labours shall have such an effect I shall think them well bestowed, and shall alwise esteem myself happy if I may in some small degree be instrumental in reforming Scotland from Hector Boyse:[1] "*Quid enim fortius desiderat anima quam veritatem?*"[2]

The short *Table of holidays*, which follows the notes, will

---

[1] See *Annals*, vol. ii. p. 224, *Note*. Justice to departed merit demands, that the reformation of Scotland from Hector Boyse, and the improvement of historic knowledge, which has consequently taken place in it, should in a great measure be ascribed to the valuable Annals and other works of LORD HAILES. I the more freely contribute my mite of the praise due to his historic merit, as even malice cannot pretend that it proceeds from any expectation of a return. Had he been alive, I should scarcely have presumed to say even thus much.

[2] Several of the notes are abridgments of essays written long ago, which have been occasionally revised and corrected during the course of many years.

sometimes save the reader the trouble of searching in calendars for dates long ago disused.

In the *Index* will be found catalogues of the Kings, Bishops, noble families, &c., every succeeding King, Bishop, or Chief of a family being distinguished by Italics; and where the succession of Kings, Earls, &c., is continuous or nearly so, the connection of each one with his predecessor, whose name is marked by the initial letter, is also ascertained, either from my author, or from the best authorities attainable. The actions of each person are arranged in order of time, and under one head, whatever variety of titles he may have had, so as to give a connected biographical sketch of his life. Thus the reader may find at one glance the whole information given by Wyntown concerning families or individuals, with the addition of their genealogical connection. Kings, Earls, &c., are also found under their own proper names in the alphabetical order; but not Bishops, they being never mentioned as concerned in any transactions foreign to their episcopal character. I have been as careful as possible not to omit any Scottish or English names.

The *Glossary*, which is usually subjoined to the author's work, is here prefixed to it, chiefly for the uniformity of the volumes, as the second would otherways be so much larger than the first, owing to the great quantity of the eighth book and the necessary appendages already mentioned.

In a Glossary it is not satisfactory to a reader who desires to judge for himself and scorns to be put in leading-strings (and to such only do I wish to devote my labours) to see one word set after another as its explanation, for the justness of which he is obliged to rely on the infallibility of the glossarist, who, perhaps without any investigation of the nature and structure of the word or of its connection with the context in a sufficient number of examples, boldly puts down whatever will make grammatical sense in the passage before him, though

PREFACE.   xxix

it may be very far from the meaning of his author. But when the reader sees before him the same word with little or no variation bearing the same meaning in the cognate languages, no doubt can remain of the justness of the interpretation.

In order to afford this satisfaction to the reader, I have selected such of the *synonyma* in the cognate or sororian languages, as are most clearly illustrative of the words to be explained. This, to be sure, is a very laborious task which I have imposed upon myself; but had I preferred sloth to exertion, and faith in others to my own endeavours to get as near to the fountain-head of knowledge as possible, I ought to have let alone the work altogether.

In selecting the kindred words I have rejected all far-fetched affinities, though many of them are ingeniously supported, and some of them may be true. I do not in any instance pretend to determine which are primitive words, and which derivative, or that any of them are *primitives*. Neither do I take any concern in the deduction of their genealogy from Noah's ark or the plains of Shinar.[1] All that I pretend to

[1] I have sometimes adduced Greek, and more frequently Latin words, as cognates; but it does not follow that the Scottish words are derived from them any more than they from the Scottish. There is reason to hope that a more rational system of philology will soon explode the schoolboy idea, which has for ages perverted the judgment of even learned men, and set them upon deriving all the languages of Europe from the Greek and Latin, but chiefly from the Greek. They surely imagined either that the Greeks peopled all Europe, or that all the nations of Europe were destitute of names for the most common things till they went to school in Greece. There is no reason to believe that a single word of the languages spoken by any of the antient nations in Britain could possibly be derived to them from the Greeks, who do not appear to have ever had any intercourse with this island. When the Christian religion was introduced, some Greek words peculiar to it and to the sciences came along with it, and these, to the best of my recollection, are the only Greek words to be found in Wyntown. Of later date are most of the terms of art, which have in like manner been received with the arts, or, from a partiality for the Greek language, been fabricated at home, the more expressive native words being discarded to make way for them: hence most

know is, that the words which I have brought together appear evidently, from their strong family likeness, to be of the same origin, or rather in most cases the very same words, when each is divested of its peculiar servile termination, which is therefore generally separated from the body of the word by a hyphen. Thus my Glossary, though containing the materials of a huge *Etymologicon*, is entirely free of etymology.

As a partial Dictionary of the language of Scotland, this Glossary, however inferior in other respects to the excellent one compiled by Mr. Ruddiman for Douglas's Virgil, has this material advantage of it, that most of the words in it belong to the genuine language of the country; whereas a very great proportion of the other consists of foreign words fabricated by Douglas himself.[1] Such words as occur in both Glossaries

of the books describing the fruits of the earth or the diseases of mankind, subjects which ought to be level to every comprehension, though they bear English titles, cannot be read by any, who have not studied these sciences, without the help of a Greek Lexicon.

The naturalizing of Latin words, perhaps through the medium of the French, was common in England, and most probably also in Scotland, long before Wyntown's time. The judicious reader will find no difficulty in distinguishing those which are descended of the Latin by the manner of their formation, from those with which it is only cognate; and here it is proper to observe, that many modern words, which we have received from the Latin, are in reality Gothic, an example of which is shewn in the Glossary, vo. *Thole*.

I beg leave to close this note with a childish story of myself. Soon after I began to learn Latin, another boy and I having been told that the most of the English language was derived from it, set ourselves to find out the words so derived; and we discovered that the English adjective *secure* was from the Latin noun *securis*, *an axe!* How many hundreds of pompous etymologies have no better foundation ?

[1] Douglas's translation of Virgil's Æneid is the Scottish work best known to the learned beyond the limits of Scotland, having been often quoted and referred to as the standard of the Scottish language, even before the publication of Ruddiman's Glossary ; and a wonderful work it is, being, according to Warton [vol. ii. p. 281], the first complete metrical translation of Virgil's Æneid (and indeed of any classic writer) done in Britain, and also in the opinion of several good judges the best. No part of his merit, however,

(and these are not near so many as might be expected) frequently have very different explanations, it being the business of a glossarist to give only those meanings of a word in which his author uses it. The little identity to be found in the two Glossaries is a circumstance which adds to the utility of both.

The *General Rules*, which precede the Glossary, also differ considerably from Mr. Ruddiman's, owing to the superior purity of the language in Wyntown's time, which will be obvious on a comparison of the vocables and construction with those of the Mœso-Gothic, Anglo-Saxon, and Islandic, some instances of which I have observed in the notes, and many more may be found in every page of the Glossary.

I have no doubt that the candid reader, considering this Glossary as an attempt, in which, I may say, I have had no predecessor, and moreover as being only an appendage, will think it entitled to some indulgence for its errors and deficiencies. The critic, who finds these very numerous, will do

consists in presenting a genuine specimen of the language, as will be obvious to any one who compares the language of Barber and Wyntown with his, and all of them with the most antient and genuine specimen of the Gothic preserved in the precious Gospels of Ulfila. Douglas was sensible that the use of exotic words was not a merit, but an inevitable defect in his work [*see his preface*, pp. 5, 9]; yet some of his admirers affect to praise him for this defect, which they call enriching the language. So the wine-makers of this country enrich the genuine juice of the grape with sloe-juice and other heterogeneous poisons.

It may be agreeable to those, who love to trace the history of literature, to see the following notice of a translation at least a full century before Douglas (but whether from a classic or not is unknown), which is in our author's Chronicle, B. I. ch. viii.

"In Ynd ar othir ferlyis sere,
That I lewe for to rekyn here;
For tha ar tyl yhowre knawlage
Translatyde welle in oure langage."

Q. If the original of this now lost translation was Solinus, in whose description of India there are many wonders; or the pretended letter of Alexander to Aristotle, *De situ et mirabilibus Indiæ*, said to be translated by Cornelius Nepos from the Greek, which was a very common manuscript?

a good service to the republic of letters if he will furnish a complete one; in doing which he may perhaps find even my poor attempt of some assistance to him. Those, whom their own studies have qualified to judge of such an undertaking, well know, that to do complete justice to it requires the assiduous labour of many years devoted to the study of philology, together with the abilities of an IHRE.

I wish it were in my power to give any thing which might deserve to be called *the Life of Wyntown;* but from want of materials I can do little more than draw into one point of view what may be gathered from his own work.

ANDROW OF WYNTOWN appears to have been born about the middle of the long reign of David II., as he complains of the infirmities of old age when engaged in the first copy of his Chronicle.[1] It is quite unknown of what family he was, though conjecture might venture to suppose him a relation of Alane of Wyntown, whose marriage with the heiress of Setown, mistaken by the historiographer of the family, and misrepresented or omitted by the compilers of peerages, is related by him [*see* B. VIII. ch. xli. *and note*], and from him by Bower.[2]

---

[1] See B. IX. Prol., which is the same in the Cotton manuscript transcribed from the first copy.

[2] Besides this Alane and his posterity, mentioned by the transcriber of the Cupar manuscript of the Scotichronicon [*v. Sc. Chr.* vol. ii. p. 337, *note*], I find the following men of the name, who were all cotemporary with our author.

Ingrame of Winton, appointed by David II. keeper of the castle of Kildrummy in 1362 [*see* B. VIII. ch. xlvi. 7165].

Willielmus de Wintonia, who died on his pilgrimage to Mount Sinay. [*Rot. Scotiæ*, 37mo. *Edw. III. apud Ayloffe*, p. 226.] If this be not the son of Alane and the Lady of Setown, and his death is too early for him to be called " veteranus " [*v. Sc. Chr. ut supra*], the pilgrimage to the holy land may be said to have been a family disease among the Wyntowns.

Eymunde de Wyntona, witness in a charter by the Earl of Ross, conveying the lands of Gerloch to Paul Mactyre, dated at Delgheny 5th April 1366.

PREFACE. xxxiii

He was a Canon regular of the priory of St. Andrews, which was so great and flourishing, that it had under its jurisdiction the priories of St. Serf's insh in Loch Levin, Portmoak on the north bank of the same Loch, both in Kinross-shire, Pittenween in the east part of Fife, the isle of May in the Firth of Forth, and Monymusk in Aberdeenshire. The Prior of St. Andrews was moreover entitled to take precedence in parliament, not only of all Priors, but even of all Abbats, in honour of the supremacy of the episcopal see, with which he was connected. [*Sc. Chr.* vol. i. p. 367; *and note on* B. IX. ch. vi. 555.] In or before the year 1395,[1] our author was by the favour of his fellow Canons elected Prior of the monastery of St. Serf's insh in Loch Levin, one of the most ancient religious establishments in Scotland, which was founded by Brud, son of Dargard, King of the Pichts, probably about the year 700, and enriched

Johannes Wenton, Armiger de Scotia, who has a safe conduct from Henry v. to come to the presence of him and his dear cousin James, King of the Scots, in London, 4th October 1421 [*Fœd.* vol. x. p. 154].

Out of these a genealogist would easily find relations and frame a pedigree for our Wyntown, which might with some degree of probability be grafted on the Earls of Winton or Winchester, in England, who, by the marriage of Alan of Galloway's daughter, got vast possessions, and the important office of Great Constable in Scotland. It is certain that the cadets of a great family often assumed the title of their Chief as a designation or surname, and the fiery dragon born by the Earls of Winchester in England and the Earls of Winton in Scotland is, according to the rules of heraldry, a presumption of affinity. Whether a partiality for the family of Winchester induced our author superfluously to detail their genealogy, along with that of Alan's daughters, who were of the royal blood, I know not.

The only family of the name mentioned in *Nisbet's Heraldry* [vol. i. pp. 142, 363] is stiled *of Strathmartin.*

[1] In 1395 "Andreas de Wynton, Prior insule lacus de Levin" was present with others at a perambulation for dividing the baronies of Kirkness and Lochor "in presentia serenissimi principis Roberti Ducis Albanie." In 1406 he is designed "Canonicus Sancti Andree, Prior prioratus insule Sancti Servani infra lacum de Levin.' These notices are partly from the Chartulary of St. Andrews, and partly from extracts taken from a quarto volume of manuscript collections belonging to Mr. Henry Malcolm, an episcopal minister

with many ample possessions by the Kings of Scotland and Bishops of St Andrews.[1]

Schyr Jhone of the Wemyss, ancestor of the Earls of Wemys, was one of his particular friends, to whom he appears to have considered himself as under great obligations. It was at his request that he undertook his Chronicle [B. I. *Prol.* 54], which was finished between the 3d of September 1420 and the return of King James from England in April 1424, as appears by Robert Duke of Albany being mentioned as dead, and the prayer for the prosperity of his children in B. IX. ch. xxvi. 2782, et seqq. Indeed, from the tenor of this chapter, it is pretty evident that it was written very soon after the death of Duke Robert, and that it once stood as the conclusion of the work; for the chapter following it, which is quite foreign to the history of Scotland, may be presumed to have been added afterwards, especially if the marriage of John of Bavaria was not earlier than 1424. [*See Notes*, B. IX. ch. xxvi. 2849, *and* ch. xxvii. 3321.]

While our author was engaged in his work, some unknown person of a genius similar to his own, sent him the history

at Ballingry before the revolution, who died at Cupar in Fife about the year 1730, by George Chalmers, Esq., whose communication of both of them, and of the notice concerning Eymund de Wynton in the preceding note is a part of his many kind attentions to this publication and to me.

Innes [*p.* 622] mentions "several authentick acts or publick instruments" of Wyntown as Prior from 1395 till 1413 in Extracts from the Register of the Priory of St. Andrews in the possession of the Earl of Panmure. These concurring testimonies make it certain that he was Prior in 1395; and yet in Extracts from the same Register in the Harleian library, No. 4628, f. 2 b, there is noted a charter "per Jacobum priorem S. Andree de Loch Leven, anno 1396," which must be a mistake; and indeed this manuscript is very carelessly written, so by no means to be set in competition with the copy examined by Innes.

[1] See B. I. Prol. B. V. ch. xii. 5228, and Excerpts from the Earl of Panmure's manuscript of the Register of the Priory of St. Andrews, published in *Crawford's Officers*, pp. 428 *et seqq.*, containing the donations and some curious notices concerning antient manners and customs extracted from an old volume written "*antiquo Scotorum idiomate.*"

from the birth of David II. to the death of Robert II., apparently written, or rather finished, in the beginning of the reign of Robert III. [*See* B. IX. ch. x. 1118], which having examined and approved, he gladly incorporated into his own work. [*See* B. VIII. ch. xix.; B. IX. ch. x. 1153.] This ample contribution is composed in the same style and same kind of verse with his own work; so that without the least breach of uniformity, it gives us the singular advantage of having the last eighty-three years of the history composed by two writers, who lived during the greatest part of the time which they wrote of.

Before Wyntown's time the history of the Scots had been plunged into confusion almost inextricable by an insatiable and ignorant rage for antiquity, which placed the reign of Fergus 1200 years before that of Kenneth Mac-Alpin, whom they made only the tenth in descent from him, thus involving themselves in the monstrous absurdity of allowing 120 years to each generation. Wyntown saw and felt the dilemma, but not having sufficiently informed himself from antient records, he could see no way of getting rid of it, and fairly gave it up to "othir of mare sufficians." [*See* B. IV. ch. viii. xix. *in V. R.*]

Having afterwards obtained better information, he found it expedient to give a second improved copy of the Chronicle with the important correction, which by enumerating the years of Fergus and his successors reduces his æra pretty near to the truth, being even a little below it;[1] though at the same time he could not drop the notion that the Scots were in Scotland 245 years before the Pichts. But he knew nothing of the

---

[1] The reigns contained in B. IV. ch. viii. amount to 195 years; the reign of Ewan or Heatgan by *Reg. S. And.* is 16 years, which numbers subtracted from 741, the year in which Ewan died, place the accession of Fergus in 530, which is too late by 27 years.

The transcripts from this corrected copy of Wyntown are much scarcer than those from the first one. Innes, who had examined many, never saw any but the one in the Royal library. The Harleian manuscript is another.

forty-four or (thirty-nine) Kings preceding Fergus, nor of his interpolated successors, and in short has the happiness to be ignorant of many of the stories, which have long been deemed essential points of faith in Scottish history, but are now vanishing like mist before the increasing sunshine of reason.

Fordun, our author's cotemporary and fellow labourer (though they were unknown to each other) fell upon a method of settling the chronology of Fergus very easily by fairly splitting him into two Kings, one of whom he places 100 years before his due time, and the other 330 years before the Christian æra, leaving however the names, actions, and characters of the Kings between his two Fergusses to be supplied from the "fine fancy" of Hector Boyse, though he is particular enough in the history of the imaginary Kings, interpolated among the successors of Fergus, which he in vain attempts to authenticate from Bede and other authors of credit. These fictitious Kings constitute the grossest fault in Fordun's work, which, except in this instance, where the ambition of false antiquity *for the honour of Scotland* has carried him off his feet, is in general faithfully compiled from the best materials he could obtain.[1] From a comparison of Fordun and Wyntown, who may be considered as two witnesses ignorant of the evidence given by each other, we may obtain a pretty just view of the unsettled and inaccurate idea, which the Scots entertained about the conclusion of the fourteenth century of their early history.

It is probable that Wyntown did not very long survive the final conclusion of his work; for, as I have already observed, he reckoned himself an old man when engaged in it; and in-

[1] The reader will please to advert, that I speak of Fordun's own work, as published by Hearne, and partly by Gale, but not of the *Scotichronicon* published by Goodal, which the continuator has made almost his own by interpolations and additions. This distinction ought to be carefully attended to by all who study the history of Scotland.

PREFACE. xxxvii

deed he could be no less, for he had then presided over his priory about thirty years, perhaps longer; and we may take it for granted that he was not a young man when he was elected to that dignity.

The character of Wyntown as an historian is in a great measure common to the other historical writers of his age, who generally admitted into their works the absurdity of tradition along with authentic narrative, and often without any mark of discrimination, esteeming it a sufficient standard of historic fidelity to narrate nothing but what they found written by others before them. Indeed, as connection of parts, uniformity of subject, and strict investigation of authorities were little known or studied in those ages, it is very fortunate that they did compile their works in that crude manner, for thereby we have the advantage of often finding in these authors genuine transcripts from more antient authorities, of which their extracts are the only existing remains.[1] Had they, who after Wyntown assumed the office of historians of Scotland, followed his example in adhering strictly to authorities, and expatiated less in the enchanted wilderness of "*beautiful genius and fine fancy,*" the history might have run in a much clearer stream than it does at present.

The early writers of various ages and countries seem to have agreed in a lazy custom of referring their readers to the works of others for 'great portions of the history which they themselves professed to give. Thus Ennius omits the relation of the first Punic war, because it had already been written by Nævius, who lived about forty years before him. So Robert of Glocester (p. 487) and Robert of Brunne (p. 205), the two earliest writers of English history in English, refer their readers to the romance of *Richard Coeur de Lion.* So Barber (p. 340)

---

[1] See Montaigne's approbation of these simple historians, and particularly of Froissart. *Essais,* L. ii. ch. 10.

passes over the particulars of a battle because then sung in songs by the young women. In like manner Wyntown passes lightly over the history of Alexander the Great, the wars of the Saxons with the Britons, the actions of William Walays and of Robert the Brus, and the origin of the Stewarts, because they are

"Contenyd in othir bukis sere."

This way of sending the reader to other books for some of the most important parts of the work proposed must have been particularly distressing, where books were so scarce and inaccessible, as they undoubtedly were in Scotland before the invention of printing.[1]

A contrary fault may perhaps be objected to Wyntown, that he sometimes runs into descriptions more minute and diffuse than are consistent with the rules of writing history; in answer to which it is sufficient to say that these rules were unknown in his age. Such descriptions were the defect perhaps more properly speaking the beauty of several early historians: by them Snorro, the venerable Herodotus of the north, and Froissart, the history-painter of France, England and Scotland, who, like our Wyntown, had the courage to write history in their native languages, bring us home to the scenes they

[1] Books, and particularly historical ones, were very scarce in Scotland in the ages preceding our author, as appears by the small number of authorities quoted by him (which are subjoined to the preface [to be given in vol. iii.]) and his lamenting the little assistance he had in his general history from preceding authors (see B. I. *Prol.* 115): nor are the historians quoted by Fordun in his own work very numerous, though he is said to have travelled through England in quest of books and materials for his history. This need not be wondered at, when we observe, how very scarce books were even in England and France at the same time. (See *Warton*, vol. i., *Preliminary Dissertation* ii.) Printing was not yet invented, nor had the Turks, by taking possession of Constantinople, driven the treasures of Greek and Roman literature into the western parts of Europe. A modern reader surrounded by his library of many thousand printed books must compassionate the distress of those poor authors who attempted to rear up an historical fabric with so few materials.

describe, and make us take an interest in the characters they draw. If the succession of Kings and the relation of their battles be the body of history, the progress of the human mind in arts and knowledge, and a true delineation of manners so different from our own, as appears, for example, in the justing at Berwick in 1388, unquestionably constitute the very soul of it.

If we except one severe sentence extorted from him by the cruelties of Edward I., and a reflection upon the English in consequence of the seizure of Prince James, Wyntown nowhere runs into that abuse and contempt of the enemies of his country, which disgrace the writings of many of his cotemporaries; but takes every occasion to bestow due praise on their gallantry and bravery in war. The same liberality of sentiment induces him to mention other writers, and particularly Barber, in the most respectful manner. If he shows himself a very zealous son of the Church, in taking all occasions to advance the power and dignity of the clergy, and to maintain that superiority over the civil power, which they claimed as a divine right (see B. VI. ch. ii. iv. ix., etc.); we must remember that in that age even the laity considered devotion to the Church as the quintessence of religion and virtue, and the surest passport to the joys of heaven.

Historians have frequently declined bringing their works quite down to the time of writing, and perhaps it was rather dangerous for truth to tread too close upon the heels of time.[1] Whatever was his motive, Wyntown has concluded his Chronicle of Scotland at least fourteen years before the time of writing the twenty-sixth chapter of the ninth book.[2]

[1] "Tiberii, Caiique et Claudii ac Neronis res, florentibus ipsis *ob metum falsæ;* postquam occiderant, recentibus odiis compositae sunt."
[*Taciti Annal.* lib. i. c. 1.]
[2] In the same manner Bower breaks off at the death of James I., though he appears to have been engaged in his work in the fourteenth year of James II.:

Hitherto I have considered Wyntown only as an historian, in which character he certainly stands higher than as a poet; but as his work is in ryme, he is also classed among the poets of Scotland, and he is in point of time the second of the few early ones whose works we possess, Barber being his only extant predecessor.[1] Though his work in general partakes little or nothing of the nature of poetry, unless ryme can be said to constitute poetry, yet he now and then throws in some touches of true poetic description, and paints the scenery of his battles with so exact a pencil, that a person who is on the spot may point out the various scenes of each particular action; and sometimes like Homer, whose poems he never saw, he bestows a portion of his work in expatiating on the achievements of a particular hero, as in B. VIII. ch. xxxvi., where the actions of William Douglas are related.

Wyntown's verse consists of eight syllables, though, like his cotemporaries in England as well as in Scotland, he does not adhere strictly to his measure, lines even of ten, and others of only six syllables, frequently occurring. In only a very few instances he uses alliteration, that dreadful fetter upon the sense of antient poetry, which about his time was so common, especially in Scotland and the north of England, that short poems, and even some of considerable length, were entirely composed in it. Neglect of equality in the lines, alliteration, and violent transpositions of the natural order of the language, which are now considered as unpardonable blemishes in poetical compo-

Mair finishes with the marriage of James III., fifty years before the time when he wrote: and Boyse concludes his first edition almost a century before his own time. Several of the English historians have also declined writing the actions of their cotemporaries.

[1] Gordon, the author of the poetical history of King Robert, in his preface mentions a manuscript poem on the same subject, which he had the use of, written in rymes like Chaucer's by Peter Fenton in 1369, and consequently a few years earlier than Barber's poem. It is worthy of remark that Wyntown, though he often quotes Barber, has never once mentioned Fenton. Q. if there is no mistake in the date.

Preface p.XI.

Specimens of the writing of the three oldest Manuscripts of Wyntown's Chronicle.

Royal M.S. 17.D.XX. f.191 b.

Quhen alexander oure kyng was dede —
yat Scotland led in luwe and le
I lay was sons off ale and brede —
Off wyne and wax off gamyn and gle

Cotton M.S. Nero. D.XI. f.139 a.

Quhen alexander our kyng was ded
yat scotland led in lauche and le
Alay was sons of alle and brede
off wyne and way of gamyn and gle

Advocates' M.S. A.7.1.

Quhen alexand our kyng was ded
yt scotland led in lauth & le
alday was sons of all & brud
off wyn & wax gawyn & glu

sition, were esteemed beauties by the antient Anglo-Saxon and other Gothic poets.[1]

Wyntown's work is entirely composed in couplets without the intervention of a single stanza. It frequently happens that two couplets together end with similar rymes, which in those days was not accounted a defect.

The Royal manuscript, marked 17, D. xx., which, as already observed, is greatly superior to all other known manuscripts of Wyntown,[2] appears to have been transcribed for George Barclay of Achrody;[3] and very soon after the autograph of the cor-

---

[1] Hickes has collected several examples of alliteration in the Greek and Roman poets [*g. as.* p. 195].

[2] See the account of this manuscript by Innes, p. 624.

[3] F. 262 b, being the outside or cover of one of the *quairs*, has no part of Wyntown's work upon it, but has the following lines written apparently by retainers of the gentleman, for whom the manuscript was transcribed, which obliged the transcriber to pass to f. 263.

At the top of the page in large writing:

>   This buik dois perteine
>   To ane rycht honora^{ll} man
>   Georg Barclay of Achrody
>   And mony wther propirly
>   Brother german is he
>   To Sr Patrik of Tollie
>   Cheiff of Barclays in Scotland
>   And mony guid deid hes haid
>   in hand

Under which in a small and very bad hand are the following:

	Barclay
The mariage of that Lady	Sr Patrik˄of Tollie
Indenit w$_t$ guid qualitie	Cheiff of that name I testifie
Movit hir husband Toly than	As in his Scheild ye may sie
Into his armis to d	Twa Corsis weiris he
Q^r corsis twa befoir hand	The thrid be resone quhy
For he was	That hous marit properly
. . . . . the thrid to bere	Ane dochter of Gartly
	W^t gryt honor^r and dignity
	Q^{lk} than was Barclay
	& was ane Kny^t ry^t worthy

The left hand column, which is to be read last, is in some places so blotted as to be unintelligible.

rected copy, as several good judges of manuscripts have pronounced it to be of the beginning of the fifteenth century, and some have placed it even before the year 1400. As we know that it could not possibly be written earlier than in 1420 or 1421, the opinion of these gentlemen may warrant a belief that it is not latter than 1430, and no manuscript in the language of Scotland older than it is known to be extant. To enable the reader to compare the writing with coeval monuments, a specimen of the hand is herewith given.[1]

The writing, of which a specimen is engraved, continues till the last chapter of the eighth book, after which two different transcribers have been employed, who wrote worse hands; and both, particularly the last one, have taken the common liberty of modernizing the language, whence the last part of it is sometimes inferior to the Cotton manuscript for purity. The Rubrics, which are in red and in a hand like black print, are also the work of a more modern writer, at least if we may judge from some innovations in the spelling. This kind of hand, wherever it appears, is distinguished in the edition by black letter, which, though disagreeable to the eye when long continued, is useful as a distinction. The illuminated letters of the manuscript are, as already observed, represented in the edition by open capitals. There is no punctuation in the whole manuscript.

The volume consists of sixteen *quairs*, each containing eighteen leaves in folio of thick paper, inclosed in a sheet of

[1] In this writing many of the letters are of the same form with others, e.g. *l*, *el*, and *w*; *c*, *t*, and sometimes *i*; *b* and *v*; *y* and *th*; *bb* and *lb*; *f* and *s*; *ft* and *s*; *b* and *l*; *m*, *n*, *u*, *v*, *i* not to be known but by the sense; *ff* generally written for *f*, e.g. *ffuffe*; *ll* for *l*, e.g. *bllyssyn*; and the character for *s* so like *ss*, that *Ross* to a reader unacquainted with the writing will seem *Rosss*. These confusions of the letters, and the frequent contractions, account for the prodigious discrepancies we find in manuscripts, and show how necessary it is for a transcriber to know the language and the subject. The custom of writing *ff* for *f* was common with old men in the present age.

vellum, having at the bottom of the last page the first words of the following one for a direction to the binder, like the signatures in printed books; for no numbers of the folios were originally marked.[1] Thus, at the end and beginning of the *quairs* there are alwise two leaves of vellum, which in the edition are marked with V added to the number of the folio on the margin. Though now bound in one volume, it has formerly been in three, the first and third of which have been damaged by water on the edges of the leaves.

Wyntown's Chronicle is followed by a short Chronicle of Scotland in Scottish prose, written by an unknown author about 1530;[2] and after that there is a Scottish translation or paraphrase of the letter pretended to be written by Prester John to the Emperor Frederick which concludes the volume.[3]

Several other names besides that of George Barclay, are written in this book; but whether they have been owners of it

---

[1] Some person has numbered a few folios at the beginning; and I have numbered the rest with black lead, writing with ink on books belonging to the Museum not being permitted.

[2] The age of this Chronicle appears from an observation in f. 302, that the Conquest of the Pichts in "aucht hundyr xxx and od" was 700 years ago. This brings it after 1530: but 700 being a round number we cannot pretend to say that the computation is accurate. This author is most ample, where he has no foundation to go upon, in the fabulous settlement of the Scots, which, he contends, took place long before the birth of Brutus, or even the Trojan war: he more rationally explodes the conquests of Arthur, who, he observes, could not defend his own; and he takes notice of the hereditary right of the Scottish Kings as heirs of Edmund Ironside, to the crown of England. Having got through the anti-historical part, he gives brief notes of remarkable events with their dates down to the year 1482.

[3] This letter begins thus:—" John callit Prest King amang all the Kingis of the Erde tyl ane nobyl man Frederik Empriour of Rome salutis gretyng."
—He invites him to be his Steward and Viceroy, and tells him that he is both King and Priest, but values himself chiefly on his priestly character. Then follows an account of a palace built of gold and jewels by his father, which satisfies the hunger of those who enter it without the use of food: after which he describes the neighbouring nations, viz., a nation of canibals subject to him, whom Alexander the Great shut up between the hills Goth

is unknown, and of little consequence. In the early part of the last century it has belonged to Sir William Le-Neve, when he was York Herald, whose signature and arms appear in several places of it.[1] After him, but whether immediately or not, I know not, the King became proprietor of it, from whose library it came with many others into the British Museum, where it now is.

The manuscript in the Cotton library, marked Nero, D,XI, is, after the Royal, superior for age and purity of language, not only to all other manuscripts of Wyntown, but even to all others extant in the language of Scotland.[2] Its being posterior to the Royal can only be inferred from the proper names and the language being in many instances more modern, examples of which may be found in the contents of the seventh book, in the prologue and contents of the eighth, and in the various readings; for the writing, of which a specimen is given in the plate, though very different from that of the Royal, is in

---

and Magoth: these he sometimes turns out against his enemies, and then shuts them up again between the hills, where they are to remain till the coming of Antichrist. Another people in the sandy desert have "the clwis of ane hors." In the desert is also "the Vemon land" or land of the Amazons, who are 100,000 warlike ladies on horse besides foot. His whole land is surrounded by the river Gihon, which flows from Paradise; and beyond it is the land of the pigmies, "mennikynis lik barnes of fyẅe or sax yeris ald," who are Christians. Near them are monsters half men and half horse, and other monsters called Sagittaris, who eat raw flesh and sleep upon trees. In another desert there are Unicorns, which can be caught by none but a virgin.——The end is wanting. There is a copy of this letter in French in the King's library, 20, A, XI; and there is a quotation from it in the Chronicle of Melros, p. 237 of the edition.

[1] In order to ascertain the identity of the signature I went to the Herald's college, where Edmund Lodge, Esq., Lancaster Herald, with great politeness took the trouble of shewing me many signatures of this gentleman in the official books.

[2] The next to it for antiquity is probably either the manuscript of Barber, dated 1489, in the Advocates' Library; or the translation of the Psalms in Scottish metre, No. 278 of the manuscripts bequeathed by Archbishop Parker to Corpus-Christi College in Cambridge.

the opinion of judges not distinguishable from it in point of antiquity; and indeed the difference of a few years in writing cannot be ascertained by the inspection even of a *Casely*. In this copy the lines are divided by a short sloping mark, not for the grammatical division of the sense, but for a kind of musical rest in reading, examples of which may be seen in the various readings, B. IV. ch. viii. xix. The book is written in folio, on paper folded so as to make a long and narrow page. It has been in very bad keeping; several leaves at the beginning and at the end are lost [*see V. R.*] and the writing at the bottoms of many leaves, which have been rotted with water, is supplied by a latter hand upon slips of paper pasted on. When it was rebound by Sir Robert Cotton, most of the inner margins have been strengthened with guards and some marginal notes, which however appear to have been of no value, have been partly cut off.[1]

The next manuscript of Wyntown in order of time is that which is marked A, 7, 1 in the library of the Faculty of Advocates at Edinburgh. It is written in folio upon paper; and the writing, of which a specimen is given in the plate, is supposed to be of the beginning of the sixteenth century. It varies greatly in the numeration of the chapters from the Royal, as it does also in many parts of the text, and in the orthography, which has been much *mended* by the transcriber. Unfortunately it has lost many of its leaves, particularly from the middle of the sixth[2] to near the end of the seventh[3] chapter, and all after the middle of the tenth[4] chapter of the ninth book.

---

[1] This is the Scottish manuscript, from which Selden and Hearne have published extracts; [*See Notes*, B. VI. ch. vi.; B. VII. ch. ix. 2641] and which Smith in the Catalogue of the Cotton Library, Nicolson [*Scottish Hist. Lib.* p. 129] and Mackenzie [*Lives of Scottish Writers*, vol. i. p. 475] describe as a history of the Kings in old Scottish verse. For want of the beginning none of them knew the name of the author.

[2] Ninth.   [3] Twenty-first.   [4] Twenty-third in the Royal.

It came into the library, while it was under the care of the learned Mr. Thomas Ruddiman, and has probably been purchased by him :[1] but nothing is known of its former owners, further than that the name of John Ærskine is written on a vellum leaf at the beginning.

Next to this is another manuscript belonging to the same library, and marked A, 1, 13, which is in folio, neatly written on paper about the end of the sixteenth century. It is abridged in many places, and more modernized and corrupted throughout than A, 7, 1. The transcriber, though he wrote the author's division of his work into nine books, has neglected it, and carried on the series of chapters, 212 in number, to the end. Annexed to it is the short Chronicle in prose, which is subjoined to the Royal. This manuscript was the property of Sir James Balfour, and is marked, as all his books were, with *Denmilne*, the name of the place where he kept his library : it afterwards belonged to Sir Robert Sibbald, after whose death it was purchased by the Faculty of Advocates, and was for some time the only copy they had.[2]

These three manuscripts have been transcribed from the first unimproved copy of Wyntown's work.

Another manuscript, though not deserving notice for its age or correctness, yet must be noted as being perhaps the only

[1] Ruddiman's quotations of Wyntown, as appears particularly from his note on Buchanan's history, p. 159, A, 11, are from the manuscript A, 1, 13, and show that this one had not come into his hand in 1715.

[2] This is the manuscript so erroneously described by Mackenzie in his life of our author, as being in nine books. The notes by Sir James Balfour which he mentions in a manner that must make us suppose them very interesting, are chiefly marginal contents, and of no value. See Note on B. VI. ch. vi.

The account of these two manuscripts is taken from the very obliging communications of Alexander Fraser Tytler, Esq., to whom this work is also indebted for many collations from them (accompanied with an attestation of their accuracy by Mr. Brown, the librarian), which have enabled me to correct some errors of the copies in the museum.

one, besides the Royal, which contains the author's improvements, and as having been of some little use in the present edition. It is No. 6909 of the Harleian library in the Museum, and has been written about the middle of the last century, upon sixty-seven sheets of coarse paper in quarto. The transcriber has taken great liberties in altering and abridging. Along with the foreign matter he has omitted the short notices of the Pichtish Kings, the reign of Macbeth, and some other parts of the history of Scotland, his idea of which has led him frequently to correct Wyntown from Hector Boyse. This manuscript seems to have been copied from one written in the abbey of Kelso; for in the rubric of the chapter answering to B. VII. ch. vi., King David is called "St. David our founder," and the one answering to B. VIII. ch. xxvi. informs us, that William of Dalgernow, Abbat of Kelso, was tutor to David II. during his residence in France; a piece of intelligence which I find nowhere else.[1]

These are the manuscripts, from the first of which as the standard text, and the others as occasional auxiliaries, THE ORYGYNALE CRONYKIL OF SCOTLAND is now for the first time presented to the public. I am persuaded, that, notwithstanding all my endeavours to execute the work with propriety, many mistakes and omissions must have escaped my attention,

---

[1] There have been, and perhaps there are now, many other manuscripts of Wyntown. (See *Innes*, pp. 624, 683.) There was one in the possession of Mr. Kirton, a clergyman of Edinburgh; one at or near Venice (see *Note* I. *prol.* 57); and Mr. Macleod, a clergyman in the north part of Scotland, is *said* to have an excellent one; but the author of my information does not speak of it with certainty, and one can never be too cautious in reports concerning manuscripts. In consequence of a report, that there was a copy of Wyntown in the valuable collection of manuscripts belonging to the Marquis of Lansdown, I applied to his lordship for permission to collate some passages, who had the goodness to send a messenger to inform me that if he had had such a manuscript I should have been welcome to the use of it; but that, from a search made in consequence of my application, it appeared, that there was no manuscript of Wyntown in his possession.

PREFACE.

and I am confident that those who know what a labour it is to do justice to such a work, and consequently are most capable of discovering my errors, will be the most ready to look upon them with indulgence, and to consider them as the effect, not of carelessness, but of that imperfection to which all human undertakings are liable, and perhaps none more than the first publication of a work in an obsolete language with proper elucidations.

[DAVID MACPHERSON, 1795.]

THE FYRST BUKE

OF THE

ORYGYNALE CRONYKIL

OF SCOTLAND.

THE
ORYGYNALE CRONYKIL
OF SCOTLAND.

[Heir followis the Prolog, but faill
Off the Cornykillis callit Originale.]

Fol. 1.
As men ar be thare qualyteys
Inclynyd tyl dyẅersyteys,
Mony yharnys for tyll here
Off tymys that befor thaim were,
The statys chawngyde ande the greis.
Quhar-for off swylk antyqwyteys,
Thai that set hale thare delyte
Gest or story for to wryte,
Owthir in metyre, or in prose,
Fluryside fayrly thaire purpose 10
Wytht queynt and curyous circumstance,
To rays hartis in plesance,
And the heraris tyll excyte
Be wyt, or wyll, tyll thaire delyte.
 As Gwido de Columpna qwhille,
The poete Omere, and Vyrgylle,
Fayrly fowrmyde thaire tretis,
And curyowsly dytyde thare storis.
Sum oyside bot in plane manere

The dedis dwne, and thare matere 20
To wryte, as Dares of Frygy
Wrate of the Trojanys the story,
Bot in to plane and opyne style,
But curyous wordis or suttyle.
   Allsua set I myne intent,
My wyt, my wyll, and myne talent,
Fra that I sene hade storis sere
In Cronnyklys, quhare thai wryttyne were,
Thare matere in tyll fowrme to drawe
Off Latyne, in tyll Ynglys sawe. 30
For Romans to rede is delytabylle,
Suppose that thai be quhyle bot fabylle,
And set tyll this I gawe my wylle,
My wyt, I kene, swa skant thare-tylle,
That I dowt sare thaime tyll offende
That kane me, and my werk amende,
Gywe I wryte owthir mare or les
Than the storys berys wytnes:
For, as I sayde, rwde is my wyte
And sympyll to put all in wryte, 40
And clerly bryng thame tyll knawlage
Off Latyne in tyll owre langage,
Tyll ilke mannys wndyrstandyng
For syndrynes of thare chawngyng:
Swa throuch ffolly or nycete,
I dowt confowndyt for to be.
   Bot Lordys, gywe youre curtasy,
Forbere me in this juperty,
And fra thaire lethe walde me defende,
That kane reprowe, and wyll noucht mende, 50
Hawande excusyde my sympylnes,
Syne that I set my besynes

Tyll all yhoure plesans generaly :
Fol. 1. b. Suppos this tretys sympylly
I made at the instans of a larde
That hade my serẅys in his warde,
Schyr Jhone of the Wemys be rycht name,
Ane honest Knycht, and of gude fame,
Suppos hys Lordschype lyk noucht be
Tyll gret statys in eqwalyte :   60
He mon of nede be partenere
Off qwhat kyne blame, that I sulde bere ;
Syne for byddynge at hys cownsalle
Off det I spendyt my traẅalle ;
For all honest det sulde be
Qwyt wyth possibylyte :
And bowsumnes, that as the wys
Sayis, bettyre is than sacrifyis :
For in sacryfyis, the slayne,
And noucht the slayare, mon thole the payne : 70
Swa that the slaare haẅe the mede,
The payne is soft, he tholys, in dede.
Than sulde hys mede wytht rycht be mare,
That suffiryde in hym self the sare,
Quharë bowsumnes mays fredwme threlle
Lykyng wndyr awe to dwelle,
Noucht as bondage wndyr lawe,
Bot that lykyng grace sulde knawe.
I than, set in lyk assay,
Wylfull is my det to pay :   80
Sympyll or sufficeand, quhether it be,
To bowsumnes ay yhelde I me.

And for I wyll nane bere the blame
Off my defawte, [this] is my name

Be baptysyne, ANDROWE of WYNTOWNE,
Off Sanctandrowys a Chanowne
Regulare, bot noucht for-thi
Off thaim all the lest worthy:
Bot off thare grace and thaire faẃoure
I wes, but meryt, made Priowre   90
Off the Ynche, wythin Lochleẅyne;
Haẅand tharof my tytill eẅyne
Off Sanctandrowys dyocesy,
Betwene the Lomownde and Bennarty.

The tytill of this Tretis hale,
I wyll be caulde ORYGYNALE:
For that begynnyng sall mak clere
Be playne proces owre matere.
As of Angelis, and of Man
Fyrst to rys the kynde began: 100
And how, eftyr thare creatioune,
Men grewe in tyll successyowne,
Wyde sprede in to thare greys,
Thare statys, and thare qwalyteis,
Tyll the tyme at Nynws Kyng
Ras, and tuk the goẅernyng
Off Babylon and Assyry.
Fra hyme syne dystynctly
It is my purpos tyll afferme
This Tretis in tyll certane terme,   110
Haldand tyme be tym the date,
As Cronyklerys be-for me wrate,
Reqwyrande the correctioune
Off grettare of perfectyoune.
For few wrytys I redy fande,
That I couth drawe to my warande:

Part off the Bybyll wytht that, that Perys
Comestor ekyde in hys yherys;
Orosius, and Frere Martyne,
Wytht Ynglis and Scottis storys syne,   120
And othir incedeyns sere,
Acordand lyk tyll oure matere.
To this my wyt is walowide dry
But floure or froyte; bot noucht for-thi
To furthhyre fayrly this purpos
I seke the saẅowre of that ros
That spanysys, spredys, and evyre spryngys,
In plesans of the Kyng of Kyngis.

The Chapterys off the Fyrst Buke.

i. BE dywÿsiownys of this Tretis.
ii. Off Angelis.
iii. Off Mannys fyrst creatioune.
iiii. Off the slawchtere of Abelle.
v. Off Kayinnys generatyown.
vi. Off Sethys generatyown.
vii. Off Geawndys.
viii. Off the Arke off Noe, and off the Spate.
ix. Off the foure Kynrykis pryncipale.
x. How Ynde and othir landys lyis.
xi. How othir sindry Lauddys lyis.
xii. How Egipe and othir landdys lyis.
xiii. How the land off Affryk lyis.
xiiii. Howe the landys of Europe lyis.
xv. How Brettanne and Irlande lyis.
xvi. The fyrst chawngyng of the Twngis.
xvii. The fyrst matere of Poesy.
xviii. The fyrst matere of Mawmentry.
xix. A Genology discendande.

CHAP. I.

[The diwisionis of all this Buke
In to this nixt Chepture ye luke.]

In honowre of the Ordrys nyne
Off haly Angelys, the quhilk dyẅyne
Scrypture loẅys, on lyk wys
I wylle departe now this Tretis
In Nyne Bukis, and noucht ma.

And the Fyrst Buke of tha
Sall trete fra the begynnyng
Off the Warlde, quhyll Nynus kyng
Off Babylon and Assyry
Tuk wpe the lordschype halily;
That wes in to Abrahammys dayis,
As off that the story sayis.

The Secound Buke sall be fra than,
Quhill Brutus come in Mare Bretan,
The wys can the story telle,
Quhen Jugis jugyd Israelle.

The Thryde sall contynwyde be,
Quhille made of Rome wes the cité;
That wes quhen Achas Kyng
Judam hade in goẅernyng,
And the prophet Ysay
Made and prechide hys Prophecy.

Fol. 2. b.   The Ferde, tyll the Incarnatyown,
That made oure Salvatyowne ;
And Octovyane wytht honoure
Off all the warlde was Emprioure.

The Fyft, quhyll the Scottis
Put out of Scotland the Pychtis ;
That wes in to gret Charlys dayis,
As off that the Corneklis sayis.   30

The Sext, quhill that Malcolme ras,
That weddyt wytht Saynt Margret was.

The Sewynd, quhylle Alysawndyre, oure Kyng
The thryde, of hys dayis made endyng.

The Auchtande, quhyle the tothir Robert
Oure Kyng wes crownyde efterwert.

The Nynde sall contynuyde be
In hym, and hys posteryte.

CHAP. II.

[Off Angellis, now sall yhe heir
In this followand nixt Cheptere.]

SAYNT Gregor in ane Omely
Thus sayis of Angelys opynly ;   40
The kynde of angelys and of men
God made of noucht hym for tyll ken ;
And for he walde that kynde sulde be
Ay lestand in eternyte,
Tyll hys schape and hys lyklynes,

Man and angell fourmyd wes.
Off angelys ordrys thrys thre,
In tyll hys wryt rehersys he.
The name of angelys for to dewys
Is noucht of kynd bot of offys ;   50
Ane messynger sulde ane angell be
Quhen chargyde oucht to say is he.
Angelis yhe may spyritis call,
Bot angelis ar noucht thare spyritis all.
Thre Angelis we fynd wsuall
Tyttlyde be namys spirytualle.
The fyrst cald is Mychaell,
Gabryell syne, and Raphaell.
Off Angelis nature and thare state
I trowe fer bettyr than I wate,   60
And bettyr is that we all comend
Tyll Gode that we can noucht defende,
Syn na thyng is that he na may
Than folyly we sulde oucht say,
That may noucht in ws consaywyde be,
Na prowyde be auctoryte,
For-thi fra this I turne my style,
Off Mankynde for to carpe a quhylle.

CHAP. III.

[How God maid Adam and Eve his maik,
And how He for his syne tuk wraik.]

OFF Adame oure orygynale,
And all oure kynde is cummyn hale,   70
That in the felde of Damask fayre,

Off nature and off nobyll ayre,
Or in the wale of Ebron,
As sum haldis opynyon,
Lyk made to Gode and schapyne wes
In Hys schape and Hys lyklynes,
And say fourmyde at dewys
Translatyde wes in Paradys;
And thare lywand in that schape

Fol. 3. Slepand quhylle he tuk a nape,   80
Out of hys syde wes tane a ryb,
Thar of tyll [him] bathe lyke and sybe
That woman wes made that Eve we call,
For scho wes modyr of ws all.
Than thaire state wes innocent,
And all thyng bowyd tyll thair entent.
And name till bestis Adame gawe,
Swylk as yhit thai halde and hawe;
And Eve he cald thare a woman,
Syn scho wes of hys fles and bane.   90
Off matrymony the sacrymcnt
Than rase in that state innocent,
And of all thyngis at thare plesance
Thai hade large abowndance;
Quhill that thai bathe brokyn hade,
The byddyng that God thaim bade,
And myskend thare Creatoure.
Than fell thai swne fra gret honoure,
Kennand that thai nakid ware,
And of clethyng gret mystare;   100
Thai wroucht nothir lynt na wowlle
Bot levys of the tre can powle,
Quhare-of array wes made that tyde,
Thair nakyde membrys for tyll hyde;

And wes put out of Paradys,
A propyr place at all dewys,
Abowndande in all delyte,
Bathe of plesaunce, and profyte,
Off froyte, and foule, and feldis fayre,
Off arbuste, erbys, and of ayre,   110
Off buskis, bankkis, and of bewys,
Off clyfftis, craggis, and of cluys;
The tre of lyf thare-in is set,
Off that froyt quha mycht get
He sulde in lyf ay lestand be,
But seknes or mortalyte.
 This terrestre Paradys
In to the est of Asy lyis:
Quhen Adam wes wythin that quhille
Put out of that stede in exile,   120
To kepe it than, and lat nane in,
Before it set wes Cherubyn
(That may be wndyrstandyn rycht
A stwff of angelis blyth and brycht),
And a swerd as fyre all rede
Wes set thare als to kepe that stede;
Wythin that propyre place, but pere,
Thare is a welle of wattyr clere.
Out of that welle cummys fludis foure
Till moyst the erde quhar thai ryn oure;   130
Ane of thir watterys is cald Ganges,
Syne Tyger, Nyle, and Ewfrates.
Nyle wes hattyn Gyon
As Ganges fyrst wes calde Phison.
In Paradys thai ar wnkend
Bot wytht-out thai brek on ende,
At the hylle of Oskobares;

In Ynde the hewyde is of Ganges
Agayne the est the streme is gane,
Swa rynnand in the Occeane,   140
Be-syd ane hylle is cald Accland,
Off Nyle the ryware is spryngande;
Bot syne the erde it swellis in,
Quhar throucht all hyd it oysis to ryn
[It] brystys out syne at the strande
That by the Rede Se lyis strykande.
All Ethiop it rynnys a-bowt,
And throucht all Egypt rynnys out;
Departyde syne in fyffe and twa
Syndry partis rynnys swa,   150
By Alexawnder that cite
It entrys in the Mykyll Se.
Tyger syne, and Ewfrates,
Off Armeny thai tak thair res;
Agayne the sowtht thai ar rynnand
Swa to the Se thare streme strekand.

   Hard wyth mankynde than it stude
Adam worthyde to wync his fude
Off the Erde, that waryde wes,
In hys werk and his besynes,   160
And wytht his swat till ete hys brede,
Drywand hys lyf till dulefulle dede.

CHAP. IV.

**This Chapiter sall yhow tell
How Cayin hys Brodyr slew Abell.**

On Eve Adam gat sonnys twa,
Kayin and Abell callid war tha;
How that thai lywyde, and on quhat wys,
To God thai made thair sacrifice,
Abell wytht gude devotioune,
Kayin wyth indignatyoune,
The Bybyll tellys it opynly,
Thar-for I lat it nowe ga by: 170
Bot the sawmpyll is rycht fellowne,
Quha doys noucht wytht devotyoune
Hys det to God, in hys serwys,
Offerand teynd or sacrifice,
Bot makis hys excusatyone
Wyth ire and indignatyowne;
Howe may he luk tyll other end
Than Kayin dyde, bot gyve he mende,
Will and wawerand to be ay
In dowt and dwle till his end day   180
Off quham that may hym fynde of case
In hyddlys or in opyn plase,
Cowardly to tak hys dede,
Disparyde of all gud remede.

CHAP. V.

**This Chappter makkys descriptyowne
Off Caynis generatioune.**

<blockquote>

THIS Kayin to sone Enok gat,
The quhilk gat Jarede, efter that
Enoch a towne gert byggyt be,
And gart call Enoch that cite:
This Jarede gat Mawlaliale,
The quhilk that gat Matussaele: 190
Matussaele he gat Lamech;
Quha that likys of hym to spek,
He wes the fyrst fand bygamy,
Throucht lykyng lust and lychery;
Tyll hym alane wes wywys twa,
That Ade wes callyde, and Sella.
He wes the fyrste at schot in bowe,
Wyth vyre or bolt or wyth arowe.
Swa happnyd as he faylhyde lycht,
For celd had myrknyd all hys sycht,   200
A chyld bade hym he sulde draw nere,
Quhar that, he sayde, he sawe a dere;
Wytht that the takyll wp he drewe,
And wytht that schot he Kayin slewe,
That lurkand lay in tyll a buske;
Than tyll that boy he gawe a ruske,
All brayne-wode in to that stede,
He dang hym wytht hys bowe to dede.
   This Lamech Jabel gat on Ade;
He wes the fyrst at gart be made   210

</blockquote>

Fol. 4.

Tentys to be borne a-bowte,
As catell lesowyde in and oute,
Quhar hyrdys mycht in herbry be,
Nycht and day, to kepe thare fé.
He gert dissewÿr fyrst and kepe,
As yhe se now, the gayt fra schepe.
The brukyd bestys and the wayre
He gert depart fra quhyt and fayre.
The yhownge he partyde fra the awlde
And oysyde thaim to bowcht and fawlde. 220
Syne be craft and be delyte
Off mylk and wole he gat profyte.

 This Lamek gat on Ade wyth all
Ane othyr sowne wes callyde Jubal.
The story gerrys ws wndyrstande,
He wes the fyrst at musyke fande
Wyth hammerys clynkand on a stythy,
Quhar men war wyrkand in a smythy.
Jubal, quhen he herd Adam tel
In prophecy, as efter felle, 230
That fyre and flwde sulde all oure-ga
And wndo that thai mycht oure-ta;
Off swylk matyr as he hade
He gert twa pillars sune be made :
Off tylde or plastyr wes the tane
The tothir wes made of marbyll stane,
The tane to sawffe be fra the flwde,
The tother fra fyre thoucht it war wowde ;
And in tha twa he gart full tyt,
All the art of musyke wryte, 240
Swa that it mycht haldyn be
Wnfaylland in posteryte.

 Josephus sayis, in tyll his buke,

Qwha can well that story luke,
That yhit in to [the] Surry lande
The pyllare of marbyll is standand.
   This Lameke gat yhit on Sella
Twbalkayin and Noéma.
Twbalkayin delytyt haile.
Be oysyde craft to wyrk mettalle.   250
Irne and stele, lede and tyn,
To yhet, or bete, or grawe thairin.
Hys systyr than cald Noéma
Scho begowth on hand to ta
Wewyng that nevyr than before
Wes oysyd be cavale na reduore.
   Off Kayniys generatioune,
Na off thar successyowne,
Is na ma fyndyn in story,
Thar-for I lat thaime now ga by.   260
Fol. 4. b. Sum story sayis that Noeys flude
Drownyd thaim that tym that lywand stude.

CHAP. VI.

Off Sethis generatioune here
Next folowys in this Chapitere.

ADAM murnyd a hundyr yhere
Abel hys swnnys slauchter dere,
And quhen that slawchtyr wes foryhettyn
On Eve Adam Seth has gettyn:
Seth gat Enos that oysyde to call
On Gode, in till hys dedys all,
In prayer and in orysowne

And specyalle devotyown. 270
Enos gat, the buke can tell,
Caynan, that gat Malalyell;
Malaliel he Jeryt gat,
The quhilk gat Enoch efter that.
This Enoch fand, as I herd tell,
Fyrst wyth lettyrys for tyll spell,
And syne he tuk in tyll delyte
To sett togyddyr faste and wryte.
In tyll hys tyme bukys he wrate
That drownyde ware in Noeys spate. 280
Tyll God he wes in all plesand
Tharfor he is yhit quyk lywand,
Bydand the Antecrystyes come
Befor the mykyll day of dome.
Off Enok come Matussale,
Off quham Lamek that gat Noe.

Nowe the fyrst Eeld endys here
In to the quhilk ar, yher be yhere,
Sexten hundyr sexty and sewyn,
Gyff that the Hebrewys rekknes ewyn 290
The ten and sexty Clerkes wys,
As thai fynd in thare storys
Twa thowsand and twa hundyre yhere,
And four and fourty passyd ar clere
Thai oysyd to cownt in thare reknyng
Than fra the warldys begynnyng
Gyff ony letterys than thai wrate
Thar oys wes than to set thaire date;
As we now fra the byrtht of God
Reknys yherys ewyn or od, 300
Swa reknyd thai in thaire cowntyng
Than fra the Warldys begynnyng.

CHAP. VII.

This Chapitere tellis off Geawndis
Fyrst grew and sprede in mony landys.

IN TYLL this tyme at I off telle
Was Geawndys walkand fers and fell
That lyk tyll men ware in fygure,
Bot thai war largear of stature.
On quhat kyn wys and quhat manere
Thir ilk geawndis gottyn were,
Syn syndry haldys oppynyown,
I wyll mak na conclusyown.   310
Sethys swnnys, sum oysyde to say,
Luwyde Kayinys dowchtrys, stowt and gay,
And gat on thaim bodely
Thir geawndis that worthyde sa forssy;
Or syndry spyrytys on thair wys
Slepande women walde supprys
Wyth maystry, qweyntys, or wyth slycht,
That gat thir geawndis mykyll of mycht.
Bot howe that ever thai gottyn be
Geawndys name in propyrte,   320
Off the erde is halely
That Geos wyttnesys werraly.
The Grekys in thar langage all
Geos the Erde thai oysyd to call.
All thare sort that lywande stude
Drownyd war in Nocys flude.
Sum men haldys oppynnyown
That in the wale of Hebrown

Fol. 5.

Eftyr that grewe geawndis ma'
In Egypte sum men sayd alsua,   330
Geawndis grewe, and [of] that kynd
Come Enathym, and off hys strynd
Come Golyath, that Davy yhyng
Slewe wyth the stane cast of a slyng.
  Thai past and spred fra land to land,
And Brwyt in Bretayne of thaim fand
Coryne that of hys cumpany
West mast, and aucht the seyhnowry :
Off Cornwalle fyrst had grete lykyng
To cast thai carlys in werslyng.   340
Amang [thame] wes ane mykyll of mycht
Goemagog hys name wes rycht.
Ane ake wes na mare in hys hand
Than now in owrys ane hesylle wand;
He wes twelf cubytys large of hycht,
Ane half elne is the cubyt rycht.
He come wyth geawyndys hale twenty,
On Brwtus and hys cumpany,
Bot yhit Coryne that tyme was
Noucht wytht Brwtus in that plas,   350
Bot Brwtus wytht thame faucht swa fast,
Quhyll thai war wencust at the last;
Thar Goemagog wes tane
And haldyn quhyk be hym allane,
To se how that this Coryne
Walde dele wyth hym in to werslyng;
And as thai met fyrst in thare gamyn
Ilkane brassyd othir samyn
Sa fast, that frek that Coryne thrystyd
Till in hys syde thre rybbys brystyde.   360
Coryne than wyth all hys mycht

Heyly hewyde that hwlk on hycht,
And tyll a crag that wes neir by
He bare hym fast and spedily
That swayne he swakyde oure that hycht,
That on hys crown he gert hym lycht
Sa doggidly hym downe he dwyhsyde,
Till bak and bowalys all to brussyde.
   Off Geawndis wyll I na mare telle,
Thare endyng thws in Bretayne fell.   370

CHAP. VIII.

In this Chapitere rede and se
The Arke, and the Spate of Noe.

NOE wes a man rycht wys,
Perfyt and lele at all dewys.
He fand fyrst throucht hys sutylte
How wyne sulde growe and wynnyn be.
Quhen mannys thoucht wes gywyn till ill
And drawyn all fra Goddys wyll,
Fol. 5. b.   He wyst at thare walde fall a Flude
All tyll wndo that lywand stude.
To sawffe hym and hys swnnys thre,
Thair wywys foure, but ma menyhe,   380
He gert, of Goddis byddyng, mak
Ane ark in maner of ane stak,
That in owre tyme oysyde we
The schype to call it of Noe,
Thowcht on hycht it narowe wes
Wndyr rowme of mare larges.
The Hebrewys sayis the sewynten day

Off that moneth at we call May,
Sex hundyr yhere quhen he was awld,
Noe, that we off befor taulde, 390
And the sewyn rekkynde ware,
In to that schyppe all entryd are.
Off byrde and best, bathe wylde and tame,
Payr be payr, and name be name,
As he byddyng had clerly,
In tyll that schype he gart herbry.
Ane hundyr dayis and fyfty gude
The wattyris wox as thai war woude
Off wellys waveryde wawys wyde
Oure hyrne and hyrst, fra syd to syde, 400
Belyde boggys than out brystyd
And ranys rethe be-for that rystyde,
Fowrty dayis wytht forsys fell
Schot out thare schowrys, scharp and snell,
Bath felde and fyrth oure-flet that flude
And wndyde all that it oure-yhoude.
That schype wes drywyn oure hyllis hic
Tyll on the hycht of Armeney
Grownd it tuk instede off hawyn.
 Than Noe fyrst send furth the rawyn, 410
Till get wyttyng and knawlage
Gyf that the flude begowth to swage.
Bot that sendyng wes in wayne,
To schype that foule came noucht agayne;
Bot fell on caryown all gredy,
Swa saw he no mare of corby.
The dow he send furth anys or twyis,
As wyttnessyde is in sere storys,
And that broucht in hyr beke belywe
A brawnche agayne of greyne olywe, 420

Be that thai kend and wndyrstude
In part that swaygyd wes the flude.
The schype has left and land has tane,
That ilk day a yhere oure gayne
That thai yhede that schype wythtin,
Man and best, bath mare and meyn.
The rayne-bowe wyth hewys twa,
Red and wattery baytht ar tha,
And at the fyrst wes seyne wyth ey;
Owth thaim in the clowdys hey.   430
Than Noe made hys sacrifice,
Plesand to God, as man rychtvys.
Froyt and gyrs thai oysyd tyll etc
As kers, or mawe, or wyolete,
Nwt, or appyl, or akhorne;
Swylk wes the lyf thai led beforne.
Than thai tuk wpe to thaire fwde
For tyll etc fleyhs forowtyn blude;

Fol. 6.   Rostyt, sodyn, or in paste,
As thaim thoucht best and daynte mast,   440
And lyve in lykyn and in es,
Allanyrly bot Gode to ples,
At swa thaire generatyown
Mycht sprede in tyll successyown.

    It hapnyde eftyr on a day
This Noe drownkyn slepand lay,
For off the wyne he wonyd hade,
He drank swa fast that he wes glede,
And nakyde wes hys harnays hare,
Bak and buttoke bath wes bare.   450
I suppos, quha than walde seke
Amang thaim all wes noucht a breke.
Than Cam, that wes the myddyll brothyr,

Saw fyrst hym before all othir;
He lewch rycht fast and wald noucht byde
Hys fadrys membrys for tyll hyde,
Bot grynnyd and gapyde wytht hys gwmys,
And skornyd fast his fadyr lumys.
The tothir twa, quhen thai come by
And sawe thare fadyr swa-gat ly,   460
Wytht eys and honowre thai hym kepid,
And cwveryde hym quhille he had slepid.
 Quhen that Noe gat wyttyng
That Came had drywyn hym tyll heythyng,
He gawe hys maledictiowne
Till Camys generatyowne;
And Sem hys [eldast] swn sulde be
Lorde of Canaan, and he
Tyll Sem and Japhet in threllage
Sulde serve, and mak thaim bath omage.   470
In [this] prys begowth to payre
Syn Kam wes eldest nest the ayre
That he suld serve the yhowyngyr brothir,
Howe evyr it happnyd off the othire.

Fol. 6.

CHAP. IX.

This Chapiter now sall tell hale
The fowr Kynrykis principale.

SEM, Cam, and Japhet, thre,
Thir ware the swnnys of Noe.
Off thir come men of mekyll mycht,
Tyll statys growande and tyll hycht,
And generaly of all kyn gre

All kynd of men come of thir thre. 480
Off Sem that wes the eldest brothir
Presthed come befor all othir.
Sum that oysyde of hym to spek
Sayde he wes that Melchysedek.
That offryde tyll Abraham wyne and brede
Quhen the kyngys foure war dede
The quhilkys Abraham swa perswyde
Hys brothir swn quhill reskwyde.
Quha lukys the Bybille inerely
Off this may fynd a fayr story. 490
   Off Semys generatyown,
Be lyneale successyown,
Wes Jhesu Cryst of Mary borne
Tyll sawffe oure lyff that wes forlorne.
Off Came the nixt, for hys owtrage,
Come serẅytywde and foule threllage.
Off Japhet the yhongast of tha thre
Fyrst come knychtys dignite.
Thir awcht the landys halyly
Off Affryk, Ewrope, and Asy, 500
And the foure Kynrykys pryncypalle
Be thare successyowne lynealle
Wes occupyid; and Belus kyng
Made in the Est hys fyrst steryng.
And that than was halily
The kynryk callyde off Assyry,
And in the west art syne anone,
The kynryk ras of Sycyone.
Bot eftyr that to name it hade,
In Grece the lordschype of Archade. 510
Thare Agelyus fyrst wes kyng
Had it hale in goẅernyng.

In the north art of Sythy
Caspnyus had the senyhoury.
Myneus kyng in the south art,
Tuk all Egipte till hys part.
In thir foure partis severale
Thir Kynrykys pryncipale
Wndyr thir four kyngys ras
Qwhen Noeyis flud all swagide was;   520
And grew in gret mycht mony yhere,
Part of thaim syne chawngide were
In othir kynrykis severale,
As thai begowth off cas to fale.

CHAP. X.

**This Chapiter tellis how Paradise,
Ende, and othir landis lyis.**

TYLL Sem, as eldast, halily
Fell all the landis of Asy,
That fra the northt throucht est out-strekys
In tyll the sowth quhyll that it rekys:
The Erd swa delt in twa partys
Asy the tane half occupyis;   530
The tothir part than delt in twa,
Ewrope haldys and Affryca;
As men may be a roundale se
Markyd to be delt in thre.
In to the [est of] Asy lyis
That propyr plas of Paradys,
The quhilk is cerklyd wytht-out
Wytht wallys of fyre beltyde abowt,

And kepyde swa wytht Cherubyn
That lyvand man may nane get in. 540
[Cherubin is to saye, ane ost
Of Angellis that it kepis, but bost.]
Be-twene Ynde and Paradys
Desert landys mony lyis,
Wytht holmys, holtys, and wyth hyllys,
Till corne or crope that na man teyllys;
For bestys wylde, batht fers and felle,
F. 7. Is nane of lywe that thar dar duelle.
Out of ane hylle cald Caucasus
The wattyr is rynnande of Indus, 550
[And eftir that watter, as we fynd,
The kynrik is callit of Ynd].
Fra north on sowth the streme it strekys
In tyll the Rede Se quhille it rekys.
Yndys Occeane, that Se
The west marche of Ynde sulde be.
Fyrst it was calde Eivlat,
And syne the name of Ynde it gat,
For the wattyre of Yndus
Rynnys throucht it fra Cawcasus, 560
[And enteris in the Occane.]
The gret Ile lyis of Taperbanc
Wytht-in that Ile ar citeis ten
Stuffyt wytht catelle, gud, and men.
Thar twa summyrys in the yhere
And twa wyntrys ar, but were,
And all tyme that Ile is sene
Wytht gyrs growand cwynlyk grene.
  Thar lyis als wythin that se,
The ilys of Kryn and Argwe; 570
Thai twa ilys, as thai say,

Off silvyr ar habowndand ay,
And of gold in gret copy,
And flwryssys alway dayntely.
Hyllys hé off golde ar thare,
Bot gryphys gret nerhande thaim ar,
And dragownys; quharfor na man may
Cum nere thaim thar be nycht or day.
In Ynde als thai sulde be
The ile of Caspis in the Se, 580
And the hylle that lyis it by
That ilke name has propyrly.
Thar Gog and Magog, at felown wes,
Closyt ar in gret straytnes.
Quhen Alysawndyr, the mychty kyng,
By that plas mad hys passyng
Wytht hys ost, as man off were,
Thai closyde than maid hym prayere,
That for hys wyrschype thai mycht be,
Owt of that presown lowsyd fre. 590
Than he speryd and herd wele telle
That fra thare God of Israel
Thai chawngyd fawsly thare fay,
And closyd tharfor thar war thai;
He prewyde wytht werk-men than thraly
Thare in to steke thaim mare straitly.
And quhen he saw all that thai wroucht
Till hys intent yhit suffycyde it noucht,
He mad tyll God hys wrysowne,
One kneys wytht gud devotyoune, 600
That that werk he walde fulfyll
Till hys lykynyng and hys wylle.
At hys prayere than, but dowt,
All the hillys thar a-bowt,

The craggys, and the rockys all,
Crape to-gyddyre in ane walle
Befor thaim, that be na way
Wyne out of that place mycht thai,
Bot mare stratly thai war thare
Than closyde na befor thai ware ; 610
And be that myrakyll lyk it was
That God walde noucht at thai sulde pas
Out off that closure, bot yhit thai
Sall get out befor Domysdaye,
And mekyll way in warld sall wyrk
Agayne the lawe of Haly kyrke.
   Syne God of mycht inclynyd was
Thus tyll a pagane, of hys gras,
Quhat walde he for ws all set,
Gyff we tyll hym walde do oure det ; 620
Bot fra hys wyll quhen that we wryth,
Quhy sulde he hys gracys kyth,
Till ws, in oure necessyte,
Oure in til bale owre bute sulde be,
Na ware hys mercy gret exced
Owre gylt and all oure wrangwys dede ;
And swa, for oure gret wrechydnes,
We mon declyne hys rychtwysnes,
And on his mekyll mercy call
In oure defawt quhen that we fall. 630
For mercy and rychtwys jugement
Ar in hym bath, but argument.
For-thi, we sulde have dowt and awe
To leve hys byddyng and hys lawe,
And yheld ws fekyll fals in fay,
Wrythand in tyl werk alway,
For dowt that or we ws repent

We mon appere in jugement,
And to cry mercy, is toe late
The wayne, than standand at the yhat. 640
    In Ynde are landys fourty and fowre
Quha that sekys it all at-oure;
And thar ar folk that callyde was
Garnyanys and Orastas,
Cotras thar woddys fayr,
Rekys on hycht wp tyll the ayre;
In tyll the hyllis of that land
The pigmaveis ar duelland
That has bot cubytys twa of hycht.
And oft wyll wytht the crannys fycht. 650
Quhen thai ar thre yhere awlde, but let,
Thair barnys all thai bere and get;
And aucht yhere thai ma noucht weylde,
Thair wapnys for febyll heylde;
Thare pepyre growys that off hewe
Is qwhyt quhill it is growand newe.
Bot for eddrys that ar thare,
Off wenyme and stangys sare,
Thar is na man that may it wyne
Wyth a fyre quhill thai it bryne, 660
Swa wytht that rek thai oys to make
Owt off qwhyt hew this pepyr blak.
Thare ar folk sex elne of hycht,
Makrobitys thai ar callyde rycht;
Thai oysis oft for tyll assayhle
The gryphys in fycht and hard batyhle.
To lyownys lyk ar thare body,
And naylys scharpe hawys certanly;
And weyngys als thai hawe, but were,
As yhe se ernys hawand here. 670

Agroit thare and Bragmanyis
Leddys thare lyff on ferly wys;
For in a fyre thai wyll thaim bryn,
Thynkand a bettyr lyff to wyn.
Thar sum wyll thare eldrys sla,
Quhen eelde thaim hapnys tyl our-ta,
And sethys the fleyhs, and gerrys the kyn
Gaddryde be, bath mare and myn,
And ettys syne halily.
A the fleyhs of that body, 680
And quha that forsakys till et
Off that fleyhs, he sall, but let,
Be forsakyn off kyne
Newyr to [be] reknyde in.
Othyr folk thare oysis tyll et
All rawe fysch that thai ma get,
And drynkys bot wattyr off the se,
Quhethyr it salt or byttyr be.
Thare ar monstrys mony sere,
Off the quhilk are nane sene here, 690
That nane can wyt in propyrte
Quhethyr thai man or best sulde be.
Sum owth thair fete thare solys hawys,
And on ilke fut aucht tayis;
And sum wytht-in thai landys thare
Lyk off hewyd tyll hwndys are,
Wyth naylys scharpe, and thai ar cled
In bestys skynnys, bak and bed,
Thaire wocys, quhen thai ar spekand,
Ar lyk tyll doggys ay berkand: 700
Sum mudrys in that land alsua
Berys bot anys, and all tha
Borne thai ar qwhyt of canys,

Bathe of heẅyd and berde at anys;
Ande in thare eelde agayne thare hare
Worthys blak in all tyme thare;
And of eelde yhit mony yhere
Excedys ws that lyẅys here:
Thare sum berys of yherys fyẅe,
And passys noucht aucht yhere of lyve.   710
Thar ar folk callyde Armaspy,
And havys bot ane ey certanly:
Thar sum folk bot a fute has,
And yhit for sped the dere our-tays;
And quhen thai ly on erde to slepe,
Fra swne and weddyr thaim to kepe,
Than that a fwt wpe thai streke
That it fra thaim the weddyr brek.

    Wytht-in Ynde in tyll sum stede
Thare lyẅys a folk wytht-owtyn hede,   720
And in the fawt of thare foret,

Fol. 8. b. Twa eyne ar in thare schuldrys set;
And in thare brestys ar holys twa,
In-stede of nes and mouth ar tha.

    Besyde the wattyr of Gangis,
A pupyll thai say lyẅand is
But othir met than of ayre:
Savorand off ane appyll fayre,
And fele thai ony stynk wytht-out
Thai dé tharof, wytht-owtyn dout;   730
And quhen thai traẅaill owcht in fere
Thai wyll wyth thame that appyll bere
To be thare mete in thare traẅaylle,
In fawt of fude at thai noucht fayle.
Thare serpentys ar sa gret, but were,
At thai wyll suelly wpe a dere,

And wyll swym all oure that sé
That Yndys Occeane callid we.
In to that land thare is alsua
A best thai call Cenocrata ; 740
That best is lyk of body made
Tyll ane as, bot he is brade
Off brest before, and in fassown
Off lym is lyk tyl a lyown,
Tyll ane hors lyk ar his fet,
And has ane horne in his foret,
Hys mowyth of kynd is ryẅyn wyde
Fra ere tyll ere on ilk syde ;
A gret bane, thai say, has he,
In that stede quhar hys teth sulde be, 750
And oysis mekyll in hys bere
Syk ẅoycys as a man dois here.
  In to that land thare sulde be
Ane othir best callyde Gale,
That is lyk all tyll ane hors,
In tyll the fassown of ane cors,
And has a gret tusk as a bare,
And taylyd as elephawntys are ;
And in hys heẅyde has hornys twa,
Ane half elne lang, ilkane of tha ; 760
And fyrst he oysis wytht the tane
Tyl hald wp fychtyng and bargane ;
The tothir on hys bak he strekys
Qwhille he that blwntys, or he brekys,
And syne it castys on his bak,
Than wyll he wyth the tothir mak
Hys bargane furth, and wyth tha twa
Hys fycht he oysis for till ma :
He is a best of mekyll pytht,

And wgly blak he is thare wytht.   770
  In that land thare is alsua
A best thai call Manticora,
Off wysage thai say lyk is he
Till a man in all degre,
Bot the teth that ar wytht-in
Hys hewyde ar set in chestyr thryn;
Off cors he lyk is a lyown,
Hys taylle is lyk a scorpyown;
Hys eyne ar yholowe, and [of] hewe
Is blwde rede, and elyke ay newe;   780
Off woyce he lyk is and of bere
As yhe here eddrys quhysstyll here;
And off spede he is mare lycht
Than ony foule is apon flycht.
He oysys mekyll for tyll ete
All mannys fleyhs that he may get.
  Thare owsyn ar wytht hornys thre
Wytht fete as here on hors yhe se.
Ane othir best thare is wytht all
That Monoceros [forsuythe] thai call,   790
He is in fassown of hys cors
Lyk in all thyng till ane hors;
Bot swylk ane hewyde thai say has he
As apon ane hert yhe se;
As elephawntys bath fete and tays,
And as a swyne a tayle he hawys;
Wytht a horne, and that is set
Ewyne in the myddys of his foret,
Armyt thare wytht [he is] als wele
As men are in to yrne or stele;   800
Off leynth foure fwte hale is that horne,
And it is wondyr scharpe beforne;

F. 9.

Thai bestys wondyr fellown ar,
And oysis wyth gret rerde to rare,
And wytht that horne he wyrkys payne
Till all that standys hym agayne.
He may be tane and slane wyth slycht,
Bot nevyr dawntyde be at rycht.

In to the wattyre of Gangys
Thai say that mony elys is 810
That ar thretty fwt of leynth;
And wormys als of hwge streynth,
Lyk to partanys her ar thai,
And on thare cors has armys twai,
And sex elne are hale of leynth.
The elephawntys thai tak wytht streynth,
And oft gerrys thame drownyd be
In wattyris depe, or in the sé.

In to the Yndys Se, thai say,
Snaylys gret ar fundyn ay, 820
And men thare makys of thare schelle
Lugyngys gret for tyll in duelle.
Thare adamant, thai say, is gude
That nevyr ma brek but bukkys blwde.
In Ynd ar othir ferlyis sere,
That I lewe for to rekyn here,
For tha ar, tyll yhowre knawlage,
Translatyde welle in oure langage.

CHAP. XI.

In this Chapitere on qwhat wys
Yhe sal se that sere Landis liis.

FRA Ynd to Tygyre, by wattyrys twa,
Lyis a land calde Parthia: 830
In it ar cuntreis thryis tene
And thre attoure stuffyt wytht men,
Off men that come of Sythya,
That lande was callyt Parthia.
Nest that land wes calde Parthy
The land lyis of Aracusy.
Off Aracus, ane hyll of hycht,
That land that name has gottyn rycht.
Nest it lyis halily
The lordschype gret off Assyry: 840
Off Semys swn that Assur was
Callyde that land that name now has.
 Nest lyis the landys of Medy,
Off Medus kyng cald rychtwysly.
Syne lyis the lordschype hale of Pers;
Quhare Perseus kyng, I herde rehers,
Gert fyrst a cyté byggyde be,
And syne that lordschype Pers calde he.
Off wertu thar ar stanys twa,
Pyr and Siles calde ar tha: 850
Pir is of wertu for to bryn
The hand that it is closyd in;
Syles waxis wytht the Mowne
And wanys agayne as dois the Lune.

In Pers wes fyrst nygromancy,
And wyche-craft, wytht sorcery;
Throuch Cam fwndyn that syn was
Be name callid Zorastas,
Kyng off Baktryanys, that Nynus slwe,
To state of lordschype quhen he drewe.   860
    Wytht hyllys hey thir landys ar,
And craggys strayt, her and thare,
Bot profytabyll to man and best,
Ewyn as a lyne fra est to west,
Betwene the gret rywarys twa,
Ynd and Tygyr calde ar tha.
Fra Tygyr syne till Eufrates,
Mesopotamya fwndyt wes,
For it wes set betwene tha twa,
It hat Mesopotamya: 870
Thar lyis the towne of Nynyve,
That Nynus kyng gert bygyt be,
Quha throwcht it passis the nerrast ways
Off leynth he fyndys thre jowrnays.
Thar nest lyis that regyown
The kynrik calde off Babylown,
Quhar that a Towre of huge hycht
Wes bygyt fyrst throwcht Nembrot wycht;
That towre Babell callyde he.
Thare lyis the land off Caldé,   880
Quhar fyrst wes fwndyn astronomy.
Nest lyis the land off Araby,
And that, that we Saba call:
In it the cens is gottyn all.
Thar is the mownt of Synay,
The hill of Oreb ner thar-by.
Moyses thare the Lawe wrate,

Quhare wytht was rewlyt the Jowys state.
Thare lyis the towne off Madyane,
F. 10. Quhar Getro, prest, wes fyrst owrman; 890
Thar ar als thir Moabytys,
Idumeys, and Ammonytys,
And Saracenys of natyowyns sere,
That ma noucht all be rekynd here.
    Fra the wattyr off Ewfrates
The land off Surry lyis, but les,
Furtht strekand to the Grekes Se
Thar lyis off Damask the cyté.
Thar lyis als Antychia
That qwhylon wes calde Reblata, 900
Commagene, and syne Phenys,
Thar Tyre and Sydon alsua lyis;
Thar is that hill thai call Lybane,
And off it cummys the flwm Jordane;
Thare is the town callyd Palestyn,
That Ascalon wes callyd syne;
Thar is the kynryk of Jude,
And all the land off Canane,
Jherusalem and Samary;
All thir ar lyand in Surry, 910
And all the land of Galyle,
Wyth Nazareth, that fayre cyté;
Quhar Gabriell, that Angell lycht,
Sayd to [the] madyn, fayr and brycht,
HAYLE, FULL OF GRACE! AND GOD WYTH THE!
IN ALL WOMEN THOWE BLYSSYD BE.
    By standys a hill is calde Tabor,
Ner that wes Sodom and Gomor,
And cyteis ma that brynt for syn
And fylth of thaim that duelt thare in: 920

Thare now is bot a Dede Se,
Wytht-owt ony commodyte;
And in that Se, for-owtyn dowt,
The watterys, that cummys rynnand owt
Off the flwme Jordane, tays entre
Qwhat wyis sa ever thai rynnand be.
Thar ar mony Saracenys,
Ysmalytys, and Agarenys,
And [thai] that ware cald Rabateys,
And dywërs othir in thare greys, 930
Off Natyownys and off ceteys sere,
That I leve now to rekny here.

Thir landys that thus reknyd ware
Fra the est ewÿn lyand are,
All strekyd to the Grekys Se,
Land be land in to thair degre;
And twelf sere Natyownys on thair wys
Oysand thair lawys, and thair frawnchys.

CHAP. XII.

𝔑ext schall yhe wyt on qwhat kyn wiis
Egipe and sere Landis liis.

A GAYNE the sowtht to thir ar knyt
All Egyp hale, as sayis the wryt. 940
Be est it lyis the Rede Se.
The west marche sulde in Lyby be,
Be north the hill of Cawcasus:
Egipt lyis all marchyde thus,
Wytht syndry Natyownys twenty and foure
Quha passys Egipt all at-owre,

Fol. 10. b.

And mony a symly cyté fayre,
Wytht towre, and stepe, and hewyn stayre.
Fyrst it callyd was Ewxya,
Off Latyne, Bona Copia,   950
Gud Plenté, that is to say;
The brodyre syne off Schyr Danay,
Egystus kyng, off ryell fame,
Gert that land Egipt have till name.
In it is all kyn habowndans
That gaynand is tyll mannys substans,
Off wyne, off wax, off oyle, and qwhete;
Off byrde, and best, batht small and gret,
Off fysch in flwde, and froyte off tre,
Thare is habowndance and plente; 960
Sa clere and lycht thare is the day
That na kyn clowde puttys lycht a-waye;
Thare ryvarys ragys noucht for rayne
Na mowÿs noucht wytht mycht na mayne,
Off nakyn stormys at may fall;
The wattyr off Nyle owre-fletys it all
Wytht mowÿr spryng, fore-owtyn spate,
Quhen Egypte nedys to be wate.
  The land off Tebys in it lyis,
And off it lord was Saynt Morys,   970
Bot Gadmws, the swne off Agenor,
Made a cyté thare beffor.
Nest Tebys lyis wyldyrnes
Quhar mony mownkys quhylwm wes.
Thar Cambyses, a kyng of mycht,
That Egypt wane throucht fors off fycht,
Made in Egypt a cyté,
And Babylon it callyd he.
Syn Alysawndyr the conqweroure

Made Alysawndyr, off gret honowre.   980
  Be northt thir landys reknyd thus
Standys the hill off Cawcasus,
On est half fra the Caspys Se
Swa rysand in tyll summyte
Northt on tyll Ewrope merchande nere,
Quhare Amazonys duelland were.
Thai war wemen wyld and wycht,
And oysyd all armyt for tyll fycht,
And in all pres war sterne and stowt,
To fycht wytht men thai had na dowt.   990
Wytht thame wes Natyownys duelland sere

F. 11. That spedys noucht to be reknyd here
Off Kolcos, and off Sarvya,
Massagetys, and othir ma.
In to that est thar is ane hyll
Seres that name [is] gewyn tyll,
Syne swa wes callyd that cuntré,
Off clathys off silk thare is plente.
The land off Babeta lyis thare by,
And till it marchys Hyrkany;   1000
Thare fowlys ar swa fayre and brycht,
Thare feddrys ar schynand all the nycht.
  Nest marchand lyis Sythia,
Till it a land cald Hunya,
Wytht Natyownys syndry fourty and foure,
Quha sekys all thai landys oure.
Thare ar alsua hillys hey
That cald ar Yperborey.
Syne is a land cald Albany,
That qwhyt betakynnys propirly;   1010
For the folk duelland thare in
Ar qwhyt of hare, batht cheke and chyn.

Nest lyis the land off Armeny,
Wytht Ararat, that hill sa hey,
Quhare Noeys schype on grownde stwde,
Quhen all swagyt wes the flwde.
  Nest lyis a land cald Ybery,
Wytht it marchys Capadocy;
Wytht out stalown the merys thar
Off the wynde consayvand are.   1020
Bot thai hors or yherys thre
Hapnys noucht to lyvand be;
For this is ferly for to here,
A clerk that tretys off this matere
Sayis, thare is in to that land
A wattyre gret, on hewyd rynnand
Depe and reche, bot noucht full wyde,
Wytht bankys hey on evryilk syd;
On the ta syde off that flwde,
The stede hors gayis in pastur gude;   1030
On the tothir half, day and nycht,
The merys ar wyth in thare sycht,
Bot it ma fall be na kyn way
That togyddyr met ma thai;
Swa waycht and wod than ar thai hors
That as be-huwys apon fors,
Fra tha capylis sudanly
The kynd ethchapys habowndanly
That swa stark is off flaweoure
That [it] raykys the revar our;   1040
And in thai merys entre tais,
That baggyd gret wytht foyle thaim mais,
And castyn syne ar qwyk gangand
Bot thai fayhle to be lang lestand.
  Syn Lytyll Asy lyis, but dowt,

Nere beltyde wytht the Se abowt.
Thare Epheson the fayre cyté
Amazonys gert byggyt be.
Now men oysis it to calle
Hawtelog in landys all.   1050
Saynt Jhon the ewangelyst thare lyis,
That plesyd tyll God in hys serẅys.
The fyrst land of Les Asia
Is calde the Mare Frygya.
Fyrst Beryke and syne Mygdony,
Bytynya, and syne the Mar Frygy.
   Thare is a cyté off gret fame
That Nycea has to name,
In it a Seyhne solempne wes sene,
Thre hundyre byschapys and awchtene;   1060
Before Sylvestere the haly Pape,
Revestyde weylle in albe and cape,
Thai exponyt [than] clerly
The trewtht that Crystynmen lyẅys by.
   There is a cyté calde Smyrna,
And nest it lyis Galachia.
Syne lyis the landys off Turky,
That fyrst wes callyd the Les Frygy;
Schyr Dardanus gert eftyr call
Dardanya that lordschype all;   1070
Syne Troyws kyng, off gret powste,
Gert reale Troye byggyt be,
Abowt ane hyll wytht in the town
Ylyon calde, off gret renown.
Nest tha landys lyis by
Lykaon and Hykary:
Thare rynnys a ryvare calde Hermes,
That famows is off gret ryches.

For in the sande besyd that flwde
Off fyne golde thare is pleute gude.   1080
Nest lyis the landys off Lydys hale,
Tyatyra, be down and dale,
That is off Lydys a cyté,
And chymys off that lande sulde be.
Nest it lyis Ysawrya,
Off wynde or ayre it cald is swa,
For hale and pwre thare is the ayre,
It hat Ysawrya sa fayre.
Nest it lyis Sylycya,
Thare is ane hill calde Amana,   1090
That sum oysis to call Tawrus.
Nest lyis a cyte calde Tarsus;
Thare Paule the Apostyle prechyde
Tyll Crystyne trewth, quhen he men techyd.
Nest lyis a land cald Lycya,
Syne Sydy, and Pamphylia;
Syne Polys, that large regyown,
Wytht mony a syndry Natyowne
Lywand wpone syndry wyis,

F. 12.   Wytht thaire lawys, and thaire frawnchys.   1100
Thare Ovyde, and Saynt Clement syne,
Ware exylyde to be dede in pyne.
  Now hawe yhe herde me lychtly
Ourehale the landys off Asy,
That tylle Sem and hys lynage
Grewe, and fell in herytage,
And it the half is off the thre
That partys off the Erde sulde be.
Fra the sowth it bakwarde strekys
In tyll the northt qwhill that it rekys   1110
The northt art, as I fynde in wryte

On [the] rycht half is the west off it,
The left halff levys at Affrica,
And the west at Ewropa,
And is beltyde nere abowt
Off thre sydys wyth the Se wytht-owt.

CHAP. XIII.

En this next Chapitere folouande
Es tauld how Affrike is lyande.

OFF Abrahammys posteryte
Affer, thai say, sulde cummyn be.
He wes a man off reale fame,
Off hym all Affryk has the name,   1120
That thryde part off the Erde sulde be
Quhen all the lawe is delt in thre,
And as the land off Affryk lyis,
The sowth art hale it occupyis.
The wattyre [of] Ynde, as sayis the wryt,
On est half is the marche off it.
And at the west off it sulde be
The strayt off Marrok in the Se,
And the cyté off Gades,
The pyllarys off Ercules,   1130
Wytht-in ane yle, in to the Se,
Wes set, and may wel knawin be.
Gades nowe, that cyté fyne,
Is calde the Sept in Balmaryne.
A gret land is cald Lyby
Lyis in tyll Affryk halyly.
Pentapolys nest is syne,

For fywe cyteis thar are fyne.
Trypyll syne off cyteis thre
Nest hande that sulde lyand be;   1140
And syne the kynryke off Cartage
That Dydo awcht off herytage:
The wallys of it in brede abowt
Off awchtene cubytys ware bwt dowt.
Syne the land off Getwly,
Nest it is lyand Nwmydy,
Wytht Yppon that cyté fyne,
Off it wes byschape Saynt Awstyne.
Nest lyis a land calde Mawrytane,

F. 12. b.   Nest Cesare, and syne Syngytane: 1150
Towart the sowth is lyand syne
Ethyope; in it a cyté fyne
Off Saba, and off that cyté
Wes that Qweyne that come to se
Salamon in to hys dayis,
As the Buk off Kyngys sayis.

   Ethiope lyis in to the est.
The tothir Ethyope in to the west;
Thar is a welle off wattyre clere,
Bot thare is nane dar necht it nere,   1160
All the nycht it is sa hat,
Syne turnys it in ane othire state,
And sa cawlde is on the day
That man na best it drynk na may
Off Ethyope; and by it nere,
Throwcht sped off fwte, men tayis the dere.
Trogedytys thai oys to call
That folk in thare langage all.
By-yhonde all Ethiope, but les,
Lyis mekyll land in wyldernes,   1170

Quhar na man dare repayre na duelle
For het off swn, and eddrys felle;
As [in] a caldrown thar, thai say,
For het of sown the Se wyll play.
  Now hawe I tawlde yhowe schortly
The landys off Affryk as thai lay,
That tyll Cam and his lynage
Grewe and fell in herytage.
Tyll Ewrope now I turne my stylle,
And thare off wyll I spek a qwhille.   1180

CHAP. XIV.

𝕿his next 𝕮hapitere folowande
𝕾all tell yhow how 𝕰wrope is lyande.

THE landys that in Ewrope lyis
The northt art all occupyis.
In to the north off Ewrope is
A ryver that hat Tanays,
Quhare that thar standys hillys he
That hat the mowyntys [of] Ryphey,
Fra the wattyre off Tanayis
Sowth on to Danoy strekyd is
A land cald Nedyre Sythya,
Ovyr Sythy lyis in Asya,   1190
And tyll it [is] marchand nere
Set thai ly in partys sere,
For-thi sum haldys that bath tha
Sulde be bot a Sythya.
In it is lyand halyly
Lectow land and Albany,

Get-land and Dacya,
Thir lyis in the Nedyre Sythia.
　Fra [the] wattyre off Danoy
Tyll Alpes, that ar hyllys hey　　　　　1200
Departand Ytaly fra Frawns,
Be marchis, merys, and distawns,
Lyis Duche-land all halyly,

F. 13.　That cald wes Owyr Germany.
Germany in propyrte
Burjownyng may callyde be;
For thare men in gret multitude
Sa growys off fowrme and fasown gud;
Quhare-for men oyside propyrly
That land to call all Germany.　　　　1210
Almayne men oysyd it to calle,
Swawyne in it is lyand alle,
West on wytht the wattyr off Ryne;
On north half it is rynnand syne
A wattyr that is callyd Alvews.
In Almane spryngys Danwbyus,
That we oys to call Danoy,
Wytht wattrys ekyd hale sexty;
Bot it is rynnand to and fra
Deviddit in partys fyff and twa;　　　1220
At Powns it entrys in the se
Off Asy; that is ane cowntre.
In Almayne is Bawayr and Respoyne,
Est-Frank, Twryng, and Saxoyne:
Syne Nedyre Germany on-ane
Strekys north in the occeane:
　In that Nethir Germany.
All Northway lyis halily,
And sum men sayis Denmark alsua,

And sum men sayis in Sythia. 1230
Fra Danoy that gret ryvere
And all abowt it lyis nere
A land that calde is Messya;
For plenté gret, men callis it swa,
Off corne that thare is habowndand;
It lyis est on ay strekand,
Marchyd wyth the Mekyll Se.
Off Boemy, the gret cuntré,
It marchys nere wyth Pannony,
That lyis nere wpon Wngary. 1240
Syne lyis a land callyd Tracya,
Tyras it awcht, and cald it swa;
In it rynnys that ryver
That calde in awlde tyme wes Hyvere;
In it alsua is that cyté
That Constantynopylle now calle we.
The lande off Setym halyly,
That Grece is cald now comownly,
Fra the Mere Medyterrane
Lyis sowth on to the occeane 1250
That is in the Mekyll Se wyth-out,
Beltand all the erde abowt;
Swa all the Erde may wele be
Calde ane Ile wytht-in the Se.

In Grece lyis Dalmatia,
Epyr, and Kapuya,
Melos land, and Ellady,
Attyke, Athenys, and Boecy.
Cadmus the swn off Agenor,
That Tebyk in Asy made before, 1260
That Boecy gert byggyt be,
And Tebys in Grece it callyd he.

The men off Tebys in Asy
Ar calde in Latyne Tebey.
Tebany thai oys to call
F. 13 b. In to Grece the Tebys all.
In Grece is Pelops and Tessaly,
And the land off Macedony,
Olympws als, the hill off hycht
That passys the clowdys eẅyn wp rycht　　　1270
Tessalonyke, and Akay,
Coryntws syne, and Arkady
That calde beforne wes Sycyon,
A stane is thare calde Albeston
That may off na wys slokyd be
Fra anys in fyre men may it se.
Syne lyis Ovyr Pannony,
Tyll Appennyne the hillis hey,
On north half rynnys that ryvere
That cald quhylum wes Hystere,　　　1280
Now men oysis for to call,
Danoy that ryver all.
　　Men oysyt to call Ytaly.
Mekyll Grece all halyly;
It rysis at the Alpis he
And haldys on to the Mekyll Se;
It namys chawngyd has syndry
Bot yhit it cald is Ytaly.
Thare Romwlus gert Rome be made,
That fassown of a lyown hade;　　　1290
In takyn at it sulde soverane be
Off all landys; as yhe se
The lyown havand seyhnowry
Off all bestys hym lyvand by;
For in tyll awlde tyme men that made

Cyteis ay in custwme hade
All lyk to bestys thaim to ma;
And this Rome wes ane off tha
That wes made in tyll fassown,
As I sayd, lyk tyll a lyown.   1300
Brwndys lyk ane hart wes made,
And Cartage als the fassown hade
Off ane ox, and Troy wes
Made as ane hors in lyklynes.
Thir townys all the fassown had
Off thir bestys, and wes made
Lyk tyll thame in all kyn gre,
As the makarys had daynte
Off thai bestys and delyt
Be fret, or oys, or be profyt.   1310
    Nere Ytaly lyis Tuskayne;
Syne lyis a land is calde Chawmpayne,
And the lande off Poyhle thare by,
Syne all the landys off Lumbardy,
Wytht mony fayre and gret cyteis
Abowndand all in tyll rycheys.
At tha Alpys thai say syne
The hevyde is off the wattyr off Ryne.
Fra thine thai [say] swlde lyand be
Sowth on strekand to the Se   1320
The kynryk off Frawns tyll Occeane,
A se betwene it and Bretane,
Be west it Lyowns apon Rone,
Be sowth it lyand is Narbone,
Wytht Arle thare-in, a fayre cyté,
And nere that thai [say] sulde be,
In to the west all Eqwytane,
That we oys nowe to call Gyan:

That land thai say is lyande fayre
Ner strekand by the wattyr off Layre. 1330
Syne lyand is the land off Spayne;
A se betwene it and Bretayne
Departys bathe thai landys thare,
As severaly thai lyand are.

CHAP. XV.

How bathe Brettane and Erlande Wyth Ewrope is liggande.

BLESSYDE Bretayne beelde sulde be
Off all the Ilys in the Se,
Quhare flowrys are fele on feldys fayre,
Hale off hewe, haylsum off ayre.
Off all corne thare is copy gret,
Pese, and atys, bere, and qwhet: 1340
Bath froyt on tre, and fysche in flwde;
And tyll all catale pasture gwde.
Solynus [sayis], in Bretanny
Sum steddys growys sa habowndanly
Off gyrs, that sum tym, bot thair fe
Fra fwlth off mete refrenyht be,
Thair fwde sall turne thame to peryle,
To rot, or bryst, or dey sum quhyle.
Thare wylde in wode has welth at wylle;
Thare hyrdys hydys holme and hille; 1350
Thare bewys bowys all for byrtht,
Bathe merle and maweys mellys off myrtht;
Thare huntyng is at allkyne dere,
And richt gud hawlkyn on rywere;

Off fysche thaire is habowndance
And nedfulle thyng to mannys substance.
　On Est half it lyis Germany,
And all Denmark halyly;
And West half Bretane is lyand
All hale the landys off Irland.　　　　　　　1360
　Fyffe wrakys syndry has oure-tayne
Off [Goddis] lykyng this Bretayne;
Quhen Peychtys warrayd it stoutly,
And wan off it a gret party;
Syne the Romanys trybute gate
Off Bretayne; and syne eftyr that
The Saxonys off Ingland hale
Wan it, and hade the governale;
Syne thai off Denmark warrayd fast,
Bot yhit thai tynt it at the last;　　　　　　1370
The Normawndys eftyr wan Ingland,
And thare ar lordys yhit ryngnand.
　Off Langagis in Bretayne sere
I fynd that sum tym fyff thare were:
Off Brettys fyrst, and Inglis syne,
Peycht, and Scot, and syne Latyne.
Bot, off [the] Peychtys, is ferly,
That ar wndone sa halyly,
That nowthir remanande ar langage,
Na [yit] successyown off lynage;　　　　　　1380
Swa off thare antyqwyte
Is lyk bot fabyll for to be.
　Be west Bretane' is lyand
All the landys off Irlande:
That is ane land off nobyl ayre,
Off fyrth, and felde, and flowrys fayre:
Thare nakyn best off wenym may

Lywe or lest atoure a day;
As ask, or eddyre, tade, or pade,
Suppos that thai be thiddyr hade. 1390
 Be northt Brettane sulde lyand be
The Owt Ylys in the Se.
Off thame ar thre pryncipale,
Suppos thare be ma in the hale:
Orknay certis ane sulde be;
The Isle off Man syne in the Se,
Betwene Irland and Bretany;
Is Wycht anens Normawndy.
Yhit thretty ylys in that Se,
Wytht-owt thir, ma welle reknyde be. 1400
And in that Se thare is an Ile,
That in tyll awlde tyme cald wes Tyle
Thare sex moneth off the yhere,
That we halde for summyre here,
Thare for-owtyn nycht is day;
The sex moneth off wyntyre ay
Wytht-in that yle is ythand nycht,
Wytht-owtyn ony dayis lycht.
Be north tha may nane erde be
Fwndyn, bot a mekyll Se. 1410
 All thir landys, as thai ly
I have ourhalyd lychtly.
Quhat I have mysdone in my spelle
Ymago Mundi kane wele telle.
 Bot all Ewrope in herytage
Tyll Japhet fell, and hys lynage:
He wes the yhoungast off the thre
Swnnys gottyn throwch Noe;
The eldest swnne off this Japhet
Wes Gomere, that gat Rygact: 1420

This Rygaet eftyre that
Gat Ysrawe, that Ysrawe gat:
Syne this Ysrawe gat Jara,
That fadyre wes syne off Ara:
Off this Ara come Doyt:
And his swne calde wes Artoyt:
Off Abywr syne eftyr that
Come Otoyr, that Mayr gat:
Off hym come Reyne, that gat Boe,
The quhilk wes fadyr tyll Toe: 1430
Agnoym wes syne fadyr
Tyll ane [swn] wes calde Etoyr:
Off Etoyr come eftyre that
Lamyne, that Cogyne-Glymyne gat:
Syne Fynyas-Farset in that qwylle
Gat a swn, wes calde Nevyle:
This ilke Nevylle eftyre that

F. 15.   To swn Gedyll-Glays gat,
That hade weddyt Scota yhyng,
Pharaoys dowchtyr of Egypt kyng.   1440

CHAP. XVI.

*In this next Chapitere yhe sall here
How fyrst the Tongis changide were.*

CAM, the myddyl off the thre
Swnnys gottyne off Noe,
Had a swn callyde Cws,
That gat Nembrot, and he Belus.
This Nembrot stalwart wes of pytht
And wayth man he wes thare wyth;

He wes the fyrst that yharnyde tyll have
Seyhnowry oure all the laẅe
That lyẅand wes in lande hym by.
Off hys cownsale halyly   1450
Babelle, that towre, biggyd was,
That off hycht hade foure thowsand pas,
In to the felde off Sennaare,
Quhare that mony gadryde ware
On set purpos to wyn thaim name
And hey thaire prys, thaire state, thaire fame,
Thai thoucht a cyté for to ma,
A Toure wythin off hycht alsua,
To clym wpe to the ayre quhen thai
Swylk maysterys lykyd till assay.   1460
This purpos thai put in tyll deyde,
And wes wyrkand wytht gud speyd;
Swa it happnyd, at the last,
As thai wroucht and travelyde fast,
Thare speke chawngyd sudanly,
And ilkane spak swa syndyrly
That nane cowth othyr wndyrstande,
As he wes on hym than blabrande.
Comestor sayis in this chawngyng
God made na wrocht, na wnkouth thyng,   1470
Tha ilke ẅoycys sykyrly.
Thai had before all generaly
Remaynyde styll wytht-owtyn lesyng,
Suppos thai ẅoycis [made] chawngyng
A worde is newe in fourmys sere
Ma than I kan reknyn here;
Qwhare before wes oysid nane
Bot Hebrew langage, it allane.
Thai cessyde than off thare byggyng,

For thai mycht bryng tyll nane endyng 1480
Thare purpos, na thare fyrst intent,
Thai had sa fers impedyment,
Qwhare-off ilkane hade ferly
Thai spak to-gyddyre sa wnkowthly,
That nane ane othir wndyrstude,
All wyll off wane fra thine thai yhwde,
Dyvysyde in to landys sere;
All thus the langagys chawngyt were.

CHAP. XVII.

𝔗𝔥𝔢 𝔣𝔶𝔯𝔰𝔱 𝔪𝔞𝔱𝔢𝔯𝔢 𝔬𝔣𝔣 𝔓𝔬𝔢𝔠𝔶
𝔗𝔥𝔞𝔱 𝔦𝔰 𝔟𝔬𝔱 𝔣𝔢𝔶𝔥𝔢𝔦𝔫𝔢 𝔭𝔯𝔬𝔭𝔦𝔯𝔩𝔶.

F. 15. b.   AWTORYS sere, in thare storys,
Oppynnyownys haldys on syndry wys 1490
Off this Nembrot, the swn off Cus;
Frere Martyne cald hym Saturnus,
Pullux swn, sum sayd, he wes,
Sum feyhneyd he wes fadyrles,
And nane sowerane our hym hade,
And all the warlde off golde he made.
The poetys calde hym Creatowre
Off all that thai dyde tyll honowre,
As Pluto, Jupyter, and Bachus,
Neptwne, Mars, and Eolus, 1500
Off batylle, wyne, wynd, and se,
Thai feyhne that thir sulde goddys be;
Yhit thir poetys feyhnys mare
Off this Saturne we spake off are
That fra he wyst be werde that he

Throwcht hys swn sulde geldyt be
He bad hys wyffe rycht straytly
Quhat byrth scho bare off hyr body
Befor hym scho sulde it set,
For that, he sayde, sulde be hys met,　　　　1510
Swa on hys barnys he sulde be wrokyn,
That that werde sulde all be brokyn.
Than Pluto fyrst hyr happnyt to bere,
And off hym, quhen scho wes lychtere,
Scho gert send hym hys fadyr to,
To se off hym quhat he walde do.
Than Satwrne dawe hym in yerde,
Swa fayhlyd in tyll hym the werde;
Thar-for hym god off erde or helle
Poetys callys in thare spelle.　　　　1520
Off Neptwne nest scho wes lychtare
And scho hym tyll hys fadyre bare,
And he hym swaykyde in the se,
Thar-off thai feyhne that god is he.
Fra scho herde this felny dwne.
Tyll Pluto fyrst, and syne Neptwne,
Scho let tyll hym be browcht no mare
The barnys that scho eftyre bare.
Syne to swn he gat Pycus,
That fadyr wes to Fernyus,　　　　1530
And hys swne wes calde Latyne.
Off Ytaly he lord wes syne,
And this Latyne langage he
In tyll fowrme gert spokyn be.
The ferde swn scho happynde to bere
Wes calde be name Jupytere;
This Jupyter all prevaly
Scho gert be fostryde tendirly,

Quhill he passid all yhowthade,
And storknyde in tyll stowt manhade. 1540
Agayne hys fadyre irowsly

F. 16. Than he ras in swylk felny,
And made on hym swa fellown chas,
Folowand hym fra place to place,
Quhill Satwrne, for sawfftc,
Flede in that ile was callyde Crete;
Thiddyr hys swn folowyde fast,
And tuk hym thare in at the last,
And presonyde hym lang tyme in pyne,
And tyte fra hym hys lumys syne. 1550
Thare thai kest thame in the se,
Wenus thare off sulde cummyn be.
Thir poetys sayis in thare fenyhyng
(Bot it is noucht all suthfast thyng)
Men may trowe full werraly,
And mystrow this all wtraly,
For in the articlys off the Crede
Is noucht off this for-owtyn dred.
Thai halde alsua this Venus wes
Off luve lady and goddes, 1560
Off all fayrhede; and for-thi
All thai that luwyd perdrwry
Made tyll hyr thare sacrifyis,
And honowryd hyr in thare serwys.
Propyrly, as scho sulde be
Thare hope, thare hape, and thare awowe.

    Thare-eftyre fra that Saturnus,
As yhe hawe herde was geldyt thus,
He buskyd off that land to ga,
That Jupyter suld noucht hym sla, 1570
Na wyrk hym mare wa na dispyte,

He gat in tyll a gala tyte,
And passyd the se sa happely
That he gat in tyll Ytaly.
Thare, as he closyd hys latyrday,
Poetys off hym noucht mare walde say,
Bot that he wes howth vs sete
To be rygnand a planete,
Hys cours haldande be hym-selwe.
In ilkane off the taknys twelve,   1580
Sex moneth and twa yhere.
Fra he entyre in the syngnyfere,
Quhill thretty wyntyr be oure-tane
Or he be qwytly all throwch gane.
The Zodiake that we call;
For that he berys the taknys all,
In hys cours wytht wyolence
Offt hapnys were or pestilence;
Swa is mankynde in gret dowte
Quhyll he hys cours hawe all made owte, 1590
 Wndir this Saturne, as Ovyde sayis,
That made the warld in tyll his dayis.
Off Gold, all state was innocent,
But plede, or ony jugement.
He gert nothyr erde na tre,
In hys tyme dolwyn na hewyn be,
Thair byrth, but thret, thai oysid bere,
Thaire wes na wylde that wyst off were,
Then wes na schype to sayle the Se,
Nowthir craere, farkost, na galé;   1600
Thare wes na cuntre mare plesande
Tyll man, that tyme, than hys awne lande;
Best and byrd, and fysch in flwde,
Had at thaire chos all lykand fwde,

The lady that tyme, Dame Nature,
Wytht hyr rewle lede all creature.
　Quhen this Saturne away wes dede,
Hys swn that ras in tyll hys stede,
Saw this golde off kynd sa brycht
All dysessfull tyll hys sycht; 　　　　　　1610
Wp that gold he tuke away;
And he the warlde made, in hys day,
Off qwhyte Sylẅyre, that wes were
Metalle than the golde beffere.
He gert bestys wndir yhoke
Thole brodys sare, and mony a knoke;
He gert fyrst men mak byggyng
And oys in hows thare dwellyng;
Hors he gert bath drwg and drawe,
And men he kend tyll ere and sawe; 　　1620
Goshawke he dawntyde and fawcownys
To tak bathe boytoure and herrownys.
　Quhen Jupyter syne wes dede,
He that succedyt in hys stede,
The golde and sylvyr he gert be hyde,
As yhit is wndyr the kyst lyd,
And all the warlde he made off Bras,
That were than gold or sylver was,
That wes all state of mare dowrnes,
Than ony tyme before it wes. 　　　　　1630
　The werst generatyowne
The ferde was in successyoune,
Quhen that prynce hys powere hade,
Off Yrne all the warlde he made.
Oẅyde sayis in to that quhyle
Wpe ras falshede, swyk and gyle,
Slycht, mycht, and ill qweyntys,

And brynnand lust off cowatyis.
The gest yharnyed wele to fare,
Mycht nowcht be sykkyre off his hoslare;   1640
Na the mawich couth noucht be
In pes wytht hys alyé;
And oftsys the ta brodyre
Walde off were be wytht the tothire;
The fadyre trowyt that the swn
Walde, for hys land, hys dayis war dwne.

CHAP. XVIII.

The fyrst matere off Mawmentry
That Clerkis callis Ydolatry.

A MAN in awlde tyme wes calde Belus,
F. 17.   Fadyr he wes to Schyr Nynus,
That wes kyng off Assyry.
Hys fadyr he luwyde sa tendirly,   1650
That quhen he wes dede before,
For tyll have off hym gud memore,
All lyk hys fadyr in fygoure
Ane ymage he mayd in fayr payntoure,
That payntyd ymage wytht colowrys fyne
In publyk place he set wp syne,
Quhare comowne acces and repayre
Men mycht have tyll that figoure fayre,
And gert oure all [his] lordschype cry,
Quha to that ymage devotly   1660
Walde cum, for gyrth or sawffte,
Na man suld swa hardy be
Hym to pres to tak or slay,

Or ony mannans tyll hym may,
For ony mys that he had dwne,
Bot thare thai sulde have succoure swne,
Qwhyll thai wytht-in the presence ware
Byddande off that fygowre thare.
Than, for caus off swylk succoure,
The men off that land dyd honoure   1670
To that fygoure, as that it ware
A god off mycht and off poware,
Othire be that ensawmpylle syne
Off novyll matere or off fyne,
Off thare frendys that ware dede.
Set wp syk fygure in thaire stede,
And gert do thame sik honowre,
As thai had bene thaire creatoure:
Sum Bell thai callyd, and sum Baall,
Sum Beelzebub, sum Belyalle.   1680
Thus fyrst begouth Ydolatry,
That we oys to call Mawmentry.

CHAP. XIX.

Off a Genealogi till here
Next folowis in this Chapiter.

YHYT sulde I telle a Genealogy
Fra Sem discendand lynealy,
Gyve I sulde my mater bryng
And my purpos tyll endyng.

In tyll the tyme I spak off thus,
Semmys swn Pedagyus
Gat a swn, wes cald Gwalé,

That syne wes fadyr tyll Adre;   1690
The quhylk gat Stermonyus,
That fadyr wes off Ermodius;
Thare eftyre hys swnne Scealffy.
That fadyre wes off Scealdy,
Hys swne borne gat Tettius,
That fadyr wes syne tyll Gettius;
F. 17. b. Godduffus eftyre gat Fynny,
That was the fadyre off Frealfy;
Fredwalde eftyre, gat Woden;
He fadyr wes off mony men.   1700
   Bot Semmys fyrst swn Arphaxat
Gat Caynan, that Ebere gat.
This Caynan wes calde Sale,
Jerusalem fyrst fwndyt he,
And off hym come thai halyly
That Ynde fyrst awcht, and Samary.
Ebere eftyre gat Phalek,
In hys tyme men begouth to speke
In tyll mony twngys sere,
As efftyre that thai chawngyd were,   1710
Off Ebrewe the langage that tyme left
Tyll Phalekys lynage lange thare-eft.
In hys tyme begouth mawmentry
That we oys to call ydolatry.
Phalek the fadire wes off Rewe,
Sum oysyde to call hym Ragewe,
In the tyme that this Rewe was
Off Sythy fyrst the kynryke ras.
This Rewe to swn Sarwke gat,
Off hym come Natore, eftyre that   1720
In this Sarwkkys tyme on-one
Off Assyry and Sycyone

The kynrykis ras in ryawte.
Off this Nator come Tare.
Babylon in tyll hys dayis
Wes byggyd, as the story sayis.
Off this Tare efftyre that
Come Abraham that Isaac gat.

 Here the Secownde Elde tayis ende,
As the Hebrwyis mays ws kende,   1730
Contenys in it yhere be yhere,
A thowsand and twa hwndyr clere,
And twa and twenty yhere, but mare.
Bot to this discordand are
The Sewynty wys interpretowrys,
For, as we fynde in thare Scriptowrys,
A thowsand sevynty yhere and sevyn,
The Secownd Elde contenys cwyn.

[𝕰𝖝𝖕𝖑𝖎𝖈𝖎𝖙 𝕷𝖎𝖇𝖊𝖗 𝕻𝖗𝖎𝖒𝖚𝖘.]

THE SECUND BUKE

OF THE

ORYGYNALE CRONYKIL

OF SCOTLAND.

THE SECUND BUKE

OF THE

ORYGYNALE CRONYKIL
OF SCOTLAND.

The Proloug off the Secund Buk
In this Chapitere now yhe luke.

Now have yhe herde on quhatkyn wyis
I have contenyt this Tretys,
Fra fyrst fourmyt wes Adam,
Tyll this tyme nowe off Abraham,
And bathe the Eldys has tane ende,
As in all storys welle is kende,
Contenand hale the three thowsand yhere
Nyne scowre and foure oure passyt clere:
The quhilkys as Orosius
In tyll hys Cornyklys tellys ws,   10
Ner foryhet ware raklesly,
Or than myskende all wtraly
Wytht thayme, that set hale thair delyte
Before than storys for to wryte.
Fra Abraham ande Nynus Kynge
All storys tays thaire begynnyng;
As Pompeus, and Justyne,
Orosius says, and Frere Martyne.

F. 18.

Nowe tharefore in to certane terme
This Tretys furtht I wyll afferme, 20
Haldande tyme be tyme the date,
As Orosius qwhylum wrate;
And off hys Storys tha wyll I
Compyle, that me-thynk mast lykly
Tyll oure Matere accordande,
And tyll yhowre heryng mast plesand,
Tyll the time, that efftyre felle,
Quhen Jugis jwgyde Israelle.
Bot wytht Orosyus we wyll discorde
In tyll oure date, qwhen we recorde
Before or fra the byrth off Gode, 30
Reknand yherys ewyn, or ode:
Beffor or fra than reknys he
The yhere, as made wes the Cyté.

The Chapiteris off the Secund Buke.

i. OFF Nynus kyng, and his slawchtyr.
ii. Off Abrahamys dayis.
iii. Off Ysaakys progenye.
iiii. Qwhen fyrst byggyde wes Rodis.
v. Off Josephis forsycht.
vi. Off Dewcalyonys Flude.
vii. Off the wrakis off Egype.
viii. Off the Scottis Orygynale.
ix. Off the Yrsche Orygynale.
x. Off ane othir Geneologe.
xi. Off Danaus and Egistus.
xii. Off Josue and hys days.
xiii. Off the Cretes and Atenyens.
xiiii. Off the Amynowtaure.
xv. Off Wersozes Kyng off Egipt.
xvi. Off the Wemen Amazones.
xvii. Off the Assege off Troye.

CHAP. I.

𝔗his 𝔈hapitere tellis how 𝔑ynus kyng 𝔥ad 𝔅abilone in governynge.

A.C. 2052.
    BEFOR that Jhesu Cryst wes borne,
    To sawffe oure lyff that wes forlorne,
    Twa thowsand hale and fyfty yhere,
    And twa yhere owre, to rekyn clere,

F. 18. b.
    Nynus kyng off Assyry,
    In lust off lordschype, and fellownly,
    Tuk wpe armys to warray
    Sere landys that abowt hym lay.
    All Asy, throwche hys cruelte,
    Wytht were and batayle dawntyde he.   10
    Fyfty yhere hys lyff he lede,
    And mekyll off sakles blwde he schede;
    All the landys off Sythy,
    And othir natyownys thare syndry,
    That oysyde to lyff, bot sympyll lyff,
    Wytht-owtyn batall, were, or stryff,
    And lathe wes bargane for to mowe,
    Or in tyll were thaire pythys prowe.
    Syk lyff he kend thame for to lede,
    That blude off men in slawchtyre dede,   20
    Thai oyside to drynk mar comownaly
    Than mylk off scheype, or gayt, or ky.
    Tyll wyncust he thaim kend sa fast,
    That he wes wencust at the last.
      Cam that calde wes Zorastes,

And kyng off Baktryanys qwhylum wes,
The fyndare off nycromancy,
Off wychecraft and sorcery;
Fyrst he supprysyt wytht hys mycht,
And slewe hym syne wyth fors in fycht.   30
It happnyd eftyre on a day,
As he abowte a cyté lay,
In tyll assege as man off were,
Assayleyheande it wytht hys powere
Sik assawtys thare he made,
That nere the towne he wonnyne hade;
Ane archare in a kyrnale stude,
That wele behelde quhare Nynus yhude,
Hawand in hys hand a bowe,
Thare in he set a brade arowe,   40
That to the hwkis wpe he drwe,
And wytht that schot he Nynus slwe.

 Than Semyramys, his wyff,
That led in lykyng al hyr lyff,
In tyll hyr chawmbyr than syttand,
Hyr hayre in wympyll arayand,
Quhen that scho herd off this cas,
Suppos in hart scho sary wes,
The tane half off hyr hare wnplet,
Scho gert plat on hyr hys basynet,   50
Wytht othire armys gud and fyne,
And lape apon a cursere syne,
And to the towne, but mare abade
Arayit wytht hyr ost scho rade,
And gert thame mak thare wpe assawte,
Wythowtyn falyhyng or defawte,
Qwhyll that scho wonyn hade the towne,
And broucht it to confusyown.

Fra thine hyr lust stwde halyly
In slawchtyr and in lychory.   60
   Fowrty yhere scho lyvyt and twa,
And wandyt na mare for to sla
Hym that scho gert ly hyr by
Than hym that wes hyr inymy,
Quhat tyme that hyr lykyng stude,
And yharnyng had for to se blude.
Off chawmbyr play scho was nevyre sade,
For all the copy that scho hade;
Scho gert oure all hyr landys cry,
Be statute ordanyt fermly,   70
That all that walde in lykyng lyve,
And tyll lust thare bodyis gyve,
Thai sulde in all be als fre
As it mycht lykand to thame be.
Tyll sybredyn haffand na knawlage
And, but all reverence off maryage,
In all apport scho prowyt man,
Suppos in fourme scho wes woman.
All Ethyope scho wane, but dowt,
And made it tyll [hir] wyndyrlowt;   80
Scho passyd in Ynd in playne bataylle,
Qwhare hyr before nane durst assaylle,
Na eftyr hyr wytht fors off fycht
Bot Alexandyr, that wyth hys mycht
Wane Mede and Pers, and Ynde allswa,
And all the lave off Asya.
Bot Ynde in tyll hyr tyme wes were
To wyn, than eftyr hyre befere,
For off nakyn wer wyth-owte
Na wytht-in thai had na dowte   90
Off inwy, na cowatys,

Na falshede that thaim mycht supprys.
Set scho lyvyt in terandry,
In governance scho wes happy,
And avysy wes off were,
And kowth weylle sé for hyr mystyre.

Hyr landys lyand hyr abowte
Scho stwffyt weylle wytht-owtyn dowt,
And gert thame weyll replenysyt be
Wytht hors, and noyt, and othir fe. 100
Off wyne and wax, oyle and qwheyt,
And all tyme scho had copy greyt.
Off froyte that grew on erd and tre
Scho had in all tyme gret plente,
Scho gert men thraly set thaire cure,
Come to wyne wytht thare culture.

F. 19. b. Off Babylone, bathe towre and towne,
Scho made gude reformatyoune,
And kyrnalyt it perfytly,
And baytaylyd it rycht propyrly, 110
And drewe in tyll it marchandys,
Bowcht and sawlde on syndry wys,
And helde in tyll it crafftys sere,
At may nowcht all be reknyt here.
Amang all othir comownaly
Scho lete hyr awne swne ly hyr by;
Swa anys as scho come hym tyll
Hyr fleschly lust for to fulfyll,
Prevaly he gat a knyffe,
Wytht that fra hyr he refft the lyff. 120

All thus qwhen scho endyt was,
Hyr swne succedyt, Nynyas,
The swne and ayre to Nynus Kyng,
And had that lande in governyng.

And efftyre hym off lynyage
Succedyt to that herytage
Fourteyne ayrys syndrely,
Be lyne descendand evynly,
Beffor that lordschype was wndone,
As yhe may here eftyre sone. 130
    This Nynus had a sone alsua
Sere Dardane, lord de Frygya,
Fra quhom Barbere sutely
Has made a propyr genealogy
Tyll Robert oure Secownd kyng,
That Scotland had in governyng.
The paganys made in thaire storys,
That is bot fabyll or fantys,
That Jupyter gat on Electra,
Sere Dardane lorde off Fregya: 140
To tell yhowe thaire-off the story
Walde do as nowe bot occupy
Tyme, and walde forthir noucht
Purpos that sulde tyll ende be browcht.

CHAP. II.

**Off Abrahame now schall yhe here
Parte wryttine in this Chapitere.**

A.C. 2010. TWA thowsand yhere and ten beforne
That Cryst wes off the Madyn borne,
Quhen that fourty yhere and ane
Fra Nynus ras ware fully gane,
That ane folowand the nest yhere,
Abraham, off quhom yhe sall nowe here, 150

        Wes borne, and than ane wes he
        Off the sonnys gottyn off Tare.
        He lewyt all tym wertusly,
        And God hym blyssyd specyally,
        In tyll hys tym he fand of newe
F. 20.   To wryt lettyrys off Hebrewe,
        (For the bokis that Enok wrate
        Drownyt all in Noeys spate).
        He kend the Caldeys perfytly,
        The scyens off astronomy,   160
        He gewe fyrst, in tyll hys dayis
        Teyndis, as the Bybyll sayis,
        To Melchesedek, that than hade
        The sowerayne ordyre off Presthade,
        That offeryt tyll Abraham brede and wyne,
        That blyssyt hym, and devotly syne,
        Quhen that he come hame agayne,
        Fra that the kyngis foure ware slayne,
        Quhare that Loth rescwyd he,
        Wytht all hys gude, and hys menyhe,   170
        He kende the Egyptis wysly,
        The scyens off geometry,
        The Circumcysiowne fyrst tuke he
        And, as we fynde, the Jubilé
        Fyrst in hys tym fundyn was,
        And nowe we call the yherys off grace.
        A sone he gat on Saray,
        That Ysaak was calde werraly.
        Ane hundreth yhere quhen he wes aulde,
        And sevynty, to the gast he yhalde,   180
        Quhen all hys tyme fulfillyde wes,
        In gud eylde and in rychtwysnes.

CHAP. III.

This Chapitere tellis clerli Off Ysaakis progeni.

Y SAAK weddyt Rebecca,
And on hyr he gat sonnys twa,
Esaw callyde the eldest,
And luwyt wes wytht the fadyre best;
Jacob callyde wes the tothire,
Off byrth he wes the yhungest brothire;
At anys the modyr, nevyrtheles,
Off thame twa delyvere wes.   190
In huntyng Esawe had delyte,
Jacob set hym for profyte
Off corne, catelle, or off fe,
Quhare-wytht he mycht sustenyt be.
Fra huntyng Esawe all wery
Come on a day, and rycht hungry,
And off the potage walde hawe hade
That Jacob tyll hys dynare made,
For hym thowcht it ane harde thrawe.
Hwngyr than in tyll hale mawe,   200
That Jacob warnyde hym wtraly,
Bot gyff he saulde hym halely,
All hys awantage and hys gre,
That for as eldest hys sulde be.
Than Esaw, for-owtyn lete,
For hungyr that he wes in sete,
For a dysfulle off potage,
Gawe wpe alle hale hys herytage.

F. 20. b.

Thus Jacob wane the eldest gre,
Thowcht yhungar in the byrthe was he.   210
Syne how this Jacob sleely
Prewenyde hys brodyre qweyntlye,
Quhen throwcht hys modyre suggestyowne,
He wan his fadyr benysowne;
How syne off thir brethire twa,
Jowys and Gentyle come alsua,
Than Gentyle was all generaly,
That come noucht discendand lynealy
Fra Jacob be successiowne,
Na off hys generatyown.   220
Jowys fra thine wes in that gre
That Cristynmen now in yhe se.
This Jacob was callyd Israelle,
Fra wytht hym wyrstyllyde the Angelle,
As in the Bybyll wryttyn is,
In to that Buk callyde Genesis.
   This Jacob on hys wyffis twa,
Rachell callyde and Lya,
Gat sonnys twelf, and Judas
Ane off thai twelff sonnys was.   230
Thir twelff, that I yhowe off telle,
The Tribus are off Israelle,
Off quhome come oure suet Lady,
Goddys modyr, myld Mary.
Tribus may be the lyniage
Propyrly calde in oure langage.
Thai had in tyll possessyowne
The land off repromyssyowne.
   [Foremus] on Nyabe
In to this tyme gat Phorone.   240
He wes the fyrst [that] in hys dawys

Ordanyt in to Grece the lawys,
And before jugys ordanyt he,
Be plede causys mot to be.
He ordanyt [als] the jugis sete
To be for that oys the markete;
Forum he gert it calde be,
Eftyre hys awne name, calde Forone.
In Latyne, that is the name yhit
Off that at we call the markyte.   250
 Ysis that was hys systere syne,
In Egypte passyde be nawyn,
And thare scho kend thame letteratur,
And corne to wyne wytht thare culture.
For-thi thai sayde that scho thare wes
Amang thare goddys as a goddes.
Apis, thai say, that he sulde be
A sone off this Forone.
He pasd the se in Egypte than,
Qwhare, thai sayde, he wes weddyt man   260
Tyll this woman calde Ysys,
And gode wes calde wyth thare fayre goddys,
And Syrapis wes eftyre callyde,
As I fynde in storys eftyre taulde.
 The madyn that tym Mynerva,
Besyde a louch in Affryca
Wes fwndyn fyrst, that [craftis] sere
Kend weylle be werk and be matere.
The wemen that tym off the land
Scho gert thraly be wyrkand,   270
And mast in wolle to keme and spyn,
And clathys wewe to be cled in.
This Mynerva that than was
Eftyre that was callyde Pallas;

In Tracya is swylke ane yle,
Thare in scho noryst wes sum quhylle;
And as scho slayne hade a geande
That to name was callyd Pallande,
Tharefor Pallas was hyre name,
That maydyn off so ryalle fame. 280

CHAP. IV.

This Chapiter now tellis
How fyrst inhabit wes Rodis.

A THOWSAND and sex hundyr yhere
Foure scor, foure les to rekyne clere,
Before the Incarnatyoune
That made all oure salvatyoune,
A folk that callyd wes Telchyses,
And Caratays that wytht thame wes,
Rase agayne Sere Foroné,
Off Argos that tyme kyng wes he.
He haid in tyll hys company
A folk than callyd Parakasy; 290
Thir landys all in Grece ar hale,
Suppos thare lordschypys be severale.
The Telchyis wencust in that fycht,
Be-huẅyd on neyde to ta the flycht,
Fra pres off men to halde thame fre
And in to pes to lyẅande be.

F. 21. b. The Ile off Rodys than tuke thai
And it inhabytyt fra that day,
Be thame and thare successyown
For trayst and fre possessyown. 300

VOL. I.   F

CHAP. V.

**This Chapyter schall tell yhow rycht
Off Josephis wyt and hys forsycht.**

A THOWSAND and sewyn hundyre yhere,
And ane and saxty reknyt clere,
Befor the Natyvyte,
In Egypte that fertylyte
Begowth to rys in Josephys dayis,
As in hys cronykyll Orose sayis,
Sewyn yher owt contynnand,
Wytht othir sevyn nest folowand
Off gret derth and hungare sare;
That had the pupylle noyit mare,   310
Ne ware that Joseph, wytht hys wyt,
Hade sene remede and helpe for it.
Jacobys sone this Joseph was,
Perfyt, and off sik connandnas
That he cowth wele bayth ken and se
Quhat land suld yhelde or fertyll be.
He wes the fyrst that dremys rede
That men seys slepand in thare bede;
Off swylk mystyk wysyownys
He mad gud exposytyownys.   320
His bredyre ten salde hym for-thi
Tyll strang merchandys for inwy.
Than had hym in tyll Egypt than,
Thare he be-come the kyngys man,
That holde hym in tyll gret daynté,
And put hys gud in hys powsté.

His brodyre than that had hym saulde,
As I to yow be-fore has talde
Slew a kyde, and in the blude
Wet the gown that he in yhude, 330
And ghert hys fadyre be that ken
That wolẅys had hym weryid then.
Neverthetes, for hys bownté,
Wytht the kyng welle lufyt wes he
Off Egypt, als and wytht the Quene.
Fra scho off hym a sycht had sene,
[Scho] walde have gert hym ly hyr by:
Bot he refoysit that curtasly,
For the wyrchype off hys larde,
That all hys gude put in hys warde; 340
Bot alanerly the Quene,
Scho raryde lowde wyth cryis kene,
Sayd Joseph wald haffe lyne hyr by,
Qwhare to [scho] wowyt hym besely.
Than was he put in hard presowne
Quhyll the Kyng gat [a] vesyown,
Slepand sawe in tyll hys bede,
That nane cowth than bot Joseph rede,
He tauld hym be that drem in all
How thai fourteyne yhere sulde falle. 350

Than made he Joseph, off hys land,
Stewarde hale and luftenand;
He ghert that sevyn yhere gadryt be
Alkyne korne in swylk plente,
That in tyll tyme off hungar sare,
The folk that full relevyde ware,
And othir mony cowntré sere,
Tyll Egypt that tym drawyn were,
To by ẅyttaylle for thare fude.

Thus Joseph, throwch hys wertu gude, 360
Stuffyt hys lord weylle off moné,
And gert the folk relewyde be,
And throwcht hys slycht, and hys quentys,
Off Egypte all the tennandrys
He redemyt thare agayne,
And mayde thame to the kyng demayne;
And in husbandry for ferme,
Ilkè yhere at certane terme,
He set thai landys and the male,
The fyft part off thare wynnyng hale, 370
Ilkè yhere, in tyll certane,
At termes to the kyng was tane;
And in tyll Egypte yhit thai say
That lawch is kepyt to this day.
And for sik wertu as he pruwyt,
Sowerandly hys lard hym lufyt,
And gawe hym large and full powere
To do that lykand tyll hym were.

   Hys brethir than come tyll hym als,
(That for inwy and cownsale fals, 380
For the dremys that he taulde,
To strang marchandys hade hym saulde,)
To by off hym wyttayle thare,
For in tyll gret dystres thai ware:
Bot knawlage off hym had thai nane,
He kend thaim nevyrtheles ilkane,
And on thame threpyt thai ware spyis,
Or to the kyng kyd innymys.
All thus he taryid thame so fast
Tyll thame behuvid at the last, 390
For tyll lewe ane wytht hym on nede,
The lawe tyll pas hame full gud spede,

And in hy tyll hym to bryng
Benjamin, thaire brodyre yhing,
Thai left than wytht hym Symeon
And hame thai passyd sone on-one.
Thai taulde thare fadyr how thai ware
Anoyid in tyll Egypt sare;
And Benjamin yhet, at the last,
Wytht thame in tyll Egypt past,   400
Mekyll agayne hys fadyr wylle,
That had his presumptyoune off thaim ille.
Yhet ware thai set in hardare pres
Fra Benjamyn thare cummyn wes;
Bot at the last Joseph thame taulde
He wes thare bruthire that thai saulde,
And for thare hele in to that land
God had hym sawyt than lefand:
Than for his fadyr he gert thame pas,
That taulde hym Joseph lewand was;   410
With that worde he was so fayne
That his speryt quyknyt agayne,
And buskyt hym delyverly
In Egipt for to pas in hy,
To se hys sone that for hym sende,
And thare hys lyff for to take end.
All thus, as yhe have herd me telle,
In Egypt fyrst come Israelle.

In this tyme Primotheus yhing,
Off Caucasus baythe lorde and kyng,   420
Wytht in the landys off Asy,
Kend thame fyrst phylosophy;
He wes the brodyre off Atland,
That kyng was than off Affrykland,
Thai fenyhe that tyme he mad men,

For caus he gert thame craftis ken ;
Figuris off men he made alsua,
The quhylkis he gart be craftis ga.
Ryngys fyrst he gert men were,
Thaim he gert the myd fyngyre bere, 430
For fra that to the hart, he sayde,
Ane [e]ẅyn strekande ẅayne wes layde ;
And alsua for mast belysyng,
Thare-on he gert thame were the ryng.
   Tritolomus, that tyme alsua
Be naẅyne passyd in Grecia,
Thare he kend thame wytht mare cure,
Than thai ware wont to ma culture.
That tyme alsua Dame Ceres,
That off corne wes callyde goddes, 440
Fyrst gert corne wytht mesure mete,
As boll, or pek, or wytht fyrlete,
Quhare befor bot in to stake,
Or hepys on erde thai oysyde to make,
Tharefor scho was callyde Demetra
In all the land off Grecya.

CHAP. VI.

**Off Dewcalyonys flude
This hillys hey sumtyme our-yhude.**

A THOUSAND and fyve hundyr yhere,
Thre score and twa, to rekyn clere,
Befor the Incarnatyoune,
In Athenys Amphytryone, 450
The fadyr than off Ercules,

That the gret geand quhylum wes,
Fra Cycrope wes the thryde kyng
That hade Athenys in governyng.
Than all the folk off Tessaly
Had nere bene drownyt suddanly
Wytht a fers falland flude,
Thai ware a fewe tyll hyllys yhude.
Wpone ane hille was callyd Parnas
Thare thai ware that sawfyt was. 460
All the landys thare abowt
Dewcalyone than aucht, but dowt
That resawyt wytht gud wylle
All tha that that tyme fled hym tylle,
The men that tyme thai said wndone,
Wes throw hym reformyd sone.

For this Dewcalion in thai dayis
Wytht hys wyff Pyrra, Owyde sayis,
Ay wpe fra hyll tyll hylle past,
And on the hyest at the last 470
Thai oure-bade that felowne flude,
And to the planys than thai yhude;
Thare thaire frendys and thare kyn
Thai myssyd all, bathe mare and myn,
Na thai couth fynd na lyvand man
In all thai landys sterand than,
Thai ware wndone so halyly,
All drownyt in that dyluwy.
Than tyll a cove Dewcalyon,
And hys wyff Pyrra, passyd onone, 480
And devotly thai mad thare
Tyll a goddes thare prayare,
Tyll wyttyre thame, for hyr pyté,
How mankynd mycht reformyt be.

Thus quhyll thai ware prayand fast.
Thai war answert, at the last,
Owt off the cove that thai sulde ga,
And thare modyre banys ta,
And tha be-hynd thame thai sulde cast.
Than owt off the cove thai past,   490
And esytyde on gret manere,

F. 23. b.   Quhat sulde betakyn this answere.
For sua the Spat had all oure-gane
That thai gat nowthire flesch na bane
Off thare modyr, and for-thi
Thai ferlyid off this hugely.
Thus quhill thai studyit this Pyrra,
The first spekyne begouth to ma;
For rydely wylis in wemen
Sunnere apperys than in men;   500
Scho sayde, "I can be na way trowe
That othir modyre have we nowe
Than the erde, and the stanys
Ar thare-off, as I trowe, the banys.
Tharefore I red that we ga fast,
And lat behynd ws stanys kast."
Wytht this Deucalyon dyde all hale,
As Pyrra gawe hym to consalle,
And off tha castys eftyre grewe
Men and wemen all off newe;   510
Swa off thare kyn thai stuffyt the land
Qwhar before thai war duelland.

    Eftyre gret mortalyteis
Yhet men thus growys in sere cuntreis.
In to the kynryc yhett off Frawnce
Is nane so redy craft no chawnce
Off [auld] kyn newe to fynde,

Than to cast stanys fast behynde.
For-thi, tyll conclusyoune
Off this reformatyoune, 520
This Ovide maide thir ilk wers,
In metyre, that I wyll rehers.
   (*Inde genus durum sumus experiens quoque
      malum:*
   Et documenta damus, qua simus origine nati.)
" Thareoff, he says, be kynd we ta
For tyll be dowre and harde alsua,
And we mak kend in propyrte
Quharoff ony kynd suld commyn be."
   All this that I rehersyt nowe
Standys yow noucht on nede to trowe,
For thare is nane that can this rede
Amange the Artikyllys off the Crede. 530

CHAP. VII.

*This Chapitere now will yhow telle
The wrakis that in Egipe fell.*

A THOWSAND and fyve hundyre yhere,
And sevyn and fowrty hale, but were,
[Before the Incarnatioun,
That was oure salvatioun]
The wrakys ten in Egypt ras,
For that Israelle anoyit was
In serwytute and fowle thrylage,
Throwcht the Kyng and hys barnage,
That in tylle Egypt ras of newe
And off Joseph no thyng knewe; 540

Bot thowcht ille in sic multitwde
That alyenys amang thame stwde.
Quhen Jacob, as yhe hard me telle,
That callyde befor wes Israelle,
Hys son Joseph for to se
In Egypt pasd wytht his menyhe,
And browcht in wyth hym, taulde and sene
Thre scor off bodyis and fyftene,
That wytht hym in tyll Egypt past
And thare syne thai grewe so fast,   550
Off industry and ingyne,
In byrth, and off wertu syne,
And off welth in sufficyans,
And ryches in tyll haboundans,
That the Egyptys for inẅy
Anoyit thame dispituisly,
And in thaire werk thayme pynowrys made
That growyn wp was in manhade,
The Kyng gert commawnd, but remede,
The knaẅe barnys sulde be put to dede   560
Off Israelytys [eẅyr]-ilkane,
Than to be borne that sauff ware nane;
Bot all the madyne barnys he
Than to be borne bad saẅfyde be.
   Thus that Kyng and hys barnage
Helde this folk in gryt thryllage,
Na wald delyver on na wys
Thame to mak thare sacrifyce
Tyll God off mycht, in wyldyrnes,
As [he] was byddyn be Moyses,   570
Quhille fyrst thare wattyre turnyt in blude,
Paddokkis syne thare land our-yhude,
Syne byttyn thai ware wytht cynyphes,

That a kynde off gleggys wes,
And alkyn kynd off gleggys als,
That gart thame yhuke baythe hede and hals.
Syne in thare bleddyris boldnyt bylys,
And alkyn bruke and scab that vyle is,
Syne comune qwalm off all thare fe,
That scheype, or nowyt, or gayte sulde be, 580
And at the last in generale
All thaire ayrys deyde hale,
Be so fers mortal[it]e,
That nane in to that lande wes fre,
Than hys eldest barne wes dede,
But ony manere off remede,
Quhyll off the land thai lete thame pas.
 Moyses than thare chyftane was,

F. 24. b. And gawe thame lawys to lyve by,
Wrytyn in the Mownt off Synay. 590
In Egypte als quha wald kene
Thare felle than wrakis ma than tene,
As sayis the Buke off Exodi,
Quha wyll it se perfytly,
But for thai war noucht all so felle,
Swa apert, na swa cruelle,
Thai ar foryhet wytht autorys sere
That mentyown mays off this mater;
Bot eftyr thame, as sum men sayis,
War notyt the forbodyn dayis, 600
In ilk moneth off the yhere,
Begynand fyrst in Januere.
Bot thai of Egypt noucht for-thi,
Swa wys ware in astronomy,
That it is noucht to trowe thai walde
All thir dayis forbodyn halde,

Na thai walde in thame begyne
And do that thai saw profyt in
As to byggyn, and to ẅyage
In marchandys or pilgrimage;   610
Bot off the elementis sere
Thai that hafys thaire matere,
Or felys thare complexiownys
Movyd be constellatyownys
Discordand, it ware noucht to skylle
That thir dayis ware kepyt tylle
The Egyptis in perplexyte,
For dowt thare land sulde peryst be,
And wytht thai ẅengeance all wndone;
Sum off thame tuk purpos sone   620
Out off [that] land all qwyt to pas;
Ane Dynys Bachus off thame was,
That for that dowt all Egypt left,
And Argos mad in Grece thareft.
He kende the men off that cuntré
Off wynys the subtylyte,
Quhare[-in] he conand was in alle;
Tharfore hym god off wyne thai calle.
That tyme als Cycrope kyng
Off Egypte drede the wndoyng,   630
In to Grece sone comyn was,
Duelland fra thine in Athenas.

CHAP. VIII.

𝕿his 𝕮hapitere sall tell 𝔭ho𝔴 all hale 𝕺ff the 𝕾cottis 𝕺r𝔶𝔤𝔶nale.

Owte off Sythy in that quhylle
In to Grece come Schyre Newylle,
That wes off deid a worthy man,
And in to Grece gryt lordschype wan:
He wes nere in the twenty degré
Be lyne discendande fra Noye,
Off his yhungast son, but lete,
F. 25.   That to name was callyd Japhete.   640
Off Sem hys brodyre come Presthade;
And off this Japhet come Knychthade.
This Newyle was fra this Noye,
As I sayde ayre, the twenty degré,
And had a sone callyd Gedyelle-Glays;
And as the story off hym says,
To wiff weddyt Scota yhing
Pharois douchtyr off Egypt kyng.
This Gedeyl-Glays was off gret pyth,
And warnyst weyle off wyt thar-wyth;   650
He gat on Scota barnys fayre,
And ane of thai sulde have bene ayre
Tyll Pharao, that drownyt was
In to the Reide Se, at that chas,
That the Egyptis maid so felle
Wpon the folk off Israelle;
Quhare all that folk our-passyd dry,
The Egyptis drownyt halyly.

This Gedeyl-Glays, quhen he sawe
The land off Egypt, hey and lawe,   660
That in all thyng wes profytabille,
And tyll hys lyvyng delytabylle,
Hys duellyng thare he thoucht to ma,
And hys awantage off it to ta,
Sen hys barnys apperyt to be
Lordis off that ryawte.
Bot the barnage off the land,
That remaynyde than lywand,
Thoucht thai ware agrevyt sare
Throw the wrakis, thai tholyt are: 670
Be that ensawmpyll, off consalle
All alienys thai banyst hale.
Quharefor this ilke Gedeil-Glays
Hys way owte off that [lande] he tays,
And throwcht the Meyre Medyterrayne
He passyde, quhille he come in Spayne;
And on the watter off Hybery
He byggyde the towne off Brygancy:
Thare nowe the towne is off Galys,
Quhare that, thai say, Sanct Jamys lyis: 680
And thai that duelt than in that land
He gert be tyll hym obeysand.

    Syne, as he passyde on a day
Throwcht that land in tyll his play,
Oure fra hym be-yhonde a sé
He kend lyand a gret cuntré.
Than speryt he thraly off that land,
Quha sulde be in tyll it duelland;
Bot ansuere tharof gat he nane,
Na nakyn knawlage in certane.   690
In hy than gert he schyppys thre

Wytht armyd men sone stuffyt be,
And gert thame pas be Se thare way
To se that land how that it lay,
And gyff that it wes eyth to wyn,
And quha was duelland it wythtin.
Wytht wynd at wyll that folk than past,
And in the land come at the last
At ane yle, wes in the se,
Off gret space and off quantyte: 700
Bot thai, that duelt in to that yle,
Wnhonest was and inutyle;
Tharefore thai, that come to spy
That land, thai dressyt wnmoderly;
For sum off thame thai slewe rycht thare
Wytht arys, sum thai dang rycht sare.
[And thay that happenit to get away
Held to their schippis, but delay.]
Syne alle that yle thai passyde abowt,
And sawe thai mycht, but drede or dowte, 710
Wyn it hally to thare wylle,
Swa that thai wertu had thare-tylle.
Thai tuk wpe sayle, and passyd in hy
Wytht wynd at wyll to Brygancy
Quhare Gedeyl-Glays wes our-tane
Off case wytht dede than subitane;
Bot his body wytht honowre
Wes put in tyll honest sepultoure
Wytht swylk oys and solempnyte,
As that tyme wes in that cuntré 720

   Thir spyis taulde hys barnys sone,
In to that Ile howe thai [had] done;
And said that it wes eytht to wyn,
For thai, that duelt that Ile within,

War sottys ẅyle off na ẅalu,
Na governyde thame be na ẅertu;
And at that land wes profytabille
And tyll all levyng dylitabylle:
Tharefor thai sayde, it wes thare wylle,
And full consaylle thai gaẅe thar-tylle, 730
For to pass that Ile wytht-in,
And it be conquest to thame wyn,
And wytht thare stuffe it occupy
For thame and tharis herytabilly;
Repruẅand thame as sottis ẅyle;
Sene thai mycht doutles, but peryle,
Tyll thame and all thare lynyage
That lordschipe wyn in herytage,
For to leve it fayntly,
And lyve as lowndreris cayttevely. 740

    A sone off Gedeyl-Glays than,
Heber, that was a douchty man,
Thoucht it wes tyll hym lyẅyng fayre,
Syne he wes noucht hys fadyre ayre;
He sone inclynyd to thare consalle,
And chesyt hym men, and gat ẅytalle,
And layde his schyppys to the Se,
And entryde in wytht hys menyhe.
He tuke wpe sayle, and furth he past,
And in the Ile come at the last: 750
Alle the men thare he slewe down,
That was noucht tyll hys byddyng bown;
Off the lave he tuk homage.
Thus all that land in herytage
He wane all hale, and maid it fre
Tyll hym and hys posteryte.
So occupyid he furth the land

Wytht all, that evyr thare-in he fand,
And Scotland gert call that Ile,
For honowre off hys modyr quhille,　　　760
That Scota was wytht all men calde,
As yhe [haf] herd before be-talde.
Hybernia thai callyd it syne
Off this Hiberus, in Latyne,
That Yrland we ws to calle
Now in to oure langage alle.
Off Hiber thai come halyly,
Tha we oys to call Yrschery;
And this lady callyd Scota
All thir Scottis ar cummyn fra,　　　770
As yhe may in this proces here,
Quhen we ar cummyn to that matere.

CHAP. IX.

On othir wiis this Chapitere
Says the Yrsche cummyn were.

BOT be the Brwte, yhit Barbare sayis,
Off Yryschry all othir wayis,
That Gurgwnt-Badruk quhille wes kyng,
And Bretayne had in governyng;
Worthy wycht and wyse wes he.
As [he] passyd anys oure the sé
Fra Denmark, that he wonnyn hade,
Be Orknay hame he tuk the trade;　　　780
And thare schyppys he fand thretty
Wytht off Spaynalys a cumpany,
That flemyt ware off thaire cuntré,

And lang ware waverand on the sé.
Partoloym, that the ledare was
Off thame, besoucht the Kyng off gras
Tyll tak thame tyll hym off duellyng,
And gyff thame land for thare wonnyng.
He send wytht thame sum off his men
Tyll Yrland, that was noucht yhit then 790
Inhabityde, bot wes wast haly:
Off this folk come the Yryschry,
That duelt in Yrland to this day,
And Yrysch off Yrland callyd ar thai.

 Yhit is thare odyre awtorys sere,
That tretis part of this matere;
Bot thai oys noucht to tell hys name,
Hys state, his gre, na yhyt hys fame,
Off quhame the Yrysch cumyn are;
Bot sayis, quhen that Egyptys ware 800
Drownyde in the Reid Se,
The lave, that levyt in that cuntré,
Banyst fra thame a gentyll-man,
That duelland amangys thame wes than;
A Sytyk he wes off natyowne,
Conand in all discretyoune.
Thai dowtyd at hys senyhoury
Suld thame abawndown halyly,
Be that ensawmpyll, that thai ware
Befor throucht strangerys noyid sare. 810
This gentyll-man and hys menyhe
Gat schyppyng sone, and tuk the sé,
And saylyd Affryk all abowt
Drewyn wytht syndry stormys stoute,
And by othire costis sere,
That spedys noucht to rekyn here;

Syne in to [the] Spaynyhe sé
He hapnyd to cum wytht his menyhe,
Quhare he tuke land; and mony yhere
He and hys thare-in duelland were: 820
Sa he and all hys progeny
Held that land ay herytabylly.
  Owte off Spaynyhe than in Irland
Thai come, and wan all hale that land,
Quhen passyd wes twelf hundyr yhere
Fra the Egyptis drownyd were
Chasand the pupyll of Israelle,
As yhe have herd me before telle,
Quha that wyll cast date to date,
As autoris in thaire storyis wrate, 830
And yhere wyll rekyn eftyr yhere,
The sowme sall be thre hundyr clere
And twa and fyfty yhere beforn
Or Jhesu wes off Mary born.
I wyll noucht hald thir oppynnyownys ale
Contrary, for thai mycht weylle fale;
Bot it is dowtews be the date,
That Cronyklaris befor me wrate,
And othir incydens sere
Accordand part to this matere. 840
Bot quhethir it be, or othir wayis,
Than all thir autoris before me sayis,
For certane yhe sall wndyrstand,
That owt off Spaynyhe in tyll Yrland
The Scottis come, that to this day
Havys it and Scotland haldyn ay.
In [the] Thryde Eylde, wytht-owtyn les
In Spaynyhe the Scottis cummyn wes.
Wythtin the Ferd Eylde, Yrland

Was to the Scottis obeyschande. 850
Syn sum off thame can occupy
Parte off the north off Brettany.
Than wes in it thre Natyownys,
Scottis, Peychtis, and Brettownys.
   Part off the Scottis yhit left in Spayn,
Quhen thai war cumyn in tyll Brettane,
And Scottis thai spekys halyly,
And yhit are callyde Navarry.

F. 27.

CHAP. X.

Or I forthire nowe procede,
Off the Genealogi will I rede.

IN the Fyrst Buk, gyffe that yhe
Wele nere the last end rede and se, 860
Thare may yhe fynd the Genealogeys,
That in tyll al parte sygnyfis,
As oure Kyng suld cumyn be
Discendand ewyn fra Noe.
And quhy that thai disseveryde are,
Yhe wyt or yhe ga forthirmare.
   In the Thryd Eylde, storys sere
Sayis, the Scottis cummyn were
Wytht Gedeyl-Glays in Spaynyhe land,
And in the Ferde Eylde in Yrland, 870
And in the Fyft Eylde lang beforne,
In Scotland, or that God wes born.
Thir Genealogyis I maide for-thi
Devysyde, as yhe se, dystynctly.
And [als] suppos I fand be name

Thame wryttyn all, yhit off the fame
Off mony, and the dowchtynes,
That lang tyme swa fordelyd wes,
Mater nane I worthy fand,
That tyll yhoure heryng were plesand   880
In tyll this Tretys for to wryte:
Swa suld I dulle hale yhoure delyte,
And yhe sulde call it bot arane,
Or that I had thame half ourtane,
Gyff I sulde tell thaim halyly,
As thai are in the Genealogy
Wytht-oute othir distynctyowne.

   For-thi was myn intentyoune
Amange the Eyldys thame to drawe,
Dyviside swa, that yhe mycht knawe   890
Quha that war orygynale,
The begynnyng pryncipalle
Off ilke cuntré, quhar that thai
Occupyde thare-eftyre ay:
[And sa] I suld excusyde be,
Gyff I mak noucht thare entre,
Quhen thare entre fyrst began
In to thai landis that thai wan,
Tyll othir statis accordand
In Rome or Israelle than regnand   900
Befor the Incarnatyoune,
For I fynde na discriptyoune.
Than I fynd sic discrepance,
That I am noucht off sufficiance
For to gare thame all acorde;
Bot sympylly for to recorde
Wytht-in the Eyldis, that than felle;
And nane othir termys telle.

And, quhare I left, now to begyn,
I have in purpos, or I blyne,   910
As in the Fyrst Buke, off Woden,
That fadyr wes off mony men;
Hys swn wes callyde Bedagyus,
That fadyr wes tyll Brondyus;
This Brondyus eftyre that
Was Fredgarys fadyr, and hym gat;
He had ane swne was callyde Frewyne,
That Wyggews gat eftyre syn;
Hys swn Gennus gat Elfeus,
That fadyr wes off Elesyus;   920
Elesyus gat Kerdycy,
That awcht West Saxone halyly;
The fyrst Kyng tharoff was he,
That it fyrst awcht in reawte:
He gat Kynrycyus eftyre syn,
That fadyr wes off Cealfyne;
Hys swn Cwtwyne gat Kude;
Cedwaldys fadyr syne wes he,
And hys sown Conrad eftyre that
Inys brodyre Inglis gat.   930

Now off thir or I tell ma,
Tyll Geddyll-Glays wyll I ga.
This Geddyll-Glays eftyre that
To sown Eber-Stiwut gat;
Eber syne, as I herd telle,
Fadyr was off Novaelle;
This Novael gat Node;
And eftyre Aldoyt gat he;
Off hym come eftyr Erkada,
That gat Doat, and he Brata.   940
Hys swne Brogyne gat Broge

That gat thare-eftyre Vcande;
Syne hys swne Myle gat
Mylet off Spayn swne eftyre that;
This Mylet eftyre had, but·drede,
Tyll son Ermeon-Malanseyde;
Off hys swn Jaer-Olphaca
Come Etoyre; and eftyre tha
This Etoyr gat Phaleke,
That fadyr wes tyl Tygerneke;   950
And hys swn eftyr Enbaca
Had a swn calde Synreca;
Fyakak-Labryn eftyr that
Eugws-Olmwrge to swn gat;
His sown Temaelle gat Den;
And Syrne-Elkạde gat Olten;
Hys swn wes Moyadade-Fael,
That gat Glays, as I herd tel;
Off hys sone Edoym eftyr that
Come Coyem-Dwff, that to sone gat   960
Symon-Breke, that off Spayné land
That Stane browcht fyrst in tyll Yrland,
That syne wes callyd mony yhere
The Kyngys Stane in Scotland here,
As yhe sall here eftyr swne,
Quhen this proces tyll it is dwne.

CHAP. XI.

*Now sal yhe here off Danaus,
And off his brodire Egistus.*

A THOWSAND and fyve hundyr yhere,
And twa and fourty full, but were,
Before the Natywyte
That wes the caus off alle oure gle,   970
In tyll Egypt Schyr Danaws,
That brodyr wes tyll Egistus,
Off dowchtrys nowmbryde had fyfty.
Egyst had sownnys sa mony.
Thai swnnys slayne war everilkane
Wytht thai dowchtrys to sauffe ane,
That gat away all prewaly.
Egystus tharfore fellownly
Gert hym off Egypt banyst be;
In Argos than aryvyd he,   980
Quhare Tenelaus than wes kyng,
That made hym curtays welcummyng,
And ressawyde [hym] in that nede
And dyde hym profyt and fordede.
Bot he dyde vylny thare agayne,
This Tenelaus he walde have slayne
And be [the] lest hym banyst he
The men all hale off that cuntré,
He enbawndownyd all hym tylle,
And maid thame bowswm tyll his wylle;   990
And swa he regnyde in hys stede,
That banyst was for dowt off dede.

Than Busyrys in Egypte als
Fellown ostlare wes, and fals,
And hys devotyoune wes welle were,
And hys relygyowne cruelere
Than ony wychcraft mycht be,
Or tyrandry in ony gre.
Quhen tyll hys gestis he maid gud chere,
And welcummyd thame on fayre manere,　　　1000
And syne to thame wald ta gud kepe,
Quhyll thai ware sadly fallyn on slepe;
Than stillely walde he to thame ga,
And scheyre thare thropyll boll in twa,

F. 28. b.　　And syne thare blud walde sacryfy
Tyll his goddys devotly,
Thynkand thai sulde be parcynere
Off mede and payne that he sulde bere;
For he sayd, that sacryfyce
Plesyde hys goddys mony wys.　　　1010
　　Tereus in that tyme alsua
Lyin had by [his] systyris twa,
Prognas callyd, and Phylomene,
Off that incest fell murthyr kene,
And ane wgsum mangery
Of wlatsum corsys and wgly;
For quhen the tane full wytting had
Hyr systyr had lessyde hyr maydynhade,
Hyr systyr twyng fyrst schare scho owt;
Hyr awyne sone syne scho slw, but dowt,　　　1020
And sethyde hym in pecis smalle,
And gert hys fadyr eyt hym alle.
　　Perseus in this tyme alsua
Come owt off Grece in Asya,
Quhare all that tyme the folk were

Rude off condityoune and off fere,
Bot he thame wan, throwcht hys trawaylle,
And fors off fycht in harde batayle,
And gert thame tyll hym buxum be;
Syn Pers he gert call that contré.   1030
On this wys, as I maid rehers,
The kynryk fyrst begouth off Pers.

 Thai fenyheid fabyllis I wyll forbere
That Ovyde tellys how Jupitere
Gert the Egyle, as we rede,
Rawys the barne Ganemede,
And bere hym wp in to the ayre
Quhare Jupitere maid his repayre,
Thare, for hys soverane bewte,
Lemman to that god wes he.   1040
And spensare alsua quhen Ebes
Removyd to that offys wes.
How Tantalus that wes as fere
Tyll goddys and alye nere,
This Ganymede on this wys reft,
Tuk and held hym lang thare-eft,
Tyll lust off this Jupitere,
Or tyll hys awn lust famelyere.
How Pelops, the sone off Tantalus,
Ras agayne Schyr Dardanus,   1050
That lord off Troy was in thai dayis.
How Perseus als, as fabyll sayis,
Wytht Tebanys and Spertanyis
Maid mony syndry jupertyis:
And how Edippus, as sayis Stace,
That slaare off hys fadyre wace,
Gat on hys modyr sonnys twa,
And was hys barnys brodyr swa:

And howe the barne Ethyocles
Faucht wytht hys brodyr Polynces,　　　　1060
In that intent that bayth ware sene
Fechtaris and manslaaris kene:
And othir fenyheid fabyllis sere,
I wyll forbere to wryt in here;
For gyff I dyde as othir wrate
In this plas I sulde set thaire date.

CHAP. XII.

**Off Josue now sall yhe here,
In this next folowand Chapitere.**

IN to this tyme that I off telle
Was Josue duk in Israel,
The wattyre off Jordane in his dayis
Was dry, as the story sayis,　　　　1070
Quhill that the folk oure passyd fre
Off Jeryco the gret cyté
And all thai that he fande tharein,
Man and best, bath mare and myn,
He wndyde and slw all down
And broucht it tyll confusioune,
Bot golde, sylvyr, and wessale
Clenly maide off gud metalle,
He gert halow wytht honoure
Tyll Goddys oys, and hys tresoure.　　　　1080
That tyme als, in that cyté,
He gert that woman sawffyt be
That sauffyt hys spyis wysly
Quhen thai come that towne to spy.

Thare Achor als the mantyll stall,
The sylver and the rewell wyth alle,
And ran in sentens off courssyng
For that he stal and brak byddyng;
Tharefore Josue, but remede,
Hym gert be stanyde thare to dede. 1090
　　Syn he passyde for tyll assay
Gyff he mycht wyn the town off Hay;
He wan wytht juperty that towne
And off it slwe twelf thousand downe.
Fra thine, wytht hys ost onone,
He past to wyn Gabaone,
Bot, throucht dyssayte, the Gabaonytys
Wes frendyt wytht the Israelytis;
For quhen thai hard that Josue
Wes to cum wytht hys ryawte, 1100
Thai dowtyt sare that he walde wyn
Thare landys, and thare cyté bryne,
As he to Jericho had done,
And tyll Hay thare efftyr sone,
Messengerys to Josue
Thai gart off consalle ordanyt be,
Wytht aulde hose and rywine schone,
And mowlyde brede in kartis done;
Be thai taknys to be kend
That thai ware off fer landis sende. 1110
On this wys the Gabaonytis
Come chargyt to the Israelitis,
And delyveryde in thare presence
Tyll Josue playnly, be credence;
And sayd, thai come off landys fere,
Quhar that thai herd off his powere,
And off thai landys that thai had

F. 29. b

Tyll Jowys wes na promissyowne maide;
Bot off thaire wyll to Josue
In serwys thai walde oblysyde be,   1120
And this, thai said, wes in thare intent
That thame in message thiddyre sent.
Tyll thir wordys Josue
Trowyd, and thame ressawyde he,
And off his ost the lardis thare
Be athe to thame all bundyn ware.
Wytht-in thre dayis eftyre that,
Quhen Josue full wyttyng gat
That he dissawyd wes, but were,
He arguyt thame on fel manere;   1130
And thai excusyd thame symply
And said, thai dyd it qwhently;
For it wes gert thame wndyrstand
That thai walde occupy thare land,
And hald it in possessioune,
And bryng thame tyll confusioune;
Sen thai ware sa thame bundyn tylle
Thai mycht do wyth thame all thare wylle.
The multitwde than wes rycht lath
For to sauff thame, for thaire ath   1140
Thai sayde, wes be surreptyoune,
Gyle, and circumventyoune,
Sworne befor that, and for-thi
Tha ware excusyd lauchfully
All thai cuchowris for to ta
And, but mercy, pyne and sla.
Bot the lordys walde noucht wndo
The band that thai war oblysyd to,
Bot said, thame thoucht it wondyre lath
For to be argwyt off thare ath;   1150

For bath to frend and fa sulde be
Fayth evynlik kepyd in leawte.
On this thai yheid all tyll consale
And sone thai delyveryt hale
To ta thare gudys, and thare towne
Hale in thare possessioune,
And mak thai men thare travalourys,
Masownys, wrychtys, and pynowrys,
And sa thai mycht revengyde be,
Excusand baytht fayth and leawte. 1160
Thus maid thai schort delyverance
And gert fullfill all ordynance.

 Off this manere Kyngys fyve,
That marchyd nere thame herde belyve,
Wytht thare ost thai come onone
For tyll assege Gabaone,
And thai wytht-in, on set consalle,
Askyt at Josue suppoualle.
Wytht hys ost thane he come on
And chasyd thai folk throucht Bethoron, 1170
For off hym thai had sic drede
That thame behuvyde [to] fle onnede;
Haylstanys gryt in to that flycht
Sa hewy thyk and hard can lycht,
That [ma] peryst in that schoure
Than swerdys stikkyt in that stowre,
And quhyll thai ware in to the chas
The swn rycht fast avaland was,
And the mwne agayne the nycht,
As in mydwaxand tuk the hycht. 1180
Than Josue wytht devotyoune
Devotly maid his orysoune
To God, and swa than gert he stand

Swn and mwne batht wnmovand,
Fra thine the space hale off a day,
That never yhit, as I harde say,
Sa lang a day wes sene beforne
Wytht al thai that that tyme wes borne;
In that tyme hys fays qwyte
Fullyly Josue discomfyte.　　　　　　　1190
All this tyme in to that chas,
Quhyll Josue fast prekande was,
He persawyde that Kyngys fyve
Crape in a cove to sawffe thare lyve;
Than off that cove the mouth gert he
Wytht stannys gryt sone dyttyde be,
Quhyll that all the chas was done,
And syne he gert, wytht-owtyn hone,
Owt off that cove thai Kyngys bryng
And thame wpone a gallows hyng.　　　1200
　　Off Josue and hys wyctorys,
And othir syndry juperdys
That was in his dayis done,
In to the Bybyll yhe may sone
F. 30. b.　Fynd thaime wryttyn in his Buk,
Gyff yhe wyll all the story luk.

CHAP. XIII.

How how that the Cretens Fawcht wyth the Attineens.

FOURTENE hundyr yher beforne
And twelf full or God wes borne
A fell were ras, as Orose sayis,

And a dispetews in thai dayis 1210
Betwene thame duelland in Crete,
That is an yle in to the se,
And the folk off Athenys,
That in to Grece a gryt towne is;
Thare slauchtyr hapnyd rycht cruelle
And bathe the partys fers and felle;
Bot the Cretens faucht sa fast
Quhylle the Grekys at the last
Mast part in that batayle qwyt
Was tane, or slayne, or discumfyt. 1220
The gentyl-mennys sonnys thare
That ayrys to thare faderys ware
Thai tuk in to that were, but dowt,
And all thare eyne fyrst thai put owt.
A Mynotawre (quhethir that he
A felowne man or best sulde be,
I wyll noucht tel yow certanly),
All thai barnys halyly
Thai gert be delyveryd tyll,
For to be swellyid at hys wyll, 1230
And to be ctyn. In that place thare
The Grekys thus reboytyt ware.

 The Laphytys and the Tessalyis
In Grece bayth thai landys lyis,
In that tyme oysyd gret trawaille
Amang thame self in hard bataylle.
In tyll a buk that Palafat
Off hys wncertane ferlyis wrate:
He sayde the Laphytys trowyd hale,
And taulde als for a certane tayle, 1240
That the Tessalyis sulde be
Yppocentawrys in akyn gre;

That is to say propyrly
Bath hors and man in a body.
Suppos that thai sik wenyng had,
Swylk a best wes nevyr made;
Bot for ay thai saw so thyk
Thare horsmen in to batayle pryk
Othir wenyng had thai nane,
Bot hors and man batht wes ane. 1250

CHAP. XIV.

Hhe sall be this Chapitere se
Qwhat the Mynowtaure schuld be.

F. 31. OVIDE tellys mystyly
In tyll his Methamorphosi,
That is the Buke off Changynge,
In tyll our propyr wndoyng,
For in it ar changys sere,
That ferlyffull ar for to here.
This Owyde sayis that Dedalus
Wes in his dedys merwalus.
Off Athenys he wes kyng
And mekyll had in governyng 1260
First tyl lordschipe quhen he drewe
Hys newo in tyll ire he slewe,
And exylid for that caus wes he
Owte off Athenys in to Creté,
That is in to the Se ane yle,
Thare Mynois regnyd in that quhyle,
He Kyng that tyme wes off Creté,
And had a wyff callyd Phasyfé,

Batht off fassowne and off face
Fourmyde fayre at full scho wace.   1270
As this Queyne apon a day
Hyr laykand in a medow lay,
A tawre, that is a bul, but wene,
Scho saw ner by hir on the grene
Gnyppand gyrs rycht gredyly;
Quhen scho beheld hym increly,
Hyr fleschly lust maid [hir] so ken
That wndyr hym scho walde have bene;
Scho pressyd to [pleysse] hym wytht all slycht
Hyr brandysand in tyll his sycht   1280
And maid hyr oft wytht hym to bowrde;
Bot that best off kynd sa lowrde
Wyst rycht noucht quhat scho wald meyne
Bot wend hyr bourd hade manans bene;
Swa ay as scho wald drawe hym nere,
Fra plas to place the bul walde stere.
Scho lufyt this best so straytly
That scho walde fayne have had copy
Off hym, gyff ony wys scho moucht
Bot kynd to that accordyt noucht.   1290
 Quhyll that scho wes travalyde thus,
Scho come off case to Dedalus,
And schawyde tylle hym hyr malady,
And syne requeryd hym specyally
That he wald se for sum remede,
Or than, but dowt, scho were bot dede.
Off this request scho wes sa thra
That scho walde na wys pas hym fra,
Quhyll that he gave hys assent,
In tyll assyth off hyr talent.   1300
Than he hyr fourmyde in a kowe

Bot that is noucht yhit all to trowe,
And the bul quhylum he sawe that,
This Mynotawre apon hyr gat,
And quhen hyr tyme wes weryd owte
Off this bysyn best, but dowt,
Scho wes delyẅyre: and quhen this
The kyng off Crete, Mynois,
Hade sene, in hart he wes full wa
That he was asschamyd swa; 1310
In tyll a stede he maid in hy
A manere place swa suttely,
And stratly closyd all abowte,
That quha wytht-in walde pres hym owte,
Than hym behuẅyd to mak entre;
And quha wytht-out wytht-in walde be,
To be thare-owte ay hym behuẅyde
Quhatkyn craft sua evyre he pruẅyde.
The Laberynt thai callyd that place,
The Mynotawre set in it was, 1320
And syne thai oysyd commonaly
To call it Domus Dedaly.
Dedalus quhen he saw this,
He was so rad for Mynois,
That off the land he walde have bene,
Gyff he couth ony way have sene;
Bot hym behuẅyd oure a Se,
And schyppyn nane to that hade he.
    Than this ilk Dedalus,
And his son Ycarius, 1330
Mad thame hally to the flycht;
Swa Dedalus than, wytht hys slycht,
For hym and his sone, maide twa
Feytheramys fayre thare flycht to ta.

In thai quhen clede wes Dedalus
And his sone Ycarius,
He bade his sone in to the flycht
Hald ewyn in tyll a rawndown rycht:
Noucht tyll hey, for dowt the ayre
Sulde melt away his fethrys fayre; 1340
Na to law, for dowt the flud
Sulde wesche away his fethrys gude.
Bot this Ycarius in his flycht
Made a cowrs so hey on hycht,
That hym behowyde on nede cum doun,
Swa hapnyd hym in the Se to drown.
Be that ensawmpyll be thir ilk wers
Ware maid that I wyll yowe rehers,
    (*Ycarii fati*
    Memores estote parati,
    Jussa paterna pati,
    Medium tenuere beati.)

F. 32.   Off the werd of Ycary,
Be ye ay thouchtfull and redy, 1350
To thole yhoure fadyr byddyng ay,
Haly men mesoure held all way.
    The bul that this Dame Phasifé
Thus lufyd, wes in propyrté
Hyr awne stewart that by hyr lay,
And on hyr gat, in chambure play,
A barne that wes prywaly
Haldyn and norysyde tendyrly.
Gret slycht, as yhe herd, scho leryde
Hyr lordys ey wytht that scho bleryde. 1360

CHAP. XV.

How Wersozes off Egipt kyng
In sowth and north made gret steryng.

TWELFF hundyr and thretty yhere beforn
And twa yhere or that God wes born,
Wersozes that off Egypt kyng
Bath sowth and north maid gret steryng,
And set his diligence ay
Batht thai arthys as thai lay,
Be land partyd, or be sé,
To ger thame bowe tyll his pousté,
Or ellys he suld thame fast assayle
Wytht felown were and hard bataylle. 1370
Thare-off message he send in hy
Tyll thame than duelland in Sythy,
And bade that thai sulde tyll hym drawe,
And oys his custome and his lawe,
And becum in-deyde his men.
To this message thai ansuerd then,
And said thame thoucht it fawklys thyng
Tyll hym that wes a mychty kyng
Agayne sa sympyll folk to rys,
Or fande in were thame to supprys; 1380
Sene werde off batayle is dowtows
And tyll all partys peralows.
Off this for tyll mak schort oure tayle,
Thai mellayde sone in tyll batayle,
Quhare the fycht wes fers and felle,
On bath the partys rycht cruelle.

Bot Wersozes at the last
Dyscumfyt wes and fled rycht fast.
The Sytykys wencust that batoylle,
And tuk wp all thare apparaylle, 1390
That wes left in to that place
Quhare that batayll strykyne was,
And chasyde the Egyptys hastyly
On hors and fute dyspytuysly.
And thai, for radnes fleand fast,
Wan fra thare dawngere at the last.
 The Sytykys than wytht thare poware
Had wastyd all that land off were.
Ne ware [the] Egyptys dykys depe
About thame drewe thare land to kepe. 1400
 The Sytykys than wytht playne batayle
Maid throwcht Asy thare trawayle,
And wan mckyll off it off were,
That thai maid to thame tributere.
Fyftene yhere thare thai abade,
Bot sum tyme yit war thai hade,
Quhyll thaire wyffys made thame kende
Be the message that thai sende,
Bot gyff thai sped thame hame but let,
That othire suld thare barnys get, 1410
[And ly with thame in ful delite,
That thai mycht stanch thair appetit].

CHAP. XVI.

**How tellis the next Chapitere
Qwhat the Amazones were.**

In the menetyme that this was,
Twa yhung men in tyll Sythy ras,
The tayne callid wes Plynyus,
The tothire Scolopetyus,
That be the lawys off the land
Mycht noucht for thare dedys stand,
Than the lordys wald thame ta,
And, be thare statutys, wald thame sla, 1420
Swa that off nede thame behuẅyd
To be banyst and removid
Fra thare gud, thare kyn, thare kyth;
Off yhung falowys thai gat thame wyth
Ane lychtheẅyddyd company,
And set thame hale wpone felony,
And maid in strayttys thare reset,
Wytht all the stuff that thai mycht get,
And sum landys nere thame by
Thai gert [obey] to thare mastry, 1430
And mony landys thai destroyit,
Thare-off the folk were sare anoyid;
Swa thai conspyryd pryvaly
Wytht marcherys that lay nere thame by,
The quhilkis maid thame swylk a trayne,
That mony off thame sone had thai slayne.
[And] all the laẅe that dowt swa drede,
That thai tyll strayttare heychtys flede;

Swa was skallyd all that rowt
That off the lawe wes had na dowt. 1440
Thare wyffys that in that cas wes dede
As wedowis wyll off a gud rede,
Movyd was in tyll gret ire,
In felny brynnand as a fyre,
To thaire cummarys thair main thai made
Menande sayre thaire wedowhade;
Than thai gadyryde thame all halle.
And made amang thame be consalle
On set purpos for to qwyt,
Wytht gret revengeans, that dyspyte 1450
Done tyll thare husbandys that ware slayn,
Set thai sulde de in to the payn.
On this thai set haille thare intent,
Bot thai kest ane impediment
Dowtows to fall in to swylk cas,
Syne faynt off kynd all women was,
And mekyll scownerand to se blude,
Quhare-in as thai thair purpos stude
Thare hart in to the deyde suld faylle
And swa thai tyne sulde thare trawaylle; 1460
And for thare full presumptioune
Thai sulde fall in confusiowne.
To this ilkane said thare intent,
And delyveryd wytht hale assent,
Bot on that poynt [of] thaire accord
I dar noucht tyll yhow now record,
For dowt that wemen wald me blame
Gyff that it twechys thare defame,
And call it myne autoryte,
Set it autentyk story be; 1470
And als the sawmpyll is rycht felle,

The propyrté thareoff to telle.
Bot Oros, in his Fyrst Buke,
Gyff that yhe wyll the story luke,
The foure and twentyid chapytere,
Can tell yhowe thare-off the manere
Quhat evyre it wes, it thai begane
And held wpon it stowtly than,
And rasyde were and playne batayle;
And stoutly made thame tyll assayle   1480
The landys lyand thame about,
And maid thaime tyll thame wndyrlowt,
And slewe thare innymys ilkane
That thare husbandys before had slayne:
All thus off were thai wan the land:
And maid it tyll thame obeysand,
Bot sum men thai gert sauffyd be
In tyme to cule thare qualyte;
And in ane yle thai gert thame ga
Amang thaim na repayre to ma,   1490
Bot qwhat tyme at thaire appetyte,
Thame movyd in lust and in delyte,
That yle ay thai walde pas tylle
Thare fleschly lust for to fullfille;
And quhat barnys ware gottyn thare
Quhen thaire modyrys delyver ware
Off knaw barnys thai walde sla mony,
The madynys thai norysyde tendyrly,
Bot away thai walde ger bryn
The rycht pape the fleyhs wythtin   1500
Leffand noucht off it a crote
For dowt it sulde let thame off schot:
Thai war callyd Amazones.
    Twa gret ladyis off thame wes

That betwene thame tuk the cure
Off howshalde and off were al-ure,
Tyme be tyme per cumpany,
Wyth thare cowrtys ay syndry,
As ordanyd wes betwene thame twa:
The tayne wes callyd Mesepia, 1510
The tothire Lampete was calde
Baytht thai ware in batayllis balde.
In Europe landys rycht mony
Thai wan, and mekyll off Asy;
Thai byggyd a cyté callyd Smyrna,
Epheson thai maid alsua;
Welth at wyll thai wan off were,
All Asy dowtyde thare powere.
Syne Lampite wyth hyr cumpany
Passyde hame agayne in tyll Sythy, 1520
And lefte behynd hyr Dame Maisepe,
Wytht hyr cowrt, the land to kepe.
The Asyanys ras hyr agayne,
And has hyr in tyll bataylle slayne.
Hyr douchtyre Synope, eftyr hyre dede,
Tuke wpe armys in hyr stede
That wyrschype prowyd in mony dede,
And deyd syn in hyr madynhede.

Sik name ras off that reall route
That landys sere off thame had doute, 1530
And out off Grece be consalle wes
To werray thaim send Ercules,
That chesyt wytht hym the wychtest men
In tyll all Grece that he couth ken,
And mony schyppys gret gert he
Wytht men and armys stuffyde be,
For perylows that were hym thoucht

And ille to purpos to be broucht,
With all thai yhit in playne batayle,
Appertly durst he noucht assayle ; 1540
Bot, on the nycht, all pryvaly
He slewe off thame a gret party
As he come on thaim wnpurwayde,
Wnwarnyst, and all wnarayid.
Twa systyrys had the guvernaylle
That tyme off the land all halle,

F. 34. Antyope and Orythya,
Thir ware the namys off tha twa,
And odyr systyrys twa had thai,
Noucht off swylk state the soyth to say ; 1550
Menalympe callyd wes ane,
Scho wytht Ercules wes tane,
And he delyveryde hyr all fre
Tyll hyr systyr Antiope,
And for hyr rawnsome tuk na mare
Than the armurys that scho bare.
The tothire systyr, Ypolytes,
Weddyde wyth Theseus wes ;
Neyst Ercules in all degre
The gretest off that ost wes he. 1560

 Thare Orythya wes dede,
Penthassale ras in hyr stede,
Hyr douchtyr and hyr ayre off ale
That tyll hyr suld off profyt fale.
This lady prowyd gret douchtynes ;
Quhen the Grekys assegeand wes
The town off Troy, wytht thare powere,
Thare wyth hyr ost scho come off were,
As in the story weill is kend.
Bot schortly nowe for to mak end ; 1570

Ane hundyr yhere thare powere stud,
And landys sere thaire mycht oure-yhude,
Westande hale wytht thaire powere,
And byggand quhar thare wyllys were.

CHAP. XVII.

The Assegis off Troye here
Next folowis in this Chapitere.

A THOWSAND ane hundyr and foure score,
And twa yher fully gane before
Crystys Incarnatyoune,
Off Troy wes the destructyowne,
That the Grekys [fully] ten yhere
Assegeand war wytht thare powere. 1580
How that began and endyt wes
Homer trettis, and Dares.
And eftyr Troyis destructyowne
And the cyté castyn downe,
Eneas gert twelff schyppys be
Wytayllyde and layde to the sé.
He and hys fadyre, Anchyses,
Askaneus als, that his sone wes,
In thai twelf schyppys tuk the sé,
Wytht all thare gud and thaire menyhe, 1590
And saylland, happynyt in the ile
That be name callyde wes Syzile;
Thare that tyme dede wes Anchyses,

F. 34. b.   And in that ile enteryde wes.
And quhen Anchyses hapnyd thus,
Eneas and Askaneus,

On set purpos fermly,
For tyll have bene in Ytaly,
Wp to [the] tope thare sayllys drewe,
And drawe on, as thame blastys blewe   1600
And quhyle on Roume lay coftys owt,
As thai war stad in stormys stout,
And quhylle lay nere for tyll have sene
Quhat land that thai had nerest bene,
And at the last thai saland swa,
Arywyt on fors in Affryca.
Quhar than off Affric Dido, Quene
Fra that scho had Eneas sene,
Resawyd hym wytht gret honoure,
And lufyd hym stratly paramoure,   1610
And gert all hyr ryawte
Tyll hym and his obeysand be.
Thare sojowrnand a quhille he bade,
Quhare alkyn welth at wylle he hade.
Bot his yharnyng halyly
Stude tyll have bene in Ytaly;
Tharefore he schyppys layd to sé,
And waytyd wynd and made entré,
And tuk wpe sayle and helde thare trade,
In Tybyr quhyll thai strekyn hade;   1620
Quhare, as Eneas slepand lay
Apon a nycht in hys galay,
A woce he herd that bad hym pas
Tyll Ewandire that that tyme was
Kyng rygnand in sevyn hyllys by,
Quhare Rome is set now werraly,
And bad he sulde mak suppowale
Tyll this Ewandire, that batayle
Gawe to kyng Latyn ythandly

For the kynryk off Ytaly. 1630
Eftyr all that hys sulde be
  Wpon that purpos passyde he
Tyll this Ewandire wytht his mycht,
And faucht wytht Latyn in tyll fycht,
And Turnus in that fycht has slayne
That kyng wes that tyme off Tuskayne,
And mawch wes to this kyng Latyn,
And weddyd hys douchtyr Dame Lavyne;
And for that caus to this bataylle
This Turnus come in suppowaylle 1640
Off Latyn kyng, and slew Pallas,
That off Ewandire sone than was;
And throuch Eneas syne was he
Slayne off fors in that mellé.

F. 35.   Eneas weddyd syne Lavyne,
The douchtyr off this kyng Latyne;
And quhen that Latyne kyng wes dede,
He succedede in hys stede,
As kyng rygnand yherys thre;
And eftyr hym, quhen dede wes he, 1650
Hys sone Askaneus tuk all hale
Off Ytaly the governayle,
And byggyd thare a gret cyté,
And Albane gert it callyd be;
And auchtene wyntyr rygnand was
Eftyr his fadyre Eneas;
For owt off Troy wytht hym come he,
Gottyn and borne in that contré.
Hys sone callid wes Sylvius,
The quhilk wes fadyr to Bruttus, 1660
That this land fra geawndys wan,
And eftyr hym wes callyd Brytan.

Off Troy quhen that Eneas
Buskyd hym wytht schype to pas,
Anthenor and his menyhe
Wyth thare nawyn tuk the sé,
And arywyde by Pannony
That marchys nere tyll Wngary,
Off Wenes he maid the gret towne
That yhit is realle off renowne, 1670
And a port off the mekyll sé,
Quhare that pylgrymys mais entre
That to Jerusalem walde fayre
The sepulkyr to wysyde thare.
Off this Anthenor come syne,
Descendand ewyn down be lyne,
Francus off sa reale fame
That Frawns off hym yhit hawys the name.
Thus thai come fyrst, halyly,
All off the gret towne off Troy, 1680
That Ytaly all occupyid,
And Frawns and Brytane inhabyid,
And othir mony landys sere
That I leve nowe to rekyn here.

[**Explicit Liber Secundus.**]

THE THRYDE BUKE

OF THE

ORYGYNALE CRONYKIL

OF SCOTLAND.

THE THRYDE BUKE

OF THE

ORYGYNALE CRONYKIL
OF SCOTLAND.

**The Proloug off the Thryde Buke
In this next Chapitere yhe sall luke.**

MOYSES, that in tyll his dayis
Broucht tyll the Jowys thare wryttyn Lawys,
Gave thame in byddyng oppynly
Thus wryttyn in Dewteronomii,
Off the Bybyl the fyfte Buke
Fra the begynnyng, quha wyll thame luke.
"*Memento dierum*, that leve yow noucht,
F. 35. b.   *Antiquorum*, bot drawe to thoucht
Ilké generatyowne,
And in thare successyowne: 10
Ask at thi fadyre, quhat at fell,
And at thine eldrys, quhat thai can telle."
The sentence off this autoryte
Suld move men to besy be,
Thare statis to kene Orygynalle,
And thame to treyt Memoryalle,
Batht off thare eldrys and thaire dayis,
As in thire wers, thus Moyses sayis;

(*Memento dierum antiquorum, cogita genera-
tiones singulas:
Interroga patrem tuum, et annunciabit tibi;
majores tuos, et dicent tibi, etc.*)
Oure eldrys we sulde folowe off det,
That thaire tyme in wertu set: 20
Off thame, that lyvyd wytyously,
Carpe we bot lytyll, and that warly.
The dayis sulde be set for terme
A certane purpos for tyll afferme:
Swa stablyst have I my delyte
Consequenter now to dyt
Wytht delytabyll incydens,
And in plesand conveniens,
The tyme that Brutus wan this Ile,
And callyd it Brytane in that quhile;   30
And the dywysiownys off it, that he
Made syne to hys sonnys thre.
Swa furth drywand my purpos
Be syndry storyis syne to clos
In it that tyme, as I can se,
That made off Rome wes the cyté.
This in fourme to sped and hast
The wertu off the Haly Gast
Be prayere off the Madyn fre
I call devotly to helpe me.   40

Explicit Prologus.

The Chapiteris off the Thryde Buke.

i. OFF the Jwgis off Israelle.
ii. Off Sampson and hys wychtnes.
iii. Quhen Brutus come in Brettane.
iiii. Off a Genealogy.
v. Off Sardanapillus.
vi. Off the successyowne off Pers.
vii. Off a Terand that dyde felny.
viii. Off Olympyas.
ix. Off the Kyngys Stane off Scotland.
x. Off Symon Brek and his Lynage.

F. 36.   Incipit Liber Tertius.

CHAP. I.

**Off the Jwgis off Esraelle
This next Chapitere schall telle.**

Q WHEN the assege off Troy felle
Jwgs ras in Israelle,
And off the pepyll chosyne was
Duk and chyfftane than Judas.
The lorde off Bezeke than was tane,
And off hys fyngrys, everilkane,
And off all his tays wytht
The utmast endys be the lyth
Qwyt was strekyn off; than he
Sayde, "This, I trowe nowe done to me   10
Be Goddys wyll, for quhylum I
Off Kyngys realle had sevynty
Wndyrneth my burddys set,
Sekand crummys for tyll ete,
Mankyd all on lyk manere,
As now my cas is happynyd here;
Tharfore off Goddys wyll, I trowe,
Is all done that I suffyr nowe."

 The kyng off Moab, than Eglon,
Had wndyr hym in subjection   20
The folk off Israell auchtene yhere,
Quhyll Ayot [Ehud] begowth to stere;
The quhilk swa agyle wes in fycht
That batht the left hand and the rycht
He ewynlike oysyde, quhen that he

In were wes stade, or in mellé;
And for that oys than gert he ma
A scharpe suerd wytht edgys twa;
Syne fra the folk off Israelle thare
He presendys and gret gyftys bare   30
Tyll this Eglon that tyme kyng,
That Moab had in governyng;
All othir off dreyth than gert he drawe
Hys charge, quhill that he suld schawe
That ilk suerd, that tyme had he,
On his rycht syde in prewate
Wndyr his gown; and syn ononc
He tuke hys rayk to this Eglon,
And sayd [at] it war his wyll
A worde he had to say hym tylle.   40
Off his cheare quharein he sat,
This kyng Eglon ras wp wytht that.
Than Ayot tyt owt smertly
Hys suerd that he bare prewaly,
And put it in his wame sa fast
Quhill hylte and plumet bath in past
And leyffyt it stekand in his belch,

F. 36. b.   The carle was fat as ony selch,
Bath gore and cres rane tyll his hand
That wytht hys suerd was hym stykand.   50
His famyle thare, wytht-owtyn dout,
That was the chambure than wytht out
Wende the kyng had syttand bene
On the priwé, bot syne, but wene,
Fra thai had bade lang tyme wytht out
Thai ware in to [the] fellare dout.
Thare eftyr sone a key thai gat
And opynyt the chambure dowre with that,

In thai come, and slayne thai fand
Thare Kyng apon the flure thare lyand.   60
All thus fra thai fand hym dede
Dyspayryd thai ware off gud remede;
But mare byddyng than tuk thai
Tyll Jordane on the nerest way.
　In this mene tyme preẅaly
Ayot chapyde, and in hy
Fled fast quhill he passyd wele
All the placys ilk[a] delle
That thare ydolys than hade
And his incummyng fyrst he made.   70
Off Israell than the pepyll alle
He gert in hy befor hym calle;
And wytht thame passyd till Jordane.
All the furdys everilkane
Off that wattyr he kepyde swa,
That tene thousand full and ma
Off the Moabytys thare
Slayne about that wattyr ware.
　Sangare, as the Bybyll sayis,   80
Slw wytht a cultyre in thai dayis
Off the Phylysteis wycht
Sex hundyr men throucht fors in fycht
Barak als and Delbora
Than made that chas on Sysara,
Quhen that Jael hym resaẅyde
In tyll hyr tent and hym dyssaẅyde;
He askyt drynk off wattyr clere
To gyff hym, gyve hyr wyllis were,
For he was for runnyne hate,
And all-owr drawkyde wete in swat.   90
Swet mylk than scho broucht hym tylle,

And bade [him] thareoff drynk his fylle,
And coweryd syne, and gert hym ly
Wndyr a tapyte prewaly,
And sayde scho sulde his wache be,
And nane suld wyt thare ware he.
Wytht that to the dure in hy,
Scho tuk hyr rayk rycht hastyly,
And fand owth that on the walle
Ane hamyr and ane nayll wytht all,   100
And syne scho waytyd and tuk kepe,
Quhill he was rowtand fast on slepe,
The nayle than on his hewyde scho set,
F. 37.   And strake on fast wytht that malyhet,
Dryfand down rycht throucht his hewyde,
Swa Sysara the lyff he lewyde.

Off the folk off Israelle than
Gedeon agayne Madian
Chesyd thre hundyre men that were
Lapand wattere as hundys here,   110
And lete all the lave ga by
That he saw drynkand than kyndly;
And wytht thai thre hundyr quite
This Madian than wes discumfyte.

Jopté than alsua Galaadyte
Awowyt gyff he discumfyte
Amon, that he sulde, but let,
Off his hous quhat evyr he mete
Nest eftyrhend his wyctory
Devotly to God sacryfy.   120
Swa hapnyd that hys douchtyr yhyng,
Wytht tympanys and wytht swet syngyng,
Met hyr fadyr, this Jopté,
Quhen cumyn fra that fycht wes he;

Than in hart set he wes wa,
Yhit syne he wes oblysyd swa
Hys sacryfice set hym to do,
And to that assentyd scho;
Bot at scho mycht murnand be
Twa moneth hyr ẅyrgynyte; 130
To that leve he gave hyr sone,
And scho thare eftyre, quhen that wes done,
Tyll hyr fadyr come agayne,
And he tyll sacryfice has hyr slayne.

CHAP. II.

The next Chapitere schall onone
Tell the wychtnes off Sampsone.

THAR eftyr wes Sampsone off renowne
And slw the quhelpe off a lyowne,
As he wytht his faddyr yhed,
And wytht his modyr in yhouthede,
Wytht a wyff to maryde be
All, but thare wyttyng, that dyde he. 140
Swa [thar]eftyre quhen he was
Weddyd wyth that wyff, off cas,
He hapnyde to cum to that stede,
Quhare that he [left] the lyowne dede,
A gret swarme off beys thare
Wele hyvyd wyth-in the chaftys ware:
Off that best, than gredyly
He tuke and ete off that huny:
Tyll his fadyre syne he yhede,
And tyll his mudyr full gud spede, 150

And gert thame off that huny ete.
Eftyr that syne at the mete
Quhare off his wyff the frendys alle
Assemblyt wes at that bridalle,
That his fadyr till hym made,

F. 37. b.   As in that land thai custum hade,
And off his wyffys kyn thretty,
The nobylest in that cumpany,
Assygnyd till hym wes to be,
As feris in all honeste; 160
Than to that thretty at the mete,
As thai ware in thaire greys sete,
He sayd, gyff thai walde wndo
A rydyll that he wald schaw thame to,
Wytht-in sevyn dayis off that brydale
Wyth kyrtylis thretty garmentys hale
He suld gyve thame to thare mede,
And falyhyde that, thai sulde, but drede,
Swylk thretty garmentys tyll hym pay;
To this than assentyde thai, 170
And bade that he suld say thaim tyll
Quhat ewÿr war lykand tyll his wylle.
"Off hym that ete the mete come owt,
And swetnes off the stark and stoute,"
Sampson sayid, and syne thai
Fra this wes sayd held on thare way,
And studyand on this rydyll were,
Quhyll thare terme wes cummyn nere,
And [qwhen] they sawe be nakyn slycht
That [this] rydyll rede thai mycht; 108
All thai thretty come on-one
Tyll the wyff off this Sampsone,
And bad scho suld, on ony wys,

Fleche hyr lord wytht swylk quentys,
Quhyll that he sulde all the dout
Off that rydyll tell hyr owt,
And to thame scho sulde telle it hale,
Swa that thai ran noucht in tynsalle,
Or ellys thai sulde hyr hous bryn,
And all that eẅyre thai fand thare in, 190
For thai sayde wytht hale assent,
Gyff thai ware in tyll that intent,
Tyll fest callyd, that thai sulde be
Dyspoylyt, it war wnhoneste.
This wyff swa on hyr husband yhede,
That hym behoẅyd apon nede
Tell hyr all the suthfastnes,
Set lang tyme that he gruchand wes,
Hym excusyde be that skylle
That it come nevyr in his wyll 200
Tyll his fadyr that to say,
Na tyll his mudyr to that day;
Tyll his wyff yhit, nevertheles,
He tauld all how it hapnyde wes.
Off the lyown, that he leẅyde
Slayne, and fand syne in his hevyde
A byk off beys, and gret copy
In it he fand off suet huny.
To thai thretty than, but bade,
Scho tauld quhat wyttyng that scho hade: 210
Swa apon the seẅynde day,
As syttand at the mete war thai,
And wes examynyt throwch Sampson,
Thai ansueryd all and sayd onone,
" Quhat than the lyowne is starkare,
And quhat than huny is suettare?"

Wytht that Sampson wyst rycht wele
He wes dessayvyde ilk[a] deylle,
He sayd, "Na had yhoure tylch bene wrocht
Wytht my qwy, yhit had yhe noucht   220
Fundyn my propositioune."
  Fra thine he passyd tyll Askaloune,
And thretty men that he fand thare
Ryche robys on thame bare,
He slw all, and thare robys fyne
He gave to thai thretty syne
That he heycht tyll warysowne
Sen thai assolyeit his questyowne.
Bot tyll his wyff he kest sik leth
That thai departyd all in wreth,   230
And wes dyspytwys and fellowne
Tyll hyr and all hyr natyown,
And on sere wys [he] thame anoyid,
And all thare cornys hale he stroyid.
For in his wayth sone eftyr that
Thre hundyr foxis qwyk he gat,
And knyt tyll all thare taylis schyre
Ane hat cole off brynand fyre,
And set thame in thare flattis gret,
Than growand grene off wyne and quheyt;   240
And thai wyld bestys than
All wode throucht thai feldys rane,
Wytht thai blesys, here and thare,
Quhyll brynt wp all thare cornys ware
Than the Phylisteis hale
[That] tholyt that scaytht and that tynsalle
Movid in tyll brynand ire
Sampsonys hous set in tyll fyre;
His wyff and hyr syre at anys

Thai gert bryn wp in to thai wauys. 250
　　Than Sampson that [na] strenthys had
In tyll a cove his duellyng mad,
And the Phylisteis off were
Sone assemblyt thare powere,
And in the land off Juda thai
Come wyth thare ost, and in it lay
And tuk gret prayis to thare mete,
And dyde in tyll it schathis grete,
And quhen the barnage off Juda
Arresownyde thame quhy [thai] dide sua, 260
Thai said [at] thai come onone
To bynd and led away Sampsone,
And to quyt hym lyl for lal.
Off Juda than the barnage alle
Thai oblysyd errare [him] to ta,

F. 38. b.　Or thai sulde be anoyid swa.
Than the Phylisteis all hale
Removyde off Juda thaire batayle.
Thre thousand wycht men off Juda
Than passyd wytht rapys new to ta, 270
And for tyll bynd this Sampsone fast.
Al thus as thai togyddyr past,
Sampsone met thame on the way
And askyd quhethir thare gat lay,
And thare ansuere wes that he
Sulde bundyn, and syne yholdyne be
Tyll his fays; [for] thai ware
For his caus than anoyid sare;
And than that thai sulde noucht hym sla,
He yhald hym tyll thame off Juda. 280
　　Thare wes he tayne and bundyn fast,
And wytht hym on thaire way thai past,

And the Phylisteis, quhen that
He wes tane full wyttyng gat,
Bolenyt all wytht brage and bost,
Agayne hym come wytht a gret ost;
Bot Sampson, quhen he sawe thame nere
Comand all on that manere,
Wytht a tyt thare [he] brak alle
Thai rapys in tyll pecys smalle,   290
And gat a chek bane off ane ass,
That in the gat thare lyand wes,
And fra he gat that in his grype
He leyt abowt hym, quhype for quhype,
Quhyll off the Phylisteis wycht
A thousand men to ded was dycht
Wytht that cheke bane off ane ass;
And Sampsone thare forfowchtyn was,
Sa hate [and] thrysty nere that he
Was in to poynt to peryst be;   300
Tyll God his prayer he mad than,
Syne throucht Hys grace he wychtnes wan,
Quhare throucht his fays he put to dede,
As than wes sene in to that stede,
He walde, gyve His wyllis were,
Grant hym his fill off wattyr clere
Quhare wyth he mycht thare slok his thryst.
Rycht hastyly than begouth to bryst
Owt off a [tuythe] off that chek bane
Wattyr clere in to gret wane,   310
Thareoff than he drank his fylle;
And fra thyne he passyd tyll
The gret cyté off Gaza,
Thare in quiet a quhyll to ta.
  Thare tyll a woman yhung and fare

He oysyd mekyll his repayre;
And quhen the Phylisteis, but lete,
Wyst he had thare his resset,
Thai enbussyd thame ner by
That womanys hous, all prewaly,   320
And set thare wachys for to se
Quhen wnarayid all was he,
That swa thai mycht hym best supprys;
And he, wnwarnyd off thare spyis,
Wytht that woman yhed to bede,
As he noucht off that buschement drede.
Bot that nycht or it wes day
Thare was made hym so hard assay,
Quhyll to the yhattis off fors he past
That lokyt wer and barryd fast,   330
And thare he made than rak for rak
Quhyll conyhe and rabet bath he brak,
And ruschyde wp thai yhattis thare,
And on hys schuldrys wp thame bare
To the hey hyll outht Ebron;
All thus eschapyd than Sampson.

Syne oysyd he repayre to ma
Tyll a queyne callyd Dalyda,
And scho amang thare preweteis
Counsaylyde throwcht the Phylisteis,   340
In hyr flethyng thraly mowyde
And askyt oft, as he hyr lufyde,
Quhar in hys fors stud and hys pyth,
And quhat that he ware bundyn wyth
Sa fast mycht [hald] than that he
Mycht at his fays lykyng be.
Quhen that he sawe thare that he wes
Sa thraly, throuch hyr wantownes,

Infesteyde than that hym behuẅyde
Mak hyr ansuere he contruvyde 350
A fenyheyd ansuer, and he sayde,
"Wytht sevyn corddys newe layde
Off hert cynownys noucht all dry,
But a party, fast ware I
Bundyn, doutles I war than
Bot as ane othire comoune man."
Quhen the Phylisteis herd that,
In hy thai tha corddys gat,
And scho thame helde, and tuk gud kepe
Tyll he was sadly fallyn on slepe, 360
And wytht ane hank than bath his handys,
Fast scho festynyde wytht thai bandys,
And cryit syne lowde, wytht a schowt,
"Now all thi fays ar thé ahowt."
Sampson off his slepe wytht that
He stert wp, and [on] solys gat,
And wytht a rug thai rapys all
He crakyde in to pecys smalle.
Quhen this queyne all this had sene,
Scho mulyd fast, and maid hir tene, 370
And off hyr werdys wykyd plenyheyde,
For in tyll falshede luffe he fenyheyde
Tyll hyr that, for his luffe all hale,
Had put hyr body to tynsale.

F. 39. b.   Bot in thare flechyng syne agayne,
Quhen Dalyda made hyr to frayne
Off the mater off his pyth,
And off hys wndoyng, wyth
That hym behuẅyd on nede to ma
Ansuer tyll hyr, he sayd; "Quha 380
Walde bynd hym wyth twa bandys grene

And now, that nevyr in werk had bene,
He sulde be na wychtare than
Than anothir comoune man."
Than wytht thai rapys scho hym band
Fast, in his slepe, bath fute and hand,
And wyth a schout scho cryid on-one
"Thi fays are on thé nowe, Sampsone."
Thare in his walknyng, wytht a brayde
[Than thai] twa rapys newe layde   390
He brak, and gat wpon his fete.
Wytht that scho brystyd out off grete,
And menyd hyr wykyde werdys sare
That broucht and band hyr in that care,
That scho couth nevyre leve Sampson
To be made lady off Sydon.
It is suet lykyng and na payne
To luffe and [to] be lufyt agayne;
But for luff to yheld fenyhyng,
It is to lele hart a throwyng.   400
Swylk [is the werde] off Dalyda,
That changyd, scho sayd, welle for wa,
Off hart and body, kyn and kyth,
And off all warldys welth thare wyth,
For Sampsone scho had mad chaynge,
And he tyll hyr was alway strange,
And had hyr in tyll myslewyng,
That for lele luffe he yhald fenyhyng.
Yhit thus murnand, nevertheles,
Scho fraynyde fast off his wychtnes   410
Quhar in it stude, and how that he
Mycht lychtlyest our-cummyn be.
Than he sayde, "Gyff scho wald bynd
Sevyn harys off his hewyd behynd

Wytht a threde tyll a spykyn,
And in the erde fast styk it syne;
Than ware he febyll and off na pyth,
Na had noucht for tyll helpe hym wyth,"
That the thryd tyme scho assayid,
And off his slepe syne hym affrayid, 420
And he tyt wp that nayle wyth pyth,
And left bayth hare and threde thare wyth.

   Quhen scho saw hyr the thryd tyme swa
Dyssavyde, than scho mad gret wa,
That scho lyk wes tyll have bene dede
All thus dyspayrid off remede.
Than Sampson, movid in peté,
Tauld hyr, all in prewaté,
That gyve sevyn harys off his hewyde
War schawyn off, nane off thame lewyde, 430
He war off pyth and wychtnes than
Bot as ane othir commoune man.
And quhen his hevid was lyand
Apon hyr skyrt, and he slepand,
Scho gert slely a barbare
Off hys hevyd schawe all the hare,
And the Phylisteis in hy
Scho gert cum on him suddanly.
Thai tuk hym and his eyne put owte,
And thare eftyr, wytht-owtyn dowt, 440
Thai kyst hym in a presowne.
Sa lang he lay in that dungeowne
Quhill on his hevid the hare grewe,
And his pyth worthyde fresche and newe.

   The Philysteis on thare wys
Tyll Dagone mad thare sacryfice
Apon a day, wyth gamyn and gle,

F. 40.

Wytht myrtht, and wytht solempnyté,
And in thare halle, as thai were set,
That day to-gyddyr at thare mete,   450
A boy thai gert [gang] onone
To bryng amang [tham] in Sampson,
That he mycht thare bowrdoure be,
In ekyng off thare gamyn and gle.
And quhen he was amang thame alle
Led in to that mekyll halle,
The boy that hym kepyd thare
He requiryt wyth fayre prayare
To thole hym, bot a lytill space,
Syne he for standyn wery was,   460
Tyll a pyllare leyne hym thare,
Quhill that he refresched ware;
Thare the boy wyth-outyn lete
Sampson at a pyllare sete,
And [he] prayid to God off mycht
That, for the tynsalle off his sycht,
A rewengeans he mycht wyn
Off all his fays that war thare in.
About twa pyllarys than, but let,
At that hows was hale on sete,   470
He kest hys armys hastyly,
And ruggyt at thame dogytly,
And sayd, "My lyff in perale ga
Wytht the Phylysteis," and swa
The post he tyt tyll hym sa fast
Quhyll downe the hous [come] at the last,
And sa smoryd all at wes thar in,
Man and wyff, bath mare and myn.
  Swa slwe he ma in his deyng
Than all that he slwe in fychtyng.   480

In Israell than wes na kyng
Bot ilkane wroucht [at] thaire lykyng.

CHAP. III.

𝔗𝔥𝔢 𝔫𝔢𝔵𝔱 𝔆𝔥𝔞𝔭𝔦𝔱𝔢𝔯𝔢 𝔣𝔬𝔩𝔬𝔴𝔞𝔫𝔡
𝔖𝔠𝔥𝔞𝔩𝔩 𝔱𝔢𝔩𝔩 𝔮𝔴𝔥𝔢𝔫 𝔅𝔯𝔴𝔱𝔲𝔰 𝔴𝔞𝔫 𝔱𝔥𝔦𝔰 𝔩𝔞𝔫𝔡𝔢.

F. 40. b.
SERE Dardane Lord wes off Frygy,
That now men callis all Turky:
He, as the story tellys ws,
Had a sone callid Erictonus,
Off quham Troyus, that Troy made,
And off hym that name it hade:
He gat Ylus, that Ylion
Fwndyt, and gat Leamydon, 490
That [Priame] gat, and Anchises
That Eneas fadyr wes:
And this [Priame] nemmyde befor,
That fadyr wes to gud Hector,
That was sa wycht and sa worthy,
That nevyr yhit na chevalry
Héar yhed than his persowne,
Tharfor yhit lestys hys renowne.
 Eneas sone Askaneus
Had a sone callyd Silvius, 500
That Brut[us] gat, quham off beforne
Wes devynyd, or he wes borne,
That off gret wyrschype [he] suld be,
And rys to state and dignyte;
Bot he suld fadyr and mudyr sla.
And off cas it fell rycht sua:

For his mudyr at hys beryng
Deyd; [and] quhen that he wes yhing
Off fyftene yhere eld off case
Slwe his fadyr at the wanlas; 510
And tharefor owt off that cuntré
Fra kyth and kyne wes flemyd he.
Quhen that this Brutus flemyd was,
Furth toward Grece the way he tays,
Quhar mony off Troy a wele lang quhille
Had bene in thryldome and exyle:
Fra thai gat wyttyng thare, that he
Be leneage was off thare cuntré,
Thai maid hym thare duk and ledare;
And fra he wyst welle howe thai ware 520
Demaynyd into foule thrildome,
He movyde wes for thar fredome.
Swa hapnyde hym to ta the Kyng
And anyd for hys rawnssownyng
For to gyff that tyme hym tylle
Schyppys and ẅyttaylle till his wylle,
And large ryches tyll his men;
And syne his dowchtyr Inogen
He gave hym als to be hys wyẅe.
He buskyt hym thare eft belyve, 530
And to the Sé has tane his way,
Quhare that he traẅalyde mony day
In wayth and were and in bargane
Quhyll that he ẅerownyd haly Spayne.
Syne, eftyr syndry gret mellé,
By Poytere in tyll Frans [come] he.
And in the tyme yhe herde me telle
Than Sampsone ras in Ysraelle.
In tyll Albyone belyẅe

F. 41.

He come, quhare nowthire man na wywe 540
To sauff geawntis thare he fand;
Tyll hym he sesyd all that land,
And realle was, and [of] gud fame,
And callyd that land eftyr his name,
And it inhabytyd wytht his men,
And gat wpon this Inogen
A sone Locryne, and othir twa,
Camber and Albanach war tha.
The eldest Locryne Ingland aucht,
Camber Walys, syne Albanacht 550
Off Scotland had the senyhoury.
Than Yngland callyd wes Locry;
And Camber, Cambry, that Wallys auch
Gert call it; and syne Albanach
Gert Albany call that land,
That now callyd is Scotland.
Thus Brute Brettane gert partyd be
Amang thir forsaid barnys thre,
And byggyd in his land a towne,
Yhit realle [and] off gret renowne, 560
And Trynovant than gert he
Call the name off that cyté,
New Troy, that is to say,
Syne quhen this Brute wes dede away,
Wytht othir namys sere, I wys,
Wes callyd, and now Londyn is.
  All thus quhen thir brethir thre
Had stedede thame in thare cuntré,
And in tyll quiete and in pes
Ilkane in his regnand wes, 570
Sodanly come oure the se
Off Hennygawys a gret menyhe:

Be naẅyne in tyll Albany
Arryẅyde all that cumpany,
And stoutly moẅyd were, and faucht,
And slwe off Scotland Albanacht,
And chasyde his men halyly,
Tyll Locryne Lord than off Locry,
That Yngland wes callyd syne,
Hys ost than gadyryt this Locryne, 580
And Cambere wytht the Welsche hale
Come to mak hym suppowale
And wytht the Henygawys thai faucht,
That slwe the Kyng Albanacht;
Thai met the wattyr off Humbere nere;

F. 41. b.
Thare, wyth the kyng and his powere,
Thai mellayd sone, and faucht rycht fast,
Quhyll thai hym ẅencust at the last;
And on that Kyng thai maid sic chas,
Quhyll in that flude he drownyd was. 590
Hys land callid was Hunia;
Hunys his men [was] callyd alsua:
And quhar sa mony drownyd were,
The wattyr callid was Humbere.

Quhen Albanactus on this wys
Was slayne, as yhe me herd deẅys,
Scotland was dyssaẅarra left,
And wast nere lyand lang thare eft,
Quhyll Scottis and the Peychtis were
In tyll it cummyn, as yhe sall here 600
In tyll this Tretis here eftyre sone,
Quhen all the laẅe tyll it is done.

This Locryne had a sone, but ma,
Madaine, and he had sonnys twa
Memprys and Malyne; bot Memprys

Smyttyd wes wytht mony ẅys;
Hys brothyr he slwe, and syn all tha,
That he couth trow that wald thaim ma
For tyll succede tyll hym as kyng.
It happynyde syne at a huntyng   610
Wytht wolẅys hym to weryde be;
Swa endyt his iniquité.

 His sone Ebrawce in hys stede
Regnyd, quhen that he wes dede;
He fwndyd Yhork that gret cyté,
And Kayrbroyc it callyd he.
He byggyd Edynburgh wytht alle,
And gert thaim Allynclowde it calle
The Maydyn Castell, in sum plas
The Sorowfull [Hill] it callyd was.   620

 Off Bruttus lyneage quha wyll here
He luke the Tretis off Barbere
Mad in tyll a Genealogy
Rycht wele, and mare perfytly
Than I can on ony wys
Wytht all my wyt to yowe deẅys.

 Bot now, forthare or I pas,
I wyll tell how that Eneas
Fra that he slwe the Kyng Latyne,
Weddyd hys dowchtyr dam Laẅyne,   630
And gat wpon hyr Postumus,
That wes callyd alsua Silvius;
He was callyd Postume [for] beforne,
Hys faddyr deyde or he wes borne;
Silvius allsua callyd wes he,
That off the wode has propyrte,
For in the wode he fostyryde was:
Hys sone was callyd Eneas;

F. 42.

He regnyd thretty yhere and ane,
Quhen all his fadyr tyme wes gane, 640
And fyfty yhere he regnyd syne.
Eneas sone was callyd Latyne.
 Gad that tyme and Natan
Prophetis ware contemporan
Tyll Daẅy Kyng off Israell.
In that tyme Cartage, I herd telle,
Dydo fyrst gert formyd be,
And wallyd welle that gryte cyté;
Hyr gudame lufyde Eneas;
Off Affryk hale scho Lady was. 650
 Heyr the Thryd Elde now tayis end,
That, as the Ebrewy mays ws kende,
Contenys nyne hundyr yhere
And twa, gyff all wele rekynyd were;
Bot the Sevynty clerkis wys
Sayis twa les, be thaire storys.
All this tyme Noe his spate
Thaire oys was for to set thaire date,
As now oure oys is in lettrys,
Monumentis, or than chartrys, 660
To rekyn fra the byrth off God,
As yheris hapnys, cẅyn or od.

CHAP. IV.

 Or I forthyr now procede,
Off the Romanys I will rede.

LATYNE kyng off Ytaly,
Eftyre the dede off Sanct Daẅy,

Gat Alba Sylvius onone,
In to the tyme off Salamon:
In Rome he regnyd fourty yhere.
All thir that thus rekynyde were
Discendand fra Postumus,
To surname wes callyd Sylvius.　　　　670
Athis, that callyd wes Egyptus,
And had till surname Silvius,
In Rome foure and twenty yhere
Regnyd, quhen devysyt were
Off Israel the kynrykys and Juda;
Jeroboam had ane off tha:
He kyng wes, and in hys dayis
That scisim fel, as the story sayis;
Kyng off Israell than wes he
Roboam regnyd in Judé.　　　　680
Capis Silvius, but were,
In Rome aucht and twenty yhere
As lord regnyd, quhen Asa
Wes kyng rygnand in Juda.
That tyme in Chawmpayne he
Gert fownd and mak a gret cyté.
In Rome Carpent eftyre that
Regnyd, quhen that Josaphat
F. 42. b.　　Was off Juda lord and kyng.
　Syne off Rome the governyng　　　　690
Tiberius tuke, and wes off it
Nyne yhere lord, as sayis the wryt.
Than Octosias off Judé
The kynryk had in propyrte.
The wattyr of Tybir than alsua
Callid be name wes Albula,
Bot for this Tyberius,

As sayis Tytus Lyvyus,
Drownyde wes in that ryvere,
Thai callyd it Tyber syne, but were. 700
In Rome syne regnyde Agryppa,
Quhen Acab regnyd in Juda,
And Homere, as the story sayis,
Wes in to Grece in to tha dayis.
Syne regnyd in Rome Armulus
That had to surname Sylvius,
Nyntene wyntyr regnyd he,
Quhen Joas kyng was off Jude
Thre and thretty wyntyr syne.
Eftyre hym regnyd Awentyne. 710
In his tyme Amasias
Kyng in Juda rygnand was.

CHAP. V.

𝔒𝔣𝔣 𝔖𝔞𝔯𝔡𝔞𝔫𝔞𝔭𝔦𝔩𝔩𝔲𝔰 𝔶𝔥𝔢 𝔰𝔞𝔩𝔩 𝔥𝔢𝔯
𝔈𝔫 𝔱𝔶𝔩𝔩 𝔱𝔥𝔦𝔰 𝔫𝔢𝔵𝔱 ℭ𝔥𝔞𝔭𝔭𝔱𝔢𝔯.

AWCHT hundyr wyntyr and sextene,
Or God wes off the Maydyn clene
Borne, the land off Assyry
Sardanapillus halyly
Aucht be lyne off herytage
Ewyn descendand be lynyage
Fra Nynus, befor than kyng,
At that land had in governyng. 720
His oys wes mare wytht rok to spyne
Than landys to the crowne to wyne,
And kunandnes fer mar he had

How mony here the spyndyll made,
Than for to blasowne in to were,
As his knychtis oysid to bere,
Armys off thaire awncestry,
Or ony dedys off chewalry.
 Off Mede the kynrik than in cheffe,
Wytht alkyne serẅice and releffe,   730
Arbatus held off this kyng,
The quhilk had all tyme gret yharnyng
This Sardanapillus tyll have sene,
And off his duellyng tyll have bene,
And tyll haff had off hym reward,
Syn in to cheffe he wes his larde
Off all the kynrik off Medy,
Off kynd his hart gaffe hym, for-thi,
Befor ony othir lard
To mak him serẅys for reward.   740
Apon this purpos tyll assay
Hys lord in till gud array,
He buskyt hym rycht honestly,
And welle arayid his cumpany,
And to the towne off Babilone
Wyth his court he come onone
Innys he tuk, and bad rycht thare
And realy mad hym to fare,
Bidand opertunytte,
And tyme, his our-larde for to se.   750
 Sa in the castelle on a day
He come in tyll his best aray,
Wytht his court and his menyhe,
Commendyd off gret honeste.
Quhare that he wend for tyll have sene
Lordys cled in red and grene,

Knychtys, ladyis, and squyerys,
Haukys, hwndys and courserys,
And thare lord in fayr array
Amang thaim in to joy and play;   760
Than he fand that drowy doude
Amang a pak off karlynys loud
Flytand redy for to fecht,
As he wes wandland off his wecht;
His yharne sponnyn resawand,
And towe to spynyng delyverand.
Quhen Arbatus his lord had sene
Apon this wys, he wes full tene,
And hym removide than in hy,
And passyd agayne hame in Medy;   770
Thare his ost he gadyryt sone,
And passyd to Babilone, but hone,
And wytht the Sardanapillus fast
Faucht, and tuk hym at the last,
And gert be maid on a bale fyre
Off gret schyddys byrnand schyre,
And that fyre he gert cast in
Sardanapillus, for to bryn,
And gert thame all hale off Assyry
Mak tyll hyme homage halyly,   780
And hald thare land off hym in cheffe
Fra thine, wytht serwys and releffe
And trewage to the Medys pay,
That held off thame befor that day.
 This wes the fyrst confusioune
That ewyre yhit come to Babyloune,
That wes the mast pryncipalle
Off the fyrst foure Kynrikis hale,
And stud ellewyn hundyr yhere,

And foure and sexty passyde clere, 790
In wyrschipe growand and in state
Quhyll the tyme that Arbate
This ryffille maid, and fra that day
Babilone wes falyhand ay.
Thus in sege a sot to se,
Or do a dowde in dignite,
Sall ger standand statys stavire,
F. 43. b. And wyll bath wyt and wyrschype wavir.
   It is langsum for to telle
How mony changys that tyme felle 800
Betwene the lordys off Assyry
And the Medys syndryly,
Quhill ane, quhill othir, tributere,
As werd off were maid thaim to stere.
   Procas than off Ytaly
Had the lordschype halyly.

CHAP. VI.

This Chapiter sall yhow rehers
The successyowne off Pers.

SYNE eftyre that tyme [Arbates]
Lord and syre off Medys wes,
And regnyd twa and twenty yhere
Assayid oft [in] werys sere. 810
Tyll hym succedyd Diocles,
That in all dedys douchty wes;
Sere landys lyand hym aboute,
Tyll Medys he maid wndirlowt.
Astrages syne eftyre that

Off Medys all the lordschipe gat,
That ayrys male off his body
Gat nane; off that land, for-thi,
Hys douchtyr sone hys ayre he maid,
To propyr name that Cyrus haid, 820
And he wytht fycht and hard batayle
Forbare na thyng for tyll assayle
Hys eldfadyr Astrages,
And he than in his reklesnes
Foryhet the mys that he had done
Tyll Arpallus, quhen he his sone
Had slayne, and syne gert hym be set
Before his fadyre at the met,
In quartarys lyand on a weschelle,
Wytht precyous spycys farsyd welle. 830
Bot he gert all rawe be lewyde
The twa handys and the hewide,
The quhilk he gert the fadyr se,
Quhen off the body full wes he,
And luche at hym dispytwysly
In hethyng off that mangery.

All the cure off his batayle,
And off his ost the governaile,
He lippynyd to this Arpallus
The quhilk be tresowne tyll Cyrus 840
Yhald thaim. Than Astrages,
That in his hart all angry wes,
Hys ost assemblyd hastyly,
And on the Perseis doggydly
He duschyd on quhyll that in fycht
Mony dour to ded wes dycht
Cryand fast that he suld dé
F. 44. Quha ewyr hym maid on bak to flé.

Thare the Medys war so felle,
And on the Perseys sa cruell,   850
That mony douchty thai gert dé,
The lave on bak begouth to fle,
The Medys nere had hade the felde
Na ware the wyẅys, that behelde
And sawe the Perseys in batayle,
How fayntly thai begouth to fayle,
To stand thai maid thaim fayre prayere,
And consalyd thaim on fayr manere.
Bot the Perseys war sa rad,
For the pres thai war in stad,   860
That thai dowtyd all to de;
For-thi, thai maid thame all to fle.
Than all thai wyẅys wytht a cry
Reprovand thaim dispitwysly,
Tyt wp thare clathis outh thaire scheyre,
And poyntyt to thaire preẅa gere
That betwene thaire lymys stude;
And wytht a schout, as thai war wude,
" In here, in here, syne yhe ar rade,
And in sa staverand state ar stade,   870
Yhone folk ar felowne for the nanys,
(Thai rowpyd wytht a rare at anys,)
Sen othir succoure have yhe nane,
Na yhe can sé na bettyr wane,
Gyve yhe wyll yhoure lyvys kepe
In tyll oure cutkane nowe yhe crepe;
And here in, gyve yhe hyd the hevid,
Thare owt mon all the lave be leẅyde."
The Perseys than aschamyd were,
And turnyd agayne wytht thare powere,   880
And wytht the Medys faucht sa fast

Quhill thai thame wencust at the last
And off thame slw a gret party
And wan the feld rycht dowchtily.
    Thane thaire wes tane Astrages,
Tyl Cyrus he delyverid wes,
The quhilk maid hym halyly
Lord and syre off Hyrcany,
Bot Medy and the landys thare
To Pers fra thine wes tributare;   890
Bot thare wes cyteis syndry,
That aucht trewage to Medy,
The quhilkys in to Cyrus dayis
Payid noucht thare for alwayis.
This Cyrus wes in gret trawayle,
And mowand were and hard batayle.

CHAP. VII.

How sall yhe here in till hy
Off a Tyrane gret felony.

F. 44. b.   FALARYS off Cyzile than
Wes in hys dedys [a] felown man;
The Agrigentynys halyly
He wndyde wytht his felowny.   900
Agrigent wes a regyowne
Famows and off gud renowne,
In to the Se wytht in that yle,
That is the kynryk off Cyzile.
This Falarys wes off dedys fell,
And off intentys rycht cruelle,
Till hym wes bath indifferent,

Culpabile in payne, and innocent;
For ay in a delyt wes he
Men towrmentid in payne to se, 910
And for to se thaire kowntenans
That thai wald mak in thaire pennans.
He ay in to this lykyng stude,
Swa nere hym by a smyth wes gude,
Perillus callid, wythin his land
This smyth ay duelt, hys craft oysande,
And set all hale his diligens
Till have had the benyvolens
Off thys tyrand, that wes were
To wyne na tyne all owt befere, 920
As nowe lardys be renowne
Ar comoune off condityoune.
This smyth that kend to this tyrand
Quhat thyng war till him mast plesand,
He made in hy a bull off bras,
Large and hole wyth-in it was,
And sa rowmé wyth-in wes it
That eẅyne wp rycht a man mycht syt
Wytht-in, for it wes made sa wyde,
Wytht a dure opynand on the syde 930
Ordanyt all for thare entré
That wytht-in sulde pynyde be,
And to be stekyd fast wytht-owt;
Syne a gret fyre made abowt
Sulde ger the pynyde wytht-in rare
All lyk a nowte thoucht man he ware.
This lume mad apon this wys,
Polyst fayre and rycht fetys,
This smyth broucht in to presand,
It for to gyve to this tyrand. 940

Falaris, that all aboute
Sawe this welle, bath in and owt,
And gert hym all the fawtys mend
That mycht be sene off it or kend,
And gert that ilk smyth in ga
To prewe the lenth and breid alsua,
And gert syne steke the dure with-out
And kendyll fyre rycht fast about
Off thornys and off schyddys gret;
The smytht wytht-in, quhen he felde hete   950
Paynand hym aye mare and mare,
Off nede behowyde thain for to rare
Swa that he like wes in to rowt
In tyll his dede thrawe till a nowte;
The fyre wyth-owt thare kendyllyt sa fast
The smyth wytht-in wes at the last,
Wytht paynys strang, but all remede,
Wytht-in hys handy werk thare dede:
Swa caus and matyr bath gave he
Tyll his dede, and tyll cruelté.   960

CHAP. VIII.

Qwhen þe constitutyon was
fyrst ordanyt the Olimpias.

SEVYN hundyr wyntyr and four score
And fully fyvtene yhere before
Or God off Mary borne was,
In Grece the Olympias,
In the honowr off Jupitere,
Wes ordanyd ilk[a] fyft yhere.

And for this caus it ordanyd thai
At tha termys, but delay,
That thai foryhet noucht be na wys,
And at the cost sulde les supprys　　　970
At tha termys than wytht in,
And he that mycht [the gre] thare wyn
Off towrneamentys, or justyng,
Menstralsy, or wersslyng,
Or quhat kyn gamyn that fyft yhere
In the Olympy cryid were,
Thare sulde be made hym na warnyng
Off quhatkyn thyng he mad askyng.
This a quhyle in oys thai hade
And syne be statute thai it made,　　　980
And fra that constitutioune
Thai made in thare descriptioune,
Evry ilke yhere be yhere the date,
In all the letterys at thai wrate,
Fra thine all thare inherdans,
Held that oys and that ordynans,
And for that Grece wes off gret fame,
And than sa realle wes off name,
Before the tyme the Romanys ras
That date in tyll all landys was,　　　990
For floure in Grece wes off clergy,
And off wyrschipe, and off chewalry.
For-thi, mony landys ware
Led be thaire oys and be thare fare.

　　Off Italy the kyng Procas
Wes ded than, and regnand was
His sone thare eft, Amylyus,
That callid wes alsua Silvius.
He regnyd fourty yhere and foure,

And banysyd his brodyre Munytoure, 1000
That had a dowchtyr callid Rea;
F. 45. b. Scho wes delyver off twynnys twa,
The tane wes callid Romulus,
The secund brodyr wes Remus.
Throuch enchantment on Rea
Gottyn, thai sayd, thir twynnys twa.
Bot be the lawys, nevyr-the-les,
In erd all quyk scho dolŵyn wes,
And thir twa twynnys fundyn were
Wndyr a bra be Tybere nere, 1010
Quhar a hyrd than apon cas,
Fawsculus that callyd was,
Happynyd to cum by that bra
Quhar that he fand thir twynnys twa,
And to Laurentia, his wyffe,
That spendyd in to lust hyr lyff,
And mekyll wyth hyr body wan,
(Quharefor scho Lupa callid wes than,
And the bordale hous was syne
Callyd Lupanar in Latyne), 1020
Thir twynnys twa he broucht in hy,
And bade hyr kepe thame tendyrly;
And wytht hyr war thai nwryst thare
Till thai to manhed cummyn ware;
And for a scho wolffe in Latyne
Is Lupa callyd, thare-efftyre syne,
In Rome quhare that thare figure
Wes sene in ald tyme, in sculpture,
Or payntyd, thai twa soukand wes
A wolf, in tyll ane liklynes. 1030
  Thir twa gadyryt off revarys,
Off theŵys, and off mysdoarys,

A gret multitud in hy,
And ras off were rycht stoutely,
And slwe Amylius that before
Banysyd thare eldfadyre, Munitore,
And restoryd thare gudsyre
Tyll his land and hys empyre.

CHAP. IX.

Qwhen the Kyngis Stane off Spanyhe Fyrst come in Erlande, and Brettanyhe.

In the mene tyme that this felle,
That ye herd off thir bredyre telle, 1040
Thare wes regnand a mychty Kyng,
That had all Spayne in governyng:
This kyng mony sonnys had,
Off ane off tha yhit mast he made,
That Symon-Brek wes callyde be name,
Ane honest man and off gud fame.
A gret Stane this Kyng than had,
That for this Kyngis sete wes made,
And haldyne wes a gret jowale
Wytht-in the kynryk off Spayne hale. 1050

F. 46. This kyng bad this Symon ta
That Stane, and in tyll Yrland ga,
And wyn that land and occupy,
And halde that Stane perpetualy,
And mak it his sege thare
As thai off Spayne did off it are.

This Symon did [than] as the Kyng
Fullyly gave hym in byddyng,

And wane Yrland, and chesyd his place,
Quhare honest and mast lykand was. 1060
Thare he made a gret cyté,
And in it syne that Stane gert he
Be set, and haldyn for jowale
And chartyr off that Kynryke hale.

Fergus-Ercson fra hym syne
Down discendand eẅyn be lyne
In to the fyve and fyfty gré,
As eẅyne reknand men may se,
Broucht this Stane wytht-in Scotland,
Fyrst quhen he come and wane that land : 1070
And fyrst it set in Ikkolmkil,
And Skune thare-eftyre it wes broucht tylle.
And thare it wes syne mony day,
Quhyll Edward gert have it away
Kyng off Ingland, and syne he
Gert it set in Lundyn be,

A.D. 1310.
Eftyre that Jhesu Cryst wes borne,
To sauffe oure lyff that was forlorne,
A thousand and thre hundyr yhere
And ten thare tyll, or thare by nere. 1080

Now will I the werd rehers,
As I fynd off that Stane in wers :
NI FALLAT FATUM, SCOTI, QUOCUNQUE LOCATUM
INVENIENT LAPIDEM, REGNARE TENENTUR IBIDEM.
" Bot gyff werdys falyhand be,
Quhare evyr that stane yhe segyt se,
Thare sall the Scottis be regnand,
And lorddys hale oure all that land."

CHAP X.

**Off Symon-Brekkis linage here
next folowys in this Chapitere.**

THIS Symon-Brek eftyre that
Fyakak-Bolgeg to sone gat;
He fadyr wes off Duat-Locres;
Eakak-Vadek his sone wes;   1090
And Usuemoere his sone gat;
Costek-Baelbrek eftyre that;
And his sone callid wes Melgé;
Jero syne thare-eft gat he,
That fadyr wes off Comata;
And his sone wes callid Elela-
Casiaclek, that eftyre then
Gat Eacak-Aldeten;
His sone Catan gat Curé;
Fyere-Elmael gat he;   1100

F. 46. b.   And hys sone Fyere-Anroet
Fadyr wes off Fyre-Roet;
Fyre-Cetaroat efftyre that
Angus-Turnec to sone gat;
Fyarak gat Neroen;
Ellala gat Earen:
Feraret to sone gat he,
That Fergo gat, and he Mawè;
Arynden wes syne fadyre
Tyll Regyne, that gat Roteyre;   1120
Hys sone Trere gat Rosyne;
And he syne fadyr wes to Fyne;

He had a sone calde Dedaa;
Jaere his sone gat Elela;
Elela gat Eogen;
Edarste-Nyl his sone wes then;
And he Conare-Moere gat;
Corbre-Fynmor eftyr that
Gat Dare-Dowrmere, and he syne
To sone gat Corbre callyd Congyne; 1130
Lugnaes-Allodeg
Gat Magalama that Stege,
That Conare gat; and he alsua
Cadak-Rydesedek-Corbre-Rygada
Gat; and syne, as I hèrd telle,
Fyacrak syne Catynelle
Gat Eacrak-Andoad;
To sone he Acyre-Cyryr had;
Hys sone syne Fideacek
Gat Crudyde, that Scancormek; 1140
Eftyre this Scancormek
Fedemet gat Rephynek;
Engus-Byntynet, but les,
Off Fedynet-as-Lugeg wes
Fadyre, and syne eftyr that
Angus-Fyere to sone he gat;
Eacak-Mourea-More
Gat Ert, and he gat Fergus-More.
 To thir or I rekyne ma,
Tyll othire matere wyll I ga. 1150

[Explicit Liber Tertius.]

THE FERDE BUKE

OF THE

ORYGYNALE CRONYKIL

OF SCOTLAND.

THE FERDE BUKE

OF THE

ORYGYNALE CRONYKIL
OF SCOTLAND.

***

In this Chapitere behald and luk
The Proloug off the Ferde Buk.

TULLYUS that of Rethoryk
A Tretys made to be publik,
Fourme off dyte and fayre spekyng
Plesand tyll oys and tyll heryng,
A garland, [said,] gottyn wyth gret peryle,
Grene suld lestand be lang quhile,
Onwalowyd be ony intervale
F. 48. Off tymys, bot ay in wertu hale.
Be this clerkis autoryte
A garland as a crowne sulde be   10
Wndyrstandyn wytht all rycht,
A takyn off wyrschype, state or hycht.
The crowne wes gyvyn for wyctory
In auld tyme; Saynt Paule for-thy
Tymotheum fayrly techid,
Off hym-self quhen thus he prechyde:

  Certamen certavi: Cursum consummavi.
  De reliquo reposita Est mihi corona.

The grene hew delyte oftsys,
Oys, or plesance signyfyis.

Quha the crowne than will hald grene,
Off thaim that has before thaim bene, 20
Drawe thar delyt till here or rede
Thare famows werkis dwne in dede:
Swa, tyll excyte yhour delyte,
I have set me now to wryte
And to trete in this ẅolume,
Quhen byggyde was, be Romule, Rome,
That his brothir Remus slwe,
Fyrst tyll that lordschipe quhen he drwe;
Wytht othir storys and incydens
Plesand lik tyll yhoure reverens, 30
That ar this Tretys tyll here or rede,
In tyll this part gyffe yhe procede
Fra end tyll end, yhe sall welle kene,
Be power off gret douchty men
That the Romanys wan the crowne,
And had in tyll subjectioune
All the warld oblyst thane
And hale subdyt tyll a man,
That wes Octoẅyane Empryoure,
Quhen Cryst wes borne oure Sawẅyoure 40
Off the maykles Maydyn brycht,
Now crownyd Queyn in heẅynnys hycht.
Till hyr suete ẅyrgynyte
This Tretys I commend, and me,
Tyll end my purpos swa to bryng,
That all redwne in hyr loẅyng.

Explicit Prologus.

The Chapiteris off the Ferd Buk.

i.	QUHEN Romulus and Remus maid Rome.
ii.	Quhen Consules governyd Rome.
iii.	The destructyoune off Babilone.
iiii.	Quhen Cyrus wan the Kyng Cresus.
v.	Off Cyrus dedis.
vi.	How Darius wes discumfyt.
vii.	How Exerces wes discumfyte.
viii.	Quhen the Scottis wes before the Peychtis.
ix.	Off Brennyus and Bellynus.
x.	Off a fell Pestylens.
xi.	Off Alysawndrys fyrst rysyng.
xii.	Howe the Tarentynys warrayd the Romanys.
xiii.	Quhen Hanyball wes discumfyte.
xiiii.	Off a Flud that the Cyte nere oure-yhude.
xv.	Quhen Hanyball discumfyt the Romanys.
xvi.	Off thre bollys off Ryngis send to Cartage.
xvii.	How Hanyball wes lettyd off his purpos.
xviii.	Quhen the Kyng Antyocus anyd wytht the Romanys.
xix.	Quhen fyrst the Pechtis come in Scotland.
xx.	Quhen Cartage wes ordanyd to be wndwne.
xxi.	Quhen the Romanys wan Achaya.
xxii.	Quhen the Romanys gert Cartage be byggid agayne.
xxiii.	Quhen mony Romanys ware slayne, and women fell wode.

F.47.b. (at viii.)

xxiv. Off syndry taknys that fell in Rome.
xxv. Off Julyus Cesare.
xxvi. Off Octoviane.

CHAP. I.

Qwhene Reme and Romule the Cite Off Rome fyrst gert biggit be.

SEVYN hundyr wyntyr and fyftene
Or God was off the Maydyn clene
Borne, and off Olympias
The sext ordyr rynnand was,
That in to Grece than was thar date
In all the chartrys that thai wrate,
Off Rome the gret cyté was made,
And off it hale the lordschype hade
Romule, that his brothir slwe
Swne fra he to lordschipe drwe,   10
And eftyr hym syne gert he
Rome be callyt that cyté,
And tyll hym that lordschipe hale
In profyt tuk, and governale,
And wallyt it rycht welle wythoute,
Wytht dykis off fale and mwde aboute.
Ane hundyr men he chesyde off eylde,
That wayk ware wapnys for to weyld,
Bot, for wyt and gud consale,
To tha he lypnyd the governale   20
Off the comoune state, and he
Tha Senatowyrs gert callyt be.
He chesyd syne a thousand hale,
Yhong and lykly to batayle,
And Knychtis he gert call all tha,
Thaire name in Latyne sowndys swa.

Romule off eylde was twenty yhere
And twa quhen he begouth to stere
In Rome, and regnand was auchtene
Yheris, [ful] in dedis clene 30
F. 48. And syne hapnyd he peryst was
Throw hard tempest and swdane cas.
 Eftyre that dede was Romulus
Numa regnyd Pompilyus
Ane and fourty yhere, and he
Fyrst gert ordane knychtis fó.
Before hym Marche wes, but were,
The fyrst begynnyng off the yhere,
Bot he gert the monethis twa,
Janwere the fyrst off tha, 40
The secund Fevyryhere, but let,
Alwayis before Marche [be] set.
In hys tyme Ezechias fre
Wes kyng regnand in Jwdé.
Sybile than Eryttea
Was in the tyme off this Numa.
 Eftyre hym regnyd Tullius,
Be surname cald Hostylyus.
In tyll his tyme Manassé
Wes kyng regnand in Jwdé. 50
He oysid mykyll for to were
Purpur, silk, and browdyn gere.
Before his tyme the Romanys hale
Lyẃyd in pes wytht-out batayle
A welle lang tyme, bot eftyre he
Gert tyll his lordschipe bowsum be
The Albanyis, that in that quhile
Fra Rome off space wes auchtene myle,
And othir natyownys mony sere,

To Rome he mad than tributere 60
In tyll his tyme mekyll off prys
Wes Sybyle Samya the wys.
The kyng than off Spartany,
The cyté maid off Bysanty;
Now thai oys in landys all
Constantynopyll that to calle.

Eftyre the dede off Tullius
In Rome regnyd the kyng Antus.
In tyll his tyme Josyas
Kyng in Jude regnand was, 70
He gert be maid a gret cyté,
And Osten it callyd he.
He regnyd thre and twenty yhere
And dyde off profyte dedys sere.

Till hym succedyde syne Pryscus,
To surname callid Tarqwynyus,
He maid a burche rownd in his dayis
Wytht-in the towne till oys thare playis
As to dans, pype, or syng,
Or to wresstyl, and mak justyng. 80
Cysternys he gert be maid depe,
Fylth or wattyr for to kepe.

F. 48. b. That all the glwt wyth-in the towne
In tymys mycht be castyne downe
Throucht thai cysternys for to ryne
The gret wattyr off Tibere in
That the cyté mycht ay be
Kepyd fra glwt in honesté.
The Capytole he [fyrst] gert ma,
And be name [it] callid swa; 90
For as thai ware the grounde rypand,
Off ane man [the] hevyde thai fand

For owtyn body, quhar-for thai
The Capytole it callid ay.
In Rome he regnyd thretty yhere
And aucht owte-oure tha passid clere;
Quhen Joachym off Judé
Had all the land in propyrté.
   Eftyr hym regnyd Servius,
Callid be surname Tullius.   100
He gert be drawyn dykis depe
Abowt the wallys, at thai mycht kepe
Thaire towne, gyff ony wald assayle
Thame wytht assawt, or wytht batayle.
He wes the fyrst kyng, as thai say,
That gert the Romanys custum pay;
Befor his tyme thai war sa fre
That thai wyst noucht quhat toll suld be.
Syne slayne was this Serwius,
Throucht ane wes cald Tarquynyus   110
The Proude, and, quhen that he was dede,
He kyng regnand wes in hys stede.
In to this tyme Sedechias
Kyng in Juda regnand was,
And Nabugodonosor he
Kyng than regnand in Caldé,
Made the gret confusioune
Off Jowis, and thare destructiowne.
   The Ferde Eylde heir endis,
The quhilk off yherys contenys,   120
As the Hebrwys reknys clere,
Foure hundyr wyntere and thre yhere;
The Sevynty clerkis sayis oure
Four hundyr yher four score and foure.

CHAP. II.

Qwhen efftire kyngis Consules
En to Rome first chosyn wes.

EFTYR the dede off Servius
In Rome proude Tarqwynyus
Regnyd, and than Cyrus kyng
Off Pers had all the governyng.
He was a man off gret felny
And wmbethoucht hym incrcly 130
With quhat tormentis men mycht be
Punysyde for thaire inyqwyte,
As fetrys or presonyng,
Stokkys, boyis, or banysyng.
He wes exilyd in his dayis
  Off Rome, as Frere Martyne sayis,
For his sonys inyquyte,
That had deforsyd a lady fre,
A gentill-woman off gud fame,
Lucretia was callid hir name. 140
Scho plenyheyd tyll hir husbandis sone
Off the defoule wes till hyr done,
Till hir fadyr and hir kyne,
Till all syne that scho mycht to wyn,
And led hyr dayis a quhile in pyne,
And slwe hyr-self for sorowe syne.
Syne this proud Tarquynyus
Saw that he wes exilyd thus,
He knyt hym to the Tuskanys,
And warrayd wytht thame the Romanis, 150

F. 49.

And wytht his ost, apon a day,
To Tybyr he come, in gud aray,
And quhen thai saw his gret powere,
The Romanys all affrayid were,
Bot syne it hapnyd thame to be
Accordyt welle be fayre treté.

Thir sewyne Kyngis regnand were
Twa hundyr foure and fourty yhere;
And fra the kyngis thus can ses,
In Rome thai chesyd twa Consules,   160
And tha twa reng sulde bot a yhere,
For dowt gyff that thai regnand were
Langare tyme, that thai suld rys
In lordschype in swa hawtane wys,
That the comownys vyleusly
Grewyt sulde be throwe thaire maistry.
And twa was ordanyd for this skyll,
That gyff ane wald set his wyll
For lykyng mesoure tyll excede,
The tothir argwe suld his dede,   170
And swa chastyid he suld be
Fra foule lust and inyqwyte.
Consules than thai maid twa,
Brute and Lucius cald war tha.

Than in Rome Pictogoras
Deyde, and Anaxagoras;
That tyme alsua Socrates
The wenum drank and poysownyd wes.
Arystotyll than, but were,
Wes off eyld bot auchtene yhere,   180
And wndyr Plato, the wytty,
Studyid and herd Phylosophy.

CHAP. III.

**How how the towne off Babilone
Wes browcht till confusione.**

F. 49. b.

F YVE hundyr yhere and aucht beforne,
Or God wes off the Maydyn borne,
The fyrst off the Consules,
Brute be name callyd wes,
The Sabynys in to stout aray
Made thame the cyté till assay,
The Romanys a dytoure made,
That oure the lawe the maystry had, 190
And the Consules be fere
He sulde excede in all powere.

In this tyme that I yhoue rehers
Cyrus that was kyng off Pers
Wan a gret part off Sythy
And mony landis in Asy,
Syne wytht his ost [he] come onone
For tyll assege Babylone,
Bot the rywere off Ewfrate
Swa reych than rysand wes on spate, 200
That he mycht noucht the towne cum nere,
Bot worthyd to byd wytht hys powere,
Quhille the weltrand wawys kene
Suld a part have swagyd bene.

Swa was in tyll his ost a knycht,
Yhong and joly, bawld and wycht,
Fayr off fassowne and fetys,
Off prowes prowyd, and off prys,

Off Capados, Schyre Alaryke,
In all that ost wes nane hym lyk,   210
Sa fayre off fasowne and swa fre,
And gentyll in tyll all wes he;
He luẅyd perdrewry dame Sabyll.
That lady then wes off Pamphile,
He paramowrys so stratly luẅyd
That perelys as playis he pruẅyde
Apon a cowrsoure poumle gray
Adressly he sat that day
In tyll a gowne eẅyn schaply wyde,
In his revel bot sadyll syde,   220
Wytht brokyn lettrys on that gowne,
Byllyde wele wes his resowne,
Susus geta, that sulde be,
Ese off consale opyn yhe:
And browdyn wele was his penowne,
Off gold rampand a lyowne,
He bar in tyll asure brycht,
Hys ger was flamand all at rycht.
Thus quhill the ost thare hoẅyng maid
And swagyng off the wattyr bade,   230
He thoucht prowes for till pruve
For hyr that he lent on his luve:
The coursoure he strake wytht the spurys
And walepand oure floys and furys.
All befor the ost he rade
Quhar stend for stend the coursere maid,
And at the bra quhare nerest was
The furde, quhar men oysid to pas,
The hors he hardynyt irwysly,
The coursere lap delyverly   240
All oure the bank in to the flude,

F. 50. The stoure fere owre thare hewydis stude.
The wawys war wode, the wattyr depe,
Be na way mycht the knycht hym kepe.
Bot for to tell yhoue schortly than
Drownyd wes thare bath hors and man.
  Than Cyrus that this sycht has sene,
For angyr off his hart, and tene
That sa hys knycht [he] lesyd hade,
Gret athys swore and wowys made   250
Tyll all his goddis, yhong and awlde,
That wynd and wattyr had in waulde,
That he sulde off that wattyr be
Revengyde in to sic degre,
And sa schalde it sulde be made
That, set a woman suld it wade,
Hyr kneys off it suld noucht be wate
For nakyne weddare, spryng, na spate.
Than gert he drawe that revere all
In to foure hundyre and sexty smalle   260
And narow swyrlis, throuch feldis brade;
That gret rewere sa schalde he made
That slyke and klay micht than be sene
Quhare wattyre depe before had bene.
  Than the ost, but mare abade,
Thare passyng to the cyté made,
Throuch the depe slyk and the clay,
Haldand on the nerest way;
And thaire he lay, wytht his powere,
The cyté quhill he wan, but were,   270
And gare cast all the wallys down
Off Babilone, bath toure and towne,
That chymys was off Assyry,
At all poynt byggid propirly,

Set in a lawnd off fresch flewowre
Off haylsum ayre, and suet sawoure,
Wytht wode and wattyre all abowte
Plesand, fayr, wytht-owtyn dowte,
A hundyre yhattis off irne gret
Fra before that mekylle yhet, 280
And ma yhit mycht rekynyd be
All abowte that gret cyté;
And fra that mekyll yhete before
Four hundyr stadys and foure score
It had in umgang all abowte,
And tha to rekyn ar, but dowte,
Ane and fyfty myle and mare,
And all abowte the wallys ware
Fyve and twenty elne brade,
Wytht sykyre syment sadly made 290
Wytht ane hundyre elne on hycht,
At alkyne poynt perfytly dycht,
And, as the clerk Orosyus
In tyll hys Cornykyll tellys ws,
It war bot fantumlyke and fabylle,
And noucht till al men yhit trowabille,
That mannys wertu, or hys wyte,
Mycht othir do or wndo it.

CHAP. IV.

This Chapitere tellis how Cyrus Wan off were kyng Cresus.

Q WHEN thus wes wonnyn Babylon,
Cyrus wytht his ost onone 300

In Lidys past, wytht playne batayle,
The kyng Cresus till assayle.
This Cresus, that I yhoue rehers,
Held Lydys off the kyng off Pers;
Bot ay till hym he wes rebel,
In were, and in all consale felle:
Bot for he wes in dedys stout,
Off hym ay Cyrus had gret dout,
For rych and mychty ay wes he,
And in all dedys awÿsé.   310
He prayid till his god Appolyne
To grawnt hym wyttyng quhat kyne fyne
Last suld fall off that discorde
That was betwene hym and his lorde.
Than wryttyn was tyll hym this wers
In Latyne that I wyll rehers.
(*Crescens perdet Alini, transgressus maxima regna;*)
" The Creyhsceand sall gret landys tyne,
The wattyr oure passand off Alyne."
This sentence off this wers wes thare
For the kyng off Lidis bare,   320
Off gowlys in to sylver brycht
Thre creyhsceandis in his armys dycht.

This awnsuere Cresus thoucht rycht gude
For othir-wayis he wndyrstude;
Than eftyrwarde the gamyn yhede,
Or werde off were, prowÿd in dede,
And said, " The landys that I sall tyne
Ar Cyrus landys, and noucht myn,
That I sall wytht myn ost oure ryde,
To fell his ogert and his pryde."   330
Hys ost than sone and hastily

He assemblid, and in hy
Oure that wattyr he passid onone,
For tyll suppowale Babilone,
Quhar Cyrus lay, as yhe herd here,
In tyll assege wytht hys powere,
And thare he schawid hym, on ane hycht,
Hys ost arayand to the fycht.
Bot quhen he saw on quhat kyne wys
Wencust were the Babilonys,   340
And the cyté wonnyn nere,
He changid purpos and mancre,
And turnyd bak, and tuk the flycht,
The Perseys lyggid on at rycht,

F. 51.   Folowand fast and egyrly,
Chasand hym dispytwysly,
And slwe hys men down, here and thare,
Quhare-evyr that thai ourtakyn were;
Hym-self eschapyd narowly,
And sauff wes fra that jwperdy.   350
   This Cresus eftyre this affray,
On a nycht in his bed lay,
And, dremand in his slepe, thoucht he
Wes in a crope set off a tre,
Quhare Jupitere wyth rayne hym wete,
God Phebus quhyle wytht sone hym het;
He thoucht in tyll his slepying swa
That he [wes] stade betwene thai twa,
All the tyme that he thare lay,
Quhille on the morne day,   360
Than Fariva, his douchtyr yhing,
He callid, and tauld [hir] his dremyng;
For scho oysid for till telle
Thyngis sere before thai felle,

As wychys dois, or nycromancerys,
Dissawÿnde men on thare manerys,
And throucht the dewyll dissavyid are thai.
Than neid the certane suth can say.
Bot throuch thame quhen that he is sua
Trawalyd, that he mon ansure ma   370
The ansuere that he to thame mayis
Offt dowbyll wnderstandyn hayis,
And sa it hapnys that men are
Dyssayvid offt on that manere;
For the thyngis that is to be
To wyt is Goddys propyrte,
For-thi thar-off the certane
Is nane can telle bot He alane.
Yhit nevyr-the-les this damysel
Tauld hyr fadyr that efftyr fell,   380
That Cyrus suld hym tak in ire,
And swayk hym in a brynnand fyre,
And thare he suld be brynt, but dowt,
Bot gyff the rayne the fyre put owt.
 Sa Cyrus wyth his ost onone
Fra he had wonnyn Babylone,
Past in to Lydis tyll assayle
This Cresus kyng wytht playne batayle.
Thare, eftyre mony juperdyis,
And syndry changyd wÿctoryis,   390
The kyng off Lydis this Cresus
Wes tane and broucht quyk tyll Cyrus,
And he gert cast hym in a fyre,
Off dry fagottis, brynnand schyre,
Thare brynt he noucht bot tholyt payne,
For it layit on sa fast off rayne
On nakyne wys that he mycht bryne

All the tyme he lay thare in.
Off Pers than the kyng Cyrus
Gert qwyte delyver this kyng Cresus. 400
Owt off that fyre, and be treté
Hym tyll hys restoryt he,
Apon this wys quhen Cresus
Wes fre delyveryde fra Cyrus,
Tyll Phanwa, hys dochtyr dere,
He tauld the cas, and the manere,
And in his hert he had gret pryde
That [he] ethchapyt swa that tyde.
But scho that saw his hawtane fere,
Apon this wys maid hym awnsuere: 410
"Wyth slycht [swa], suppos yhe slyde,
Yhoure lattyre day yhit mon yhe byde:
Before that day on nakyn wys
Yhe suld yhoure fortown happy pryis
For at the evin, or eftyr, ay
Men prysis ay the fayr day,
And quhen the lyffe off man tais end,
Than is tyme hym to comend."
And eftyre that scho had tauld hym thus,
Scho bad hym be ware that Cyrus, 420
At hym suld noucht sa grewÿd be,
That he suld hang hym on a tre,
Quhare nevyre rayne wytht mekyll wete,
Na nakyn swn mycht sauff with het.

F. 51. b.

CHAP. V.

**How this Chapitere sall tell
How the dede off Cyrus fell.**

E FTYR that this kyng Cresus
Wencust wes and wonnyne thus,
Cyrus, lord and kyng off Pers,
Off quham before I maid rehers,
Past wyth his ost, as man off were,
Oure Araxys, that rywere   430
That on hewyd rynnand is
Betwene Sytyke and Lydis;
Dame Tarnys that tyme wes lady
And quene regend all Sythy,
And quhen scho hard that the gret ost
Off Cyrus come bolnyd in bost,
Hyr consale gave hyr to ger breke
The bryggys, and alle the fwrdys stek,
And let thame passage till have fre,
Wytht swylk ane ost in hyr cwntré. 440
How evyre hyr lykyd this consale,
Scho gert bath bryg and fwrde be hale,
And lete thame oure Araxis fre
Wytht-in hyr land mak thaire entré,
And in to straytis ner thare by
Scho gert hyr sone be prewaly,
Hys awantage for to se,
And byd his opertwnyté,
To dyffend or tyll assayle
For werd is waverand off batayle. 450

And quhen Cyrus wes cumin in
F. 52.   The land off Sytyke it to wyn,
For mete thaire forreowrys thai send
And pavillownys thai gert discend,
And thare tentis swne in hy,
Be lyklynes to mak herbry,
Trumpand all the day on hycht;
Bot quhen it nere drew to the nycht
All thaire fyrys thai gert baulde,
As thai wald styll thaire herbry haulde,   460
Off wyne thai drwe and rostyd flesche,
And ete and drank thaim to refresche,
And syne dewoydid prewaly
And lete with[in] thare tentys ly
All thaire wytalle swa assayid,
As thai had yschyd all affrayid.
The Cytykys than that in the hicht
Had byddyn all the day quhill nycht,
Thoucht till hawe fwndyn wnarayid
The Perseys hale and wnpurwayde,   470
And sa thai mycht thame best supprys
In slepe, or than sum othyr wys,
To tak or sla all at thare wylle,
All thus thaire purpos to fulfille.
The Sytykys come wyth thaire batayle
The Perseys derffly till assayle
Wytht-in thaire tentis, quhare thai thoucht
That all sulde at thaire wyll be wroucht.
Off [the] Perseis nane thai fand
Wytht-in the tentys than sterand,   480
For hale the ost removyde were,
As I yhowe tauld a lytill cre;
Than thai Sytykys tuk herbry,

And ete and drank rycht gredyly
Off the wytayle that was assayid,
Thai tuk rycht fast and lytill payid;
Bot or the gammyn wes all gane
Thai payid ma than twa for ane.
Wyne and flesche thai had at wylle,
Thar-off thai tuk sa gret a fyll, 490
That qwhene wyst thare-off his awine,
How mony acris he had sawyne,
Bot foryhet thame-self all qwyte
To drynk thai had sik appetyt,
That wnwachid, suddanly,
Thai fell on slepe rycht hewyly.
Off the Perseys than the spyis
Tauld tyll Cirus on quhat wyis
He mycht hys purpos welle fulfille,
And have the Sytykys at hys wylle, 500
For all tyme thai nere thaim ware,
And saw thare manere and thare fayre.

Wyth that the Perseys hastily
Arayid thame, and come suddanly,
And fand the Sytykys all lyand
Wytht-in thare tentis still slepand;
Thar thai thaime stekid in thare slepe,
And slwe thame downe as thai war schepe,
That few echapyd fra that place
To tell all how it hapnyd was; 510
The Qwenys swn in to that stede,
And in that pres, was slayne to dede,
That yhong and aviunand was, and fayre,
And till his Modyre nerest ayre
Off all the landis off Sithy;
For-thi the barnage was sary

Off his ded; and nevyrtheles
His Modyre tuk wp sik stoutnes
And dissymlyd sorow swn,
And hyr arayid wytht-outyn hwne, 520
Wyth hyr ost in bataylis sere,
And waytand quhar the Perseys were,
And hyr aẅantage for to se
How best scho mycht revengyd be.
Hyr ost scho scalyd here and thaire,
Lyk as scho affrayid ware,
And lete the Perseys wytht thare pryde
Hyr land oure ryot and oure ryde,
Bot nere scho perswyde ay,
Quhill at the last [up]on a day 530
Scho saw thame in tha straytys thare,
Quhare all hyre ost abowt thame ware,
And scho than in hyr buschement,
That thoucht to cum tyll hyr intent,
Gert trumpe wp, and suddanly
Brak on the Perseys hawtaynly,
Wytht all hyr ost on ilk[a] syde,
Sa wmbeset thai ware that tyde
Wytht the Sytykys that nane mycht
Fra the bataile ta the flycht, 540
Bot on nede behuẅyd to byd;
Thaire thai layid on ilk syde,
And sa fell thare was the fycht,
That mony doure to dede wes dycht,
Mony a hawberk, mony a scheld,
Was all to frwschyd left in felde,
Bot the Sytykys douchtely
Wan all hale the ẅyctory.
Twa hundyr thousand thai fand dede

Off Perseys lyand in that sted; 550
The kyng Cyrus off Pers that day
Wes slayne, [and] thare amang thame lay,
The Qweyne that thoucht this mellé gude,
A fat gert fill full off thare blude,
That slayne in to that feld than lewyde,
And syne gert stryk off Cyrus hewyde,
And that fat gert swayk it in,
"Drynk thi fill now or thow blyn,
Scho sayd, "for thretty yhere and mare
Ay mannys blud thow thrystyd sare; 560
Thare thow nowe may fynd thi fill,
Drynk or lewe, quhethyr evyre thow wylle."
 Eftyr that Cyrus slayne wes,
Hys swn succedyt, Cambises,
He movyd in tyll Egipt were,
And rade it throucht wyth gret powere,
Thare all thare templys he kest downe,
And wndyde thare religiowne,
And at thare awld ceremonyis,
That thai oysid on syndry wyis 570
In to thare devotyown,
He had abhomynatyown.
Twa spaymen syne put hym to dede,
And thai succedyt in his stede.
And maid thame kyngis off [the] land,
At thare lykyn it sterand,
Syne Darius ras thame agayne,
And hawe thai bath in batayle slayne.

CHAP. VI.

How Darius throw his secundry Wes discumfit in Sithy.

FOUR hundyr wyntyr and thris twenty,
Or God wes borne off oure Lady, 580
Consentand all the barnage hale,
Darius tuk the governale
Off all Pers in propirté,
And ryngnyd in gret reawté.
Quhen he recoveryd had Assyry
And Babilone all halily,
Agayne the kyng Amprityre,
Off Sythy bath lord and syre,
He rasyd ost and mowyd were,
And come on hym wytht his powere, 590
For caus Amprytyre the kyng
Off Sythy maid hym playne warnyng
Off his douchtyr till be his wyff,
Quhen he hyr askyd for this stryff,
And this were Schyre Darius
Movyd wpon Amprytyrus.
The ost off Pers wes namyd then
Sewyn hundyre thousand armyd men,
That for the lust off a body
Wes set all in tyll jwperdy. 600
And offt in tyll gret dowt off dede,
[And] all dyspayrid off remed ;
For as thai throuch the land past,
The Sytykys handlyd thame sa fast,

        Constayand thame on ilk[a] syde,
        That nane durst fra the batayle byd,
        That the Sytykys mycht oure-ta,
F. 53. b. Than thai walde thame, but rawnsone, sla.
        And swa, be syndry juperdyis,
        Fourty thousand reknyd twyis   610
        Darius myssid off his men,
        Wytht juperdiis that slayne ware then,
        And hym-self all prewaly
        Fled off the kynrike off Sythy,
        For drede thai suld be[hynd] hym stek
        The furdys, and [the] bryggys brek
        Off Danoy, that gret rywere,
        That marchand is to Sythy nere;
        And off the skayth that he had tane,
        He maid bot lytill dule or mayne,   620
        And thoucht that tynsall was bot smalle
        For to rekyn his costys all:
        Yhit wes he noucht off litill mycht,
        That swa mony couth gar dycht,
        Apon a day in till a felde,
        Off wycht men wapnys for to welde,
        As Darius tynt in tyll Sithy
        Throuch his hawtane succuddry.

        Throucht Asy syne he past onone
        Quhen he had dantid Macedone,   630
        Yonas nere by the se,
        Wytht his nawyne warrayde he,
        And the Attenyens hale
        Ras to ma thame suppowalle,
        For-thi this Darius movid his were,
        Agaynis thame wytht hale powere;
        And thai thame purwayd off diffens,

And mad agayne thame resistens,
And wytht thare awyne cumpany
And sowdyowrys off Spertany,   640
Ellewyn thousand men, but mare,
In to the feld assemblyd ware
Agayne sex hundyre thousand hale,
Off Perseys ordanyd for batale;
In to that fycht Myltiades
Off Attenyens [a] chyfftane wes.
Bath thai ostys swne onone
In to the feld off Maratone
Togyddyr mellayd hastily,
Bot off thare fychtyng wes ferly;   650
For quha that nere had by thaim bene,
Thai mycht the ta part welle hawe sene
In batayle derffly men slaand,
The tothyr as bestys thare deand;
Twa hundyre [thowsand] Perseys thare
Slayne in the feld fundyn ware.
Darius swa thare discumfyte
Chasid fled till his schippys tyte,
And wytht his nawyne in affray
Wnslayne echapyd as that day   660
In tyll hys land off Pers, and thare
Assemblyd swne [a] gret poware
In tyll intent for tyll have bene
Revengyd off his fayis kene,
Bot in hys ost he deyd, off cas,
And swa his purpos falyhyd was.

CHAP. VII.

This Chapitere tellis how Ferces, Darius sone, discumfit wes.

F OURE hundyre yhere sevynty and sewyn,
Or Mary bare the Kyng off Hewyn,
Quhen Darius, as yhe hard, wes dede,
Hys son Cerces [Xerxes] in his stede   670
In Pers succedyt kyng regnand,
And governyd wytht his lauch the land,
And that were held wpe fyve yhere,
That his fadyr in Grece gert stere.
In tyll his ost off Perseys then
He had sevyn hundyre thousand men,
At all poynt armyd clenly;
Thre hundyre thousand he had by
Off wagyouris armyd at all rycht,
In to thare gere all flawmand brycht;   680
Twelff hundyre schyppys gret off toure,
And off les thre thousand oure,
Wyth men and wytaile thare gert he
Be stuffyd welle, and layd to se;
His gret ost swa assemblid thare
Dowtyd gyff ony wattrys ware,
Off sic abowndans, and sic plente,
That to thame all thare drynk mycht be,
Or to thare bataylle for to pas,
Ony erde to large was,   690
Or tyll thare nawyne ony se
Mycht rowme enuch or large be,

Sic ane ost yhe may welle trow
Is were for to be gaddyrt nowe
Than it was than, for to supprys
Be batayle or be juperdyis.
  Off Spartany, Leonydes
Kyng and lord in that tyme wes,
He wytht aucht thousand men that quhylle
Bade in the straytis off Termopylle.   700
Quhen Cerces thare-off hade tythyng
In tyll dispyt and pure hething,
That sa few for thare defens
Durst mak agayne hym resistens,
He gert aray his gret batayle,
In purpos thaim for tyll assayle;
Bot thaim he sped before onone
That in the feld off Maratone
In tyll his fadyre tyme had bene,
And thare thaire frendys slayne had sene,   710

F. 54. b. For tyll assayle thare inymys
Wyth batayll, or wytht juperdyis.
  Off tha schortly for to tell,
As in the fycht the fortoune felle;
The begynnyng thai ware hale,
And off that fycht the fyrst tynsalle.
Syne the grete ost wytht Cerces.
Sone to the baytell cummyn wes,
And wmbeset on ilk[a] syde
The Spartanys and Leonyde.   720
Than ras the fycht bath fers and felle,
And all the batail rycht cruelle,
Thare men mycht here bot dusche for dusch,
Rappys royd wytht mony a rusch,
Mony a penowne, mony a spere,

To rewyn, and all to fruschyd were.
On basnetys, schynand brycht,
Men mycht se pollaxis lycht,
Thare morel bayard, dun and gray,
Wyth wowndys flyngand ran away.   730
In to sic pres, wytht-owtyn dowt,
The fychtyng thre dayis lestyd owt,
But trew takyn, or departyng,
Or ony kyn othire ameyssyng,
That nane off bak the flycht mycht ta,
Na nane mycht pas to purches ma.
Thai war in to that fycht so thyke
That nane had nymbilnes to stryke,
And [sa] for-tyryd in to that thrawe,
That quheyne had cume his eynde to drawe,   740
Off slayne bodyis fundyn thare,
Hepys hey wpstandand ware.
That quha that had thame that tyme sene
Wald noucht have trowid at thai had bene
Twa bataillis off sere natyownys,
As happynys betwene regyownys,
Bot off all kyn natyoune,
Pestilens, or ded felowne.

   The ferd day quhen Leonyda
Swa wyth his fayis he [wes] set sa   750
He callyd till hym his wageoures,
His freyndis, and his sowdeoures,
Out off the pres off the bataylle
And sayd, "I gyve yowe for counsaille,
That yhe remowe owt off the fycht
And drawis youe till yhone hill on hicht,
Youe to refresche and ta the ayre,
And at owre nede syne yhe repayre

Fra that yhe refreschyd be,
For bettyr yhit I thynk to se; 760
And I wyll wytht my Spartaneys
Prowe sum othir juperdyis;
Suppos I happyn to be slayne,
And for to de in to the payne,
For it is myn honest det

F. 55.　For my land my lyff to set,
And off my-self to be rekles,
Quhyll I have gottyn my land in pes;
Na I prys, na payne apere
Myn honowre and my land to were. 770
For-thi, to yhow my falowys hale
Now I gyẅe for playne consayle,
That in lang home yhe hovyr noucht,
Bot on youre wyrschye set yhoure thoucht,
And set yhoure lyff in juperdy,
For tyll supprys youre inymy;
Na biddis noucht the dayis lycht,
Na yhoure fays quhill thai be dycht;
Bot on the nycht gyẅe we can se
That the hape mycht owrys be, 780
Wytht-in thaire tentis quhar thai ly
Cum we on thame [than] suddanly,
For swa slepand best we may
Put tham in sa hard assay
That, but perell, ma sall de
Than sall be boune to fycht or fle,
And oure renowne may nevyre be
Commendyde off mare honesté
Than to be fundyn togyddyr all,
How sa cẅyr the fortowne falle, 790
Amang oure fays wytht-in thare tentis,

Thaire pavilyhownys, or thare buschementis;
For honowr aẅis ws till assaille,
And aẅenture may offt aẅaille
And prowes pynys all perelle,
And efftyr hope hape hapnys quhille.
Than swa sall gret oppynyownys
Mak for ws excusatyownys,
And we sall sawffyd be fra blame,
And sall welle defend oure fame."   800
 To this thai assentyd hale,
And wrocht all eftyre his consaille,
And gert thaire spyis tak gud kepe,
Quhen that the Perseys fell on slepe
Wytht-in thare tentis quhare thai lay.
To this schortly for to say
Leonyde wytht his company
Come on the Perseys suddanly,
Quhen thai ware sadly fallyn on slepe,
And stekyd thame as thai ware schepe,   810
That sum wytht wowndys waknyd ware,
And sum thare gaspand granyd sare,
And sum thare stekyd stakarand stud,
And sum lay bullyrrand in thaire blude,
All thus in wodnes as thai waveryd
And stekyd swa wyth stokis staveryd,

F. 55. b. The Perseyis ilkane stekyd othire,
Sparand nothire fadyre na brodyre;
For thai war off sic multitude,
And swa thyk togyddyr stude,   820
That nane mycht mys quhare he wald mynt,
Tha nane to dede gave doubill dynt,
And mony smoryd losyde the lyff,
Wyth-outyn strak off swerde or knyff.

The Spartanys wyth-outyn chas
Thare fays all wencust in that plas,
For fra the glomyng off the nycht
Till on the morne, quhill day wes lycht,
And ane howre wes eftyre none
Gane fully, or the fycht was done. 830
　　Quhen that the Kyng off Pers was soucht
And fundyn in the feld wes noucht.
Sex hundyr thousand Perseys thare,
In to that felde dede fundyn ware,
Discumfyde in that juperdy
Wytht sex hundyr anyrly
Off Spartanys, that in that tyde
To batell come wyth Leonyde,
That slayne in to that batell wes.
Thus discumfyt wes Cerces, 840
And as on nede than hym behuwyd,
Till his schippis he hym remuvyde,
And wytht his nawyne than thoucht he
That all Grece suld dystroyid be.
　In to that tyme Temystocles
Off the Attenyens chyfftane wes,
The Yonyis quhen he saw hale
In tyll Cerces suppowalle,
And had his flot in governyng,
Syne, for thare caus, off Pers the kyng, 850
Darius, the fadyre off this Cerces.
Agayne Atenys mowid wes,
Sa thai ware caus pryncipalle
Off all this were, and this batale,
For hale the Atteneys
Wytht [the] Yonyis, in thare defens,
Agayne Darius ras off were,

Quharefore he moẅyd his powere
Agayne the Atteneys,
That mayd sa manly resistens,　　　　860
Quhill in Maratone on a day
Slayne twa hundyr thousand lay.
Thare chyfftane this Temystocles,
That saw how all this cummyn wes,
Set hale his slycht and his quentis
For to trete wytht thir Yonyis.
For hym worthyt to forbere,
As oys is amang men off were,
Entyrcomunyng in[til a] bille,
He wrate his consale and his wille,　　　　870
And said, " Me thynk yhe ar to blame,

F. 56.　That negligent ar off yhoure fame,
Set yhe wyll wyth yhoure conscience,
Ay for yhoure statis ma defence.
Yhit it is gret crualte
Rekles off yhoure fame to be,
For honoure tholys confusyowne,
And revery reẅys thare resowne,
And wyt wytht wyle thare yhe supprys
And honesté defowlyt lyis.　　　　880
Off kyndnes tharefor set yhoure thoucht,
And thynk for yhowe quhat we haẅe wroucht
In Maratone, apon a day,
Quhar slayne twa hundyre thousand lay,
And how oure frendys off Spartany,
For yhoure caus hallyly,
In till oure suppowale ras,
And how thaire kyng Leonidas
Now in to this later fycht,
Sex hundyr thousand on a nycht　　　　890

Wytht sex hundyre men has slayne.
In till gret pres, thrang, and payne,
And Leonyde alsua slayne wes thare,
That Spartane rew may evermare.
   And nowe the kyng off Pers, Cerces,
That fra that fycht echapyt wes
In till yhoure gret flot, apon Se,
All affrayid has tane entré,
For-thi, yhe qwyt ws this kyndnes,
That quhen yhe se ws set in pres,   900
And owt off hawyn yhoure schyppis be
Yhe change luffe, and turne to Se,
And lat ws wyth oure fayis fycht
Quhill that oure goddys dele the rycht."
This was his consaille and his wylle,
And he gert wryt and clos in bile,
And till a stane that wes nere by,
Quhare that he wyst rycht werraly
The Yonyis wald swne arrywe,
He gert it festnyde be belywe.   910
   The Amerale swne land·has tane
And saw this bill wpon the stane,
Fra he it red, he wyst it wes
The cownsalle off Temystocles.
In hast his crand all dyde he,
And sped hym sone syne to the se;
Temystocles yhit thare abade
And off thaire schyppys wonnyn had,
And lay arayid wytht his ost,
Ay purvayde for to kepe the cost.   920
Artymodor, than lady
And queyne off Halycarnasy,
In the suppowale off Cerces,

  Brak on this Temystocles
  Owt off hyr buschement quhare scho lay,
F. 56. b. And made rycht stout and hard assay,
  And wyrschype prowÿde, and manhade,
  Amang the cheffe off his knychthade.
  Thare woman wyle in wyt off man,
  And manhade turnyd in woman.   930
  For thare off newe scho rasyt the fycht
  Quhare mony dowre to dede wes dycht;
  The wÿctory yhit, nevertheles,
  Fell all to Temystocles,
  For thare slayne wes that lady,
  And nere all hale hyr company,
  That lypnyd all that Cerces kyng
  Suld land have tane in thaire helpyng,
  Wytht all the ost off his nawyne:
  Bot, be the consalle, and kuvine,   940
  And queyntyse off Temystocles,
  All othire wayis thare fortowne wes;
  For all the Yonyis rycht,
  As thai the fors saw off the fycht,
  Turnyd the luff, and tuk the Se;
  Than Cerces in perplexité
  Wes hard set, and his nawÿne
  Come noucht yhit al till esy syne,
  For as fraward stormys stude
  Mony drownyd in the flude,   950
  And mony etchepyd for radnes,
  Fra that the kyng anoyid wes,
  And mony als wes tane off were
  Wyth the Attenyens and thare powere.
  Than off Pers, Mardonius,
  That saw his kyng reboytid thus,

Till hym said, " I rede that yhe
Set yhowe for yhoure sauffte,
For here we thole now sa gret schame,
That I dowt ware to fynd at hame, 960
And or it swa suld hapyn thare,
In till yhoure land I wald yhe ware,
Levand all yhoure ost wyth me,
And swa, how-evyr oure fortowne be,
I sall, apon sik awyis,
Hald off were oure inymyis,
That we sall welle excus oure name,
And yhe sall sauffe be fra defame."

To the counsalle off Mardone
Cerces trowyd sone onone, 970
And delyveryd hym his men,
And made hym oure thame all cheften.
Thare, that kyng that fyrst gert byg,
Wytht schyppys, oure the flud a brige
Wyth [fewe than] off his cumpany,
Away than lurkyd prewaly,
In till a litill fysch scowte
For pres that he wes in, and dowte,
And wyntyr weddrys felle and grete
Lowsyd all his bryg off threte 980
And off the serwys off a man

F. 57. Off neyde he held hym payid than,
Quhare befor he gert the se
For his schyppys lowrand be,
For fawte off rowme his mekyll mycht
Kest down hillys hey on hycht,
And wyth the waleis evyn thai made
To schawe his ost quhare that thai raide,
To scant all rynnand ryverys were

For to be drynk till his powere. 990
All kynd off thyng than falyhyde hym nere,
As infortowne maid hym off stere,
All his futmen and archerys,
That lypnyd ware to thaire lederys,
For dowte hungyr and trawaylle,
Begowth fayntly for to faylle
And bolne, quhyll at the last, the dede
Consumyd thame wyth-owt remede.
All the landys as thai lay
Mycht na man nere thame pas the way, 1000
Than for to bryst than wald thai thynke,
The ayre sa fell was off the stynk;
The fowlis wyld and bestis fell
That couth off karyowne fele the smelle,
That fey court ay folowyd nere,
Quhill deand at thai fallyn were,
And off thare fleysch wald fill thame thare,
Or fullily all dede thai ware.
Quhen Cerses thus to Mardone gave
Off his ost all hale the lawe 1010
That remanyd hale wnslayne,
His [emys] sone mad hym sa fayne
That he hym put in pres sa fast,
Quhill he defowlyde wes at the last.
The Grekis mony discumfyte,
And wan the castell off Olmyte,
And the Attenyens besyly
He tretyde wyth his industry,
And led thame in to hope off pes,
Quhill that he sawe thare fredowme wes 1020
Off sic mycht, and sic powere,
That wounyn thai mycht be noucht off were.

Off thare cyté than in ire
A gret part he brynt in fyre.
 In Boecy wytht his powere
He past syne, as man off were,
Off Grekis ane hundyre thousand hale
All welle arayid for batelle,
Folowyd forsly this Mardone
And gawe hym batale swne onone   1030
And wytht hym faucht in fycht sa fast
Quhill thai hym wencust at the last,
And all his ost thare nere was slayne ;
Wnese hym-selff wyth mekyll payne,
Etchapyde owt off that mellé

F. 57. b.   All nakyd, wytht a few menyhe,
In swate all drawkyd, as thai were
Ane awlde schypbrokyn marynere.
Hys pavilyhownys and his tentys wes
Stuffyd welle wytht gret ryches   1040
Off the kyngis tresowre hale,
And othir that [dede] wes in the bataylle
Left gold and jowelys in copy,
And als wyth othir industry.
The kyng Cerses tresoure wan
Fra that fyrst the were began
Tyll that day that he fled, for-dowte,
In till a litill fyschare scowte.
All this Mardone had that day,
That fra the fycht [he] fled away.   1050
This tresoure all the Grekis gat
And delt it amang thame eftyre that ;
Swa throuch the partyng off that pray,
And the tresoure delt that day,
The gold off Pers in sic copy

Wes the confusiowne halily
Off all Grece, that before that day
Governyd thame wytht wertu ay.
And that day Mardonyus
In Boecy wes wencust thus,   1060
A gret part off the ost of Pers,
In Asy, as I herd rehers,
Wes discumfyt wpon [the] Se,
And put till hard perplexyté.

Here-eftyr quhen the kyng Cerses
In till his awyn land cummyn wes,
Sa ille commendyt thare was he,
And lakyde all wytht his menyhe,
That schortly thare, the suth to say,
In tyll hys halle, apon a day,   1070
The burdys wndyr clathis sete,
And wyschyn he had to ga to mete,
Hys stwart maid on hym a schote,
And tyte hym dowrly be the throte,
And wyth a knyff, wp to the hefft,
He steykyd hym quhyll the lyff he lefft.
This wes the endyng off Cerses,
In all tyme that wnhappy wes.
As Oros quhille, the clerk sa fyne,
Wrat till his mastyre Saynt Awstyne,   1080
Wndyre thire kyngis thre off Pers,
The quhilkis yhe herd me last rehers,
Reknyd wes off dede bodyis
A hundyre thousand nynty syis,
All off Perseis slayne downe,
And off nane othire natyowne.

Quhen Cerses wes endyt thus
His swne succedyt, Daryus,

The quhilk in Alexandrys dayis
Endyt, as the story sayis.   1090
F. 58.   Nowe off my purpos to mak ende,
Off Pers the storys I suspend.

CHAP. VIII.

*En this Chapitere yhe sall here,
Qwhen the Scottis beset be Peychtis were.*

F OUR hundyr vyntyr and fyfty   1093
And twa to rekyn oure evynlykly
Befor the [blest] Natyvyté,
Oute off Athenys that cyté
To Rome the Lawis broucht ware then
Wryttyn in till Tablis ten.
The Romanys yhit eftyre tha

Cotton, F. 37. b.   CHAP. VIII.

[*From* MSS. C., E. I., *etc.*]

*This next Chapter folowande heyre,
Tellis qwhen Scottis and Peychtis were.*

F OUR hundyr wyntyr and fourty   †1093
And twa, to rekkyn ewynly,
Befor the blest Natywité,
Out of Athenys that cité
To Rome the Lawis broucht war then
Wryttyn in to Tabillis ten,
The Romanys yhit eftyr tha

To thame ekyd Tablis twa.   1100
    As in oure storys wryttyn is,
Than in Scotland the Scottis
Begouth to renge, and to stere,
Twa hundyr full and fourty yhere
Fyve wyntyr and monethis thre,
Gyve that all suld rekynd be,
Or the Peychtis in Scotland
Come, and in it wes duelland.
    And now to thai I turne my stille,
Off thare lynage to spek a quhille,   1110
As in the Thryd Buke wes before,
Fra Symon-Brek tyll Fergus-More,
Is, as the Scottis lynyaly
Come downe off Yrschery.
Quhare than I lefft, nowe to begyn,
Thare namys here I will tak in.

To thaim ekyt Tabillis twa.   †1100
As in oure story wryttyn is,
Than in Scotlande the Scottys
Begouthe to regne, and to stere,
Twa hundyr fully and fourty yhere
Fyve wyntyr and monethis thre,
Giff that al sulde reknyt be,
Or the Peychtis in Scotlande
Coyme, and in it was regnande.
    Bot I wil noucht tell yow thar nayme,
Thar condiscion, na thar fayme,   †1110
For possibile supposse it be,
Difficile yit it is to me
To tel thar namys distynctly

He that wes callyd Fergus-More,
In the Thrid Buke yhe hard before,
Wes Fergus-Erthswne, that thre yhere
Made hym beyhond the Drwm to stere, 1120
Oure all the hychtis evyrilkane,
As thai ly fra Drwmalbane
Tyll Stanmore and Inchegall,
Kyng he mad hym oure thaim all.
  Dongart his swn yheris fyve
Wes till his fadyre successyẃe.
  Congal, Dongarddis swne, twenty yhere
And twa wes kyng wytht-owtyn were.
  Gowran, Dongarddis swne, allswa
Regnyd twenty yhere and twa. 1130
  Conal nest hym Makcongall

Or al thar greis severelly
That befor the Peychtis rasse;
For as our story mencion mays
Fergus Erschson the fyrst man
Was that in our lande began,
Befor that tyme that the Peychtis
Our kynrik wan fra the Scottis, † 1120
And syne tha Peychtis regnande were
A thousande ane and sexty yhere.
  And fra this Fergus, doun be lyne
Discendande eẃyn, was Makalpyn
Kenyaucht, that was aucht hundyr yhere
And thre and fourty passit cleyr
Eftyr the blest Natyẃite
Or regnande he begouythe to be
Fra the Peychtis was put out.

Fourtene yhere held thai landis all.
Thretty wyntyr and foure than
Edan regnyd Makgowran.
Hecgedbwd sex yhere and ten
Kyng wes in tha landis then.
[K]ynachker Makcolnal
Thre moneth held thai landis all.
Ferchar Makcowny sextene yhere
As kyng couth all thai landis stere.   1140
Downald Brec son [of] Hecgedbowde,
Kyng wes fourtene wyntyr prowde.
F. 58. b.   And eftyre that his dayis wes dwn,
Maldowny, Dolnawde Downyswne,
Sextene wyntyr kyng wes hale.
And nest hym tuk that governale
Ferchar-Fodys sone, and was than

The tende man, wyth-outtyn dout,   † 1130
Was Keynauche Makalpyne
Fra this Fergus eẅyn be lyne,
And sa thir ten sulde occupy,
Gif al war reknyt, fullely
Twelf hundyr wynter, and weil ma,
Bot I can noucht consaif it swa
Bot that this Fergus was regnande
Wyth the Peychtis in Scotlande,
And tha ten that regnande were
Eftyr this Fergus, yhere be yhere,   † 1140
As thai that the Cornykill wrate,
In til nowmyr set the date,
Amang the Peychtis was regnande
Wyth-in the Kynrik of Scotland,

Twenty wynter kyng and ane.
  Hecgede-Monavele-Makdongat
Downad-Brec sone eftyre that 1150
Regnyd twelfe yhere fullyly.
  Her I suspende this Geneology;
Bot I wyll spek mare thareoff swne,
Quhen all the lawe till it is dwne.

And liffit in bargan and in were
Qwhil Kenyach rase with his powere.
  Gif othir, of mare sufficians,
Can fynde bettyr accordance,
This buk at likyn thai may mende,
Bot I now schortly, to mak ende, †1150
Thynkis for to set thar date,
As Cornykleris befor me wrate,
And kest and reknyt, yhere be yhere,
As the Peychtis regnande were,
And thar dait sa set I wil
Qwhen the processe is lede thartil.

CHAP. IX.

**Of Brynnyws now schall yhe here
Rede in to this Chapitere.**

FOURE hundyr thretty yhere and sewyn
Or Mary bare the Kyng off Hewyn,
The Vegentys all war wonnyn qwyte,
And throucht the Romaynys discumfyte.
Than Brynnyus wytht the men of Sauns,

That is a lordschipe gret in Frauns, 1160
All Rome off were nere wonnyn had,
Na had bene, that a gannyr made
Sa hwge crakyng and sic cry,
That the Romanys suddanly
Waknyd, quhare thai slepand lay:
All the cyté than fand thai
Wytht thare fays nere wptane.
To sauffe the Capitole allane.
And that yhet Brennyus wonnyn had,
Had noucht that gus sic crakyng mad, 1170
That waknyd the wachis suddanly,
And warnyd the Romanys hastily.

 This Brennyus and Belyne
Bredyre ware, and knychtis syne:
Off thame quha will the certane hawe,
How that thai for Bretane strawe
Ilkane wytht othir, and for it faucht;
And how thaire modyre made thaim saucht;
How thai wan Frauns, and Lumbardy,
Tuskane, and Rome nere halily; 1180
How Brennyus syne left in Tuskane,
And Belyne come hame in Bretane;
Thai rede the Brwte, and thai sall se
Ferlys gret off thare bownté.
Saynt Awstyne sayis the Romanys ware
To geys dettyd in honowre mare
Than to thare goddis all, that slepyd,
Quhen geys thame wytht thare crakyng kepyd.

CHAP. X.

**Off a Pestilens that fell,
And how in Rome men mycht se helle.**

F. 59.

THRE hundyr yhere foure score and sevyn
Before that borne wes the Kyng off Hewyn,   1190
In to the stede off Consules
In Rome Tribuny chosyn wes.
The Romanys than wan a cyté
That callyd wes, that tyme, Penestré,
And aucht cyteis than off were
To Rome wes maid tributere.
   Grete pestilens in to tha dayis
In Rome fell, as Frere Martyne sayis:
Wytht-in the myddis off the towne
All the erd than opnyd down,   1200
Sa wgsum thare that opynnyng fell
That, throuch a rytft, men mycht sé hell,
And off the stynk come off that stede
Mony wytht-in the towne wes dede.
Wytht-in the cyté wes a man
That callyd be name wes Martyne than,
He till his goddis mad prayere
To gyff hym wyt, on quhat manere
And how, that exalatyowne,
That made sa gret infectiowne,   1210
Mast hastily mycht closyd be,
And how to succoure that cyté
Mast redy helpe war, or defens,
For that fellowne pestilens.

Hys goddys hym ansuerd, at the last,
And bad hym gang, and arme hym fast,
And at that ryfft lepe evyn down,
Gyff that he thoucht to sauff the towne.
At that answere he yhed swne,
And hastyly as thai bad has dwne, 1220
And fra he downe fell in that gape,
All that ryfft togyddyre crape;
And sa was sauffyde the cyté
Fra stynk than, and mortalité.

  Brennyus yhit all tyme then
Warrayid, wytht the Frankyis men,
The Romanys in to thai dayis,
And, as Frer Martyne tharoff sayis,
A Romane sawe a Frankys man
Abowt his hals thare hawe than, 1230
Off gold thrawyn, all lyk a les;
This Romane made than sic purches,
That [al]anyrly bot thai twa
Togyddyr suld in batalle ga,
And on na wys than suld thai twyn
Quhill ane mycht the tothir wyn,
Slayne or yhowdyn in batale,
Wytht-owt ony [othir] suppowale
Off ony othir; as it fell than,
This Roman slewe the Frankis man, 1240
And fra his nek in tyll that place
Tyt away that goldyn las,
And pwt it abowt hys awyn hals;
Fra thine he, and his lynage als,
In to Latyne callid were
Lasyd Romanys mony yhere.

CHAP. XI.

**Qwhen Alysandyre, the mychty kyng,
Begouth to rys and mak sterthng.**

THRE hundyr and sex and twenty yhere
Before the byrth off oure Lord dere,
Alysandyr Phylippy,
That gotyn was on Olympy,   1250
Be herytabill successiowne,
Begouth [to] regne in Macydowne,
And wes bot yheris twelf off eelde
Quhen [he] begouth wapnys to weelde,
And regnand lyvyd bot twelff yhere
Quhen all the Oryent he wan nere,
And hale syne set his intent
Tyll have wonnyn the Occydent;
Bot tharcoff falyhyd he, off cas,
In Babylone he poysownyd was.   1260
Off his douchty dedys sere
Contenyd in othir bukis cere;
Tharfore in this Tretis I
Now wyll our-ga thame mar lychtly.

The Romanys than grewe off mycht,
And wes in dedys stout and wycht;
The Sampnytys than, that in mydway
Betwene Poyle and Chawmpayne lay,
And in to swylk abowndans wes
Off sylvyr, gold, and [of] ryches,   1270
That all the armowris that thai had
Wes off gold and sylvyr made;
Thir Sampnytys than ras all hale

Agayne [the] Romanys in batale,
Bot the Sampnytys, sone and tyte,
Wes wyth the Romanys discumfyte,
And eftyre syne, with thare powere,
The Romanys discumfyt were;
Bot the Romanys, at the last,
Wytht the Sampnytys faucht sa fast,   1280
That foure and twenty thousand lay
Slayne in the feyld apon a day,
Off the Sampnytys, and thare kyng
Was takyn thaire in that fechtyng.
Thare chymys and thare cheffe towne
Than to the grownd wes castyn downe,
Thare was na fa in feyld sa felle
Agayne Rome than, na sa cruelle,
As wes the Sampnytys in tha dayis,
As Oros and Frere Martyne sayis;   1290
And the caus wes pryncipall
Of that were, and off that batalle,
That for [of] Chawmpayne all the land
[Was] in profytis all hawbondand,
And esyly set to the se
Wytht haẅynnys gud in gret plente;
Swa that alkyn marchandyis
Come in it apone syndry wyis.

F. 60.   Thare cheffe cyté, off gret fame,
Capuva wes callyd be name,   1300
That to Cartage or to Rome wes
Paryfyid in all liklynes.
Thir landys the Romanys thoucht
Tyll thare oys suld haẅe bene broucht;
Thare-fore fyrst ras all this were
And endyt as yhe herd langere.

CHAP. XII.

How the Tarentinis hale
Agayne the Romanys movyt battalle.

THRE hundyre yhere and thrys thre
Befor the [blissit] Natyvyte,
The Tarentynys wytht thare powere,
Agayne the Romanys ras off were :   1310
Thaire messyngere dyssatwysly
Thai defoulyde wnhonestly,
And warnyst thame rycht welle wyth-oute
Wytht all thare marcharys thame abowte,
And send for Pyrrus oure the Se,
For kyng off Grece that tyme wes he.
He broucht wytht hym off fwt men
Foure schore off thousand reknyd then,
And sewyn thousand men on hors,
Fayre off fassowne and off cors,   1320
And elephantys full twenty,
Quhare nevyr nane in Ytaly
Wes kend, na sene, before that day.
In batale sone, the suth to say,
Thai mellayid and faucht rycht fast,
The Tarentynis wes at the last
Hale discumfyte in that stede,
Wytht all thare ost; than Pyrrus flede
Wytht mekyll schame attoure the se,
In till his land wyth his menyhe.   1330
Than the Tarentynis hale
Soucht at Cartage suppowalle,

That wes the cheffe off all Affryke,
A fayre cyté nane till it lyk,
And wes before Rome, but were,
Byggyd twa hundyr and sevynty yhere.
Swa thoucht thai to defend wyth mycht,
Fra thame off Rome wyth all thare slycht,
Cyzily or odyr ylys sere,
That in the Gret Se lyand were.   1340

CHAP. XIII.

How qwhen Hanyball qwhyle Wes in Cyzell discomffite.

TWA hundyr yhere and sexty,
And nyne to rekyn fullyly,
Hanyball the eldare yhude,
Wytht a welle gret multitud
Off welle arayid and armyd men,
And elephantis tauld thrys tene;
Wytht thai be schype he tuk the Se,
In Cyzyly swa arrywyde he.
The Romanys sone gaddryd ware,
And wytht hym faucht in batale thare,   1350
And handlyd hym in fecht sa fast
That thai hym wencust at the last.
Hys elephantis thare thryis ten
Thai tuk, and slewe nere all [the] men,
And his nawyne nere tuk thai
That scantly wan hym-self away.
Ane than off the consules,
Attilius that called wes,

Tuk wytht hym a gret multitude
Off men, arayid in armys gude,   1360
And passyd wytht that ost the Se;
In Cartage sone arywyde he,
And foure and sevynty cyteis sere,
And all that in thame duelland were,
Throuch all Affryk, as he rade,
All subjecte thame to Rome he made.
And throuch the land as he rad swa
Toward the wattyr off Bagrada,
Off sex score off fute he fand
Ane eddyr, lach on erd crepand,   1370
That mony off hys men to dede
Had slayne, and swellyde in that stede.
Wytht that eddyr sa he wroucht,
That to dede [he] sone hyr broucht,
And the skyn gert fra hyr tyte,
And to Rome syne he send it.
 Thai off Cartage in this quhille
Have tretyde walde wytht this Attyle;
That he refoysyd wtrely
For caus that he thoucht halyly   1380
For till hawe wonnyn thame wyth were,
Set all thare willys had bene contrere.
Than thai off Cartage, wytht counsalle,
The Affrycanys tuk to thame hale,
And faucht wytht Attyle and his ost,
And wencust hym for all his bost.
Thare wytht thame off Affryk qwyte
The Romanys wes discumfyt,
And Attyle Regule thare chyfftane
Wes yholdyn and as presownere tane,   1390
And to Cartage, in presowne

Wes send, but lypnyng off rawnsoune.
   In Rome than Emilyus,
And his falow Fulvius,
Than off that towne twa consules,
Fra thai hard how this hapnyd wes,
Thre hundyr schyppys thai gert be
Stuffyde and layd to the se,
In Affryk tyll aryẅe onane,
For to reveng that thai had tane.   1400
The Affrykanys sone in hy
Recowntryd thame dispytwysly
Wytht schyppys thre hundyr; thare agayne,
On the Se than wes the Romanys slayne,
And thaire naẅyne takyn qwyte,
And all thare hale ost discumfyte.

F. 61.

CHAP. XIV.

This Chapiter [tellis] that a flude,
Here the Cyte owrphwde.

TWA hundyr and foure score off yhere
Befor the byrth off oure Lord dere,
A fell subversyowne and suddayne
Had hale the Cyté nere ouretane;   1410
For off Tybere the ryẅere,
Sa retht off spate wyth watrys sere
Ras, that all wytht-in the towne
The gret byggynys it kest downe
Sa qwytly than, that men wald wene
That nevyr byggyne thare had bene.
The Frankis men in to that tyde

Made thame off newe thare-for to ryde
Agayne the Romanys, bot thai
Recowntryd thame in gud aray, 1420
Sa that the Frankis men qwyte
Wes wytht Romanys discumfyte.

CHAP. XV.

Qwhen Hanybal the Romanys qwhyte fyrst in batale discomfite.

TWA hundyr wyntyr and nynteyne
Or lychtare wes the Madyne cleyne,
Hanyball wyth his empyre,
Off Affryk than bath lord and syre,
Passyd in to Spayne, and thare a towne,
Famows and off gret renowne,
Sagount be name, assegyd he,
And stratly gert it kepyt be 1430
Fra all profyte and wytale
Quhill thai wytht-in begouth to fayle,
Throuch defawte and hungyr sare,
Sa [that] on nede thai yholdyn ware,
And delyvyrid wes the towne
And he till erd gert cast it downe,
For caus in all tyme that it
To Rome wes in to frendschepe knyt.
The Romanys off thare intent
Tyll Hanyball gert message sent, 1440
Bot on na-kyn wys wald he
Thaire messyngerys wytht eyne se,
Nor off thaire tythyngys walde he here,

Na spere quhar-wyth thai chargyde were.
In Rome that tyme Publius,
Scypyon, and Symphronius,
Chosyn ware thre Consules,
And governand thare office wes
Quhen Hanyball wytht his powere
Come wyth his ost, as man off were, 1450
Out oure the hillys off Pyrreny,
The nerrast way in Ytaly.
Wyth gret trawaylle as he past,
In Ytaly, yhit at the last,
He come in wyth gret were and payne,
And wyth his ost thaire tuk the playne,
That wes fully reknyd then
Ane hundyr thousand off fut-men,
And twenty thousand men on hors,
Fayr off fassown and off cors. 1460
 Scypio, that tyme wes
Ane chosyne off the Consules,
In to that playne faucht wyth him thare,
And woundyd Hanyball rycht sare;
But to record yhow schortly,
The Romanys ware halily,
Wyth the Affricanys qwyte
In that batayle discumfyte:
Thare-eftyr quhen Symphronius
Had herd that it had hapnyd thus, 1470
Till his falowe Scypion
Wytht his ost he come onone,
Off Sythy wyth his falowis all,
And faucht rycht fast wyth Hanyball,
The Romanys yhit, nevyrtheles,
In that batayle discumfyte wes,

Swa that Symphron wes rycht fayne
That he wan fra fecht wnslayne
Hym allane, wyth-outyn ma,
As he than saw the fortoune ga,　　　　　　1480
Quhen all [this] wyctory wes done,
This Hanyball wyth his ost sone
In Tuskayne passyd wyth gret fayre,
Wytht-in the fyrst moneth off wayre,
And furth wyth his batyll syne
Toward the hyllys off Appennyne,
Quhar that sa thyk the snawe felle,
Wytht haylstanys bath scharpe and snelle,
That all his elyphantis thare,
And hors and catalle, peryst ware.　　　　　　1490
This Hanyball yhit, nevyrtheles,
Wyst welle that Schir Flamyne wes,
Quhen all the Romanys ware ourtane,
Left in the tentis hym allane,
Hastyly he turnys agayne
Hym till have [wyncust] and have slayne;
Bot Flamyne wytht his cumpany
Recountryd hym rycht stoutly,
Bot yhit, throwch frawde off Hanyballe,
He and his ost wes wencust all,　　　　　　1500
Sa that off the Romanys hale
Dede and slayne in that batale
Wes fyve and twenty thousand thare,
And sex thowsand takyne ware.

CHAP. XVI.

How thre bollis off ryngis were
Till Cartage send, now schall yhe here.

TWA hundyr yhere ellewyn and ane
Or God off Mary flesch had tane,
In Rome Lucy Mylyus,
Paule, and alsua Publius
Tarentyne, and Warro wes
In to the towne maid Consules,   1510
And till a cyté callid Canos
Wyth-in the Poyle, on set purpos
The Romanys send thame to fecht
Wyth Hanyball and his gret mecht;
Off Romanys in [to] batale thare
Foure and fourty thousand ware
Reknyd and slayne wpon that grene;
Before that day wes nevyr sene
That thai off Rome, wyth sic dispyte,
Wes sa haly discumfyte;   1520
For thare wes Emylius,
And his falowe callid Paulus,
That for the grettest that tyme wes
Chosyn to be Consules,
And off the Pretore twenty men,
And grettest off the cownsale then,
And off the senatowrys thretty thare,
Slayne in that fecht or takyn ware.
Off gentyll knychtis than off fute,
That owsyd nothyr spure na bute,   1530

Thre hundyr deyd in that batale,
And fowrti thousand othir hale
Off knychtis armyd wpon hors,
Fayre off fassowne and [of] cors,
Slayne in to that journe wes.
　　Than ane off the Consules,
That be name was Warro callyd,
As in his buk Frer Martyne tallid,
All prewaly owte off the rowte
Wytht fyfty men on hors, for dowte　　　　1540
Off hys lyff, to Wenys flede
For to be tane or slayne thai drede.

F. 62. b.　To [the] Romanys but [ony] wene
This the lattast day had bene,
Gyve Hanyball in tyll all hy,
Quhen done was all the wictory,
Had past strawcht wytht his menyhe,
For tyll have tane wp the cyté.
In takyn off that wictory,
Quhen endyt wes this juperdy,　　　　　　1550
Off gold rengys, fayre and brycht,
Tane off thare fyngrys slayne in that fycht,
Thre moys that was thre bollys mete,
This Hanyball wytht-owtyn lete
To Cartage gert in hy be send,
Quhen that this jornay had tane end.
　　Than were the Romanys sa wa,
And for this cas disparyd swa,
That thai maid thame haly bowne
For tyll have fled and left the towne,　　1560
Na hade bene Scypio Affrycane,
That off the knychtis wes chyftane,
Wyth drawyn swerd than held thame in,

And thoucht aẅantage yhit to wyne.
Off cownsalle than, wyth-outyn bade,
Off [the] threllys that thai hade,
Bowcht before off comowne prys,
Wyth-in the towne to mak serẅys,
He made knychtis in that nede,
And thaim arayid in honest wede,　　　　1570
And armwrys, that halowyd ware
To goddys in thaire tempyllis thare,
Thai tuk in that necessyte,
And in thai gert thame armyd be
All thai threllys evryilkane,
For that ensawmpyll had thai tane
Be counsale off ane [Run]yus,
That tauld thame how that Romulus
Off murtheraris he kynchtis made,
And theẅys that he in presowne hade,　　　　1580
And mysdoarys mony ma,
All wnpunysyd he lete ga
In fredome, quhill that he had hale
Sex thousand wycht men to batale.
The Romanys be this counsall sone
The lyk manyr has all done,
Sa Rome before disparyd than
Respyre in to gud hope began.
Bot yhit, as Orosius
In tyll his cornyklys tellis ws,　　　　1590
Quha that in Rome befor had bene,
And had off it the wyrschype sene,
He wald have bene all rede for schame,
Fra he had sene thare reale fame
Chawngyd, [and] thare reawte,
Than turnyd in deformyte,

For nane thare governale than had
To sauff barnys off yhowthad,
Threllys, both bownd or carle,
That oysyd before to bere and harle;
And suppos thai thai war soucht,
And all in tyll hale nowmyr broucht,
Yhit war thai noucht to sicht plesand,
Na in tyll all poynt sufficiand;
For that tyme all thaire senatowrys
That chosyn wes to thare succowrys
Behuŵyd to be in thare serŵys
Informyd and kend, as yhong noŵys.

CHAP. XVII.

*How Hanyball, throw schowrys snell,
Wes lettyde off hys purpos felle.*

TWA hundyr yhere and twys thre
Befor the [blessit] Natyvyté,
Hanybyll, wytht mekyll bost,
Off Chawmpayne moŵyd hale his ost,
And thre myle wyth-out the towne abade,
And tharefore the Romanys murnyng maid,
And all the senatowrys ilkane
Sa wytht radnes wes ouretane,
And owte off thare [wit] sa qwyte,
That thai ware, but pres, discumfyte:
Yhit the women nevyrtheles
Apon the wallis besy wes,
Layand stanys here and thare,
Quhare that thai thoucht mast lykly ware

Thame to defend in tyme off were,
Eftyr as thai saw thare mystere.
And Hanyball wyth his ost syne
Come to the yhet wes callyd Collyne;
Thare the consule Fulvyus
Saw that he wes cummyn thus,
Gaddryd all the Romanys hale
For tyll have gyvyn thare batale; 1630
And as thai suld have sammyn bene
Togyddyre runnyn on the grene,
Sa gret tempest and halestayne wycht
Fell wyth sik fors and [wyth] sic pyth,
That bathe the ostis anoyid wes sare,
Or thai wytht-in thare tentis ware.
Thus fyrst quhen that that tempest left,
For tyll have met thai trystyd eft,
The neyst tyme that thai mycht se
A day set in serenyte, 1640
On the tyme that thai that sete,
Bathe hayle and tempest were thame wete,
That wytht mare dowt etchapyde thai
Than, na thai dide the fyrst day.
Hanyball be that welle thoucht
That he be man wes lettyd noucht
To wast and wndo the cyté,
Bot throucht Goddys gret powsté,
Fra Rome than he remowyed hale
Hys ost, but fandyng off batale. 1650
Scypio that tyme Affrikane
Hade sevyn and twenty [wyntyr] gane
Off his eyld, and than he
Was prysit a man off gret powsté;
He passyde in to Spayne off were

And Cartage newe wyth his powere
He wan, and gat thaire gret tresowre
Gaddryde lang tyme thare befoure,
Sylvyr [and] golde, and thare-off he
Payid till his knychtys large fe,   1660
And thaire he tuk Magon wytht-all,
That brothire wes till Hanyball,
And to the Romanys hym send he
In presowne for till haldyn be.
Quhen Scypio wpon this wyis
Had done in Spayne thir wictoryis,
In till Affryk syne he past
And fell in fechtyng thare sa fast
Wytht the duk off Affryk thare,
That, off his adversaris, ware   1670
Fourty thowsand slayne and dede,
And he, wastand fra sted to sted,
All throucht the land in ryot rad
And in tyll it his maystry made,
Na nane fra hym mycht thame defende.
Than thai off Cartage sowne gert send
Till Hanyball, and bad hym spede
Hym hame, and help thame in thare nede.
On gretyng than fell Hanyball
For Ytaly that he left all,   1680
And all the knychtys that thare was
Off Ytaly, and wald noucht pas
Wyth hym in Affryk, but remede,
He slwe and gert be put to dede.
Syne to Cartage he come onone,
And thare, quhen he sawe Scypyon,
Off pes to trete wes all his thoucht,
Bot it fell thai accordyd noucht,

And sa behuẅyd thame on nede
Thane to fecht and batalle spede,   1690
And efftyre lang fechtyng thare,
Thai off Cartage ẅencust ware,
And Hanyball, bot wyth foure men
On hors, but ma, wes chapyd then,
And fra the batale gat away
Hys lyff [sa] sawffyd he that day.
Thus Scypyon had the vyctory,
And wytht his ost syne halyly,
Wan off Cartage the cyté,
And made in it his entré.   1700

CHAP. XVIII.

How quhen Antiochus kyng
Wyth the Romanis made anyng.

TWA hundyre wyntyr and sex oure
Or Mary bare oure Salẅyoure,
The secund batalle Affrycane
Was all done and end had tane,
And hastyly son eftyr than
The were off Macedone began,
Quhen that Flamyne, that than wes
Ane chosyne off the Consules,
Eftyr mony juperdyis,
And syndry wonnyn vyctoryis,   1710
Grawntyt pes and trwys ononc
Tyll Phylippe kyng off Macedone,
That eftyre Alexsawndyr wes dede
Succedyd kyng in tyll his stede

F. 64.

Ane hundyre wyntyr and twenty.
The captywys than halyly
Off the Romanys, all
Tane before wyth Hanyball,
Recoveryd wes throuch Scypyon,
And folowid his chare onone   1720
And gert schawe off thare hewyd the hare,
In takyn that thai delyveryd ware
Fra serwytute and threllage fre,
Passand hame in thare cuntré.

   Eftyre this it hapnyd thus
The kyng, that [tyme], Anthiocus,
Agayne the Romanys ras off were,
And come on Se, wytht his powere,
In tyll Europe off Asy,
And Hanyball than prewaly   1730
Drest tyll hym agayne Scypion
In tyll confederation,
Sa that his Amerall was he
Tyll all hys Nawyne apon Se.

   Scipio than Affricane
The Romanys wytht hym has he tane,
And fawcht wytht Hanyball sa fast,
Till he hym wencust at the last,
And mad apon hym felloune chas,
And he for dede than dredand was,   1740
All his pyth put in tyll spede
As he was artyd than on nede;
And quhen the kyng Antyocus
Swa that his werd turnyd thus,
Tretyd wpone trw onone,
And concord made wyth Scypyon.

   Off Rome ar othir batalis sere,

That, gyff thai ware all reknyd here,
I dred suld dull yhoure appetyte,
And gendyre leth mare than delyte. 1750

CHAP. XIX.

Now quhen the Peychtis in Scotlande Come, and in it wes regnande.

TWA hundyr wyntyr, and na mare,
Or that the madyn Mary bare
Jhesu Cryst, a cumpany
Out off the kynryk off Sythy
Come off Peychtis in Irland,
Quhar than the Scottis war duelland,
And wald have bene in parcenary
In to that land duelland thaim by.
That the Scottys thame denyid;
F. 64. b. Bot sayd, thare was unoccupyid, 1760
Lyand beyhond an arme off Se
Anentis thame, a gret cuntré,
That oft thai saw on dayis lycht,
Quhen that the Sone wes schynand brycht:
And that, thai said, wes profytabille
For to ma to thame habitabylle;
And counsalyd thame for to pas in
That ilk land, and it to wyn;
And thai suld rys in thare defence,
Gyff ony maid thame resistence, 1770
And thai suld mak thame suppowalle
Wytht gud, and men, and wytht wytalle.
  The Peychyts askyd the Scottis then

Weddyt to be wyth thaire wemen,
Syn nakyn women off thare kyth
Thai broucht wyth-in the land thame wyth,
Swa wytht thame till alyid be
Thai and thare posterytê.
That was accordyd on this wys,
That giff ony dout suld rys,   1780
Quha suld succede, and regne as kyng,
Quhen that the kyngis maid endyng,
He sulde be kyng off all the hale,
That cummyn war be lyine female;
And off the male suld nane succed,
Bot it ware clere, but ony drede.
This prerogatyẅe than
The Scottis fra [the] Peychtys wan,
And was kepyd welle allwayis
Amang the Peychtys in thare dayis.   1790
    Syne thai passyd that land wythin,
To thame and thairis it to wyn,
And the Northt landys occupyid.

CHAP. XIX.

[*From* MSS. C., E. I., *etc.*]

. . . .

Cotton, F. 43. Syne thai passit that lande witin   †1791
To thame and to thar aris to wyn,
And the Northe landis occupyide,
The Souythe that tyme inhabyide
Withe Brettownys of Brutus seide,

By thaim wes Scottis in that tyde,
Regnand, and the fyrst man
Off thai wes Fergus-Ercswne than :
And in the Sowth yhit as we rede
Wes Bretownys than off Brwtys sede.
   Fra Fergus be lyne
Quhill that Kyned-Makalpyne   1800
Ras as kyng, and was regnand
Wytht-in the kynrik off Scotland,
Few persownys lynyalle,

Sa in our Cornyclis, as we reide,
That Scottis war regnande mony yhere
Befor the Peychtis cummyn were
Withe-in Scotland, I can noucht ken
Qwhat thai war callit that regnyt then,   † 1800
Bot Fergus Erschson, I wisse,
The fyrst of Scottis he reknyt is
That regnyt, as the Cornyclis sayis,
Kyng befor the Peychtis dayis,
And qwha that redly se kan
He wes bot the tende man.
For to rekkyn eẅyn be lyne
Befor Kenyaucht-Makalpyne.
Othir seyr that we of reide
Betweyn tha twa, as thai succeide,   † 1810
Sum fel collateralle
And regnande our the Scottis haile,
As coursse made and qwhalite
Ayris ẅareande to be ;
Sum hapnyt to ryng throw malice,

Swm othir fell collateralle,
As cours made and qualyté
Ayrys waẅerand for to be.
Sum hapnyd to regne throuch malice,
And ilkane othir wald suppryce.
Bot fra this Fergus evin be lyne
Kynede discendyd Makalpyne.   1810
And, as we fynd in oure story,
Crwthne that tyme Makrymy
Wes the fyrst in till Scotland

And ilkan othir walde supprysse,
Bot fra this Fergus, eẅyn be lyne,
Kenyaucht descendit Makalpyne,
And was bot in the tende gre,
And yhit mere, gif yhe wil se,   † 1820
Reknys qwhat the tend liffit here,
And how lang tyme thai regnande were,
And thai al sal noucht excede
Thre hundyr yhere wyth-outyn dreide,
Qwhar in the Cornykil writtyn is
Twelf hundir, and fere mare I wis,
Fra fyrst the Scottis war regnande
Or Kynyauch Makalpyn wan the lande.
 Bot be othir Auctouris seyr
The Scottis, I fynde, begouthe to stere   † 1830
Qwhen that the Peychtis was regnande;
To that I ame accordande,
And thare date set I wil
Qwhen the processe is lede thar-til.
In til this tyme be our story
Cruthne that tyme Makryny.

Atoure the Peychtys kyng regnand;
He lyvyd, and regnyd fyfty yhere;
Bot off his douchty dedis sere
I wyll tell na mare than I wate,
F. 65. For Cornykklis, that off hym wrate,
Sayd, he wes a juge myld
Regnand oure the Peychtys wyld.   1820
   Nest tyll [hym] succedyd Gede,
And was maid kyng in till his stede
Oure the Peychtys in Scotland
Ane hundyr and fyfty yhere regnand.

Was the first in to Scotlande
Attour the Peychtis kyng regnande:
He liffit and regnyt fifty yher,
Bot of his douchty dedis seyr   † 1840
I will tell na mar than I wate;
For Cornycleris that of hym wrate,
Saide, he wes a juge mylde
Regnande our the Peychtis wilde.
   Next til hym succedit Gede,
And was made kyng in til his stede
Oure the Peychtis in Scotlande
Ane hundyr and fyfty yher regnande.

CHAPTER XX.

How Cartage, off consale,
Wes ordanyt to be wndone all hale.

ANE hundyr and fyfty yhere beforne
Or God wes off our Lady borne,
Off Rome gaddryd the senage
And ordanyd till wndo all Cartage.
Scypyo than Affrycane
Lord off the Romanys and chyftane   1830
Gert in hy befor hym call
The cytyzanys off Cartage all,
And gawe thame stratly mawndement,
But ony kyn impedyment,
Hastyly for till hym bryng
Thare wapnys all, and thare armynge,
And all thaire nawyn syne bad he
Suld tyll hym delyveryde be,
And efftyr that he bad thame mare,
Fra the se that thai suld fare   1840
Ten thowsand pasys syne, but lete;
In sorowe sare than war thai sete,
Sum nevyrtheles yhyt passyd sone,
And in all as he bad has done,
Sum chesyd errare thare pyth to prowe,
Or thai wald fra the se remowe,
And sum chesid errare to de
Than thai walde fra thare fredume flé.
Chyfftanys than thai chesyd twa,
And gert off gold and silvyr ma   1850

The armwrys, and the wapnys all,
That to thare nede wes lyk to fall,
On this wyis thai relevyd welle
All thare defawte off yrne and stelle.
Scypio than in his ire
Gert set the towne than in [a] fyre,
And in it thare the fyre brynnand
Sewyntene dayis wes ay lestand.
This wes the fyrst destructyoune
Off Cartage, that nobill towne,   1860
Quhen sevyn hundyr yhere and ane
Fra it wes foundyt qwyt wes gane.

  The thryd batale Punyk here
Tays end, and lestis bot foure yhere;
The secund batalle bath and it.
Held twenty yhere, as sayis the wryt,
Thretty thousand off men thare
And fyve and twenty thousand ware
Off women, reknyd off Cartage,
That come and yhald thame in thrillage,   1870
Servandys for tyll be alway
To the Romanys fra that day;
For dowt thai had [beyn] perysyd in
The cyté quhen thai saw it bryn;
Wytht bettyr wyll yhit othir ma
In to that brynnand fyre walde ga,
And de wytht-[in] thare awyn fre,
Than in to serwytute to be
Serwand to the Romanys ay,
Thai and thare ayrys fra that day.   1880

CHAP. XXI.

How the Romanys than Corynt and Achaye wan.

Ane hundyr and sex and fourty yhere
Before that Mary, madyn clere,
God had borne off hyr body,
Cartage delete wes halyly,
And off Coryntus than the towne
Famows and off gret renowne
In to Grece, the Romanys than
Assegyd wytht thare ost, and wan.
Wytht-in the towne sic multitude
Off symulacrys on pillaris stude, 1890
Massy, grete, welle polyst syne,
Made off gold and sylvyr fyne;
Eftyre that all that towne in fyre
Wes brynt and fallyn in colys schyre,
All the metall moltynnyd than
In tyll a qwerne togydder ran;
That metalle, mad sa pure and fyne,
Off Corynt had the tytill syne,
And all the weschall off it made
The name thare-efft off Corynt hade. 1900
   In to this tym I spak beforne,
In to Rome a barne wes borne
That had foure handys and foure fete,
Foure eyne and foure eyrys yhete,
And before had pyncillis twa.
   The fyre that tyme off Ethna,

That is ane hyll wythin Cyzile,
Brwstyd owt in to that quhille,
Sa that it brynt all suddanly
Sere landys that lay nere [thar] by.   1910
  Alsua that tyme in Cyzille
Thare ras a suddane were serville,
That breyde the Romanys als welle
As thame off Cyzille ilka delle.
Bot off thai schortly for to say
Twenty thousand on a day
Discumfyte wes, and slayne all downe,
And thare pompe browcht till confusioune.
Ay serwandys quhen that yhe se rys,
In yre thare lord[is] for till supprys,   1920
Quhat the oys is seldynyare,
It hapnys all the cruellare.
For-thi till Alexandyr the kyng,
Arystotyll, in his techyng,
Sayd, "Gyff thow thynkys for to be
Kyng to regne in reawte,
Be wyt off lordys thow suld lywe,
And thé fra lustys to wertu gywe,
Twyn-tungyd serwandys on all wys,
And wykyd fals thow sall disprys,   1930
And thai that off kynd suld be
Threll serwandys in tyll powerte,
Thow sall relew thame to na hycht,
Na put thame to na stat off mycht,
For dowt that thai, apon sic wys
As ryweris reche for rayne wyll rys,
And wavyre mare wytht wawys wude,
Than wyll a kyndly standand flude,
Ryse agayne thare lord off were,

F. 66.

Hym to supprys wyth thaire powere ;   1940
Fra thai be growyn in welth and welle,
And till wnkyndly slepand seile,
Till maistry or till mykyll mycht,
Till honour and till wnhawand hycht,
Fra reuth thai sall thare erys dyt,
And na thyng will off mercy wyt,
Bot sall wyth-draw thame fra peté,
Mare deffe than ony awsk yhe se.
The reule off resowne, nevyrtheles,
Sall ye noucht lede in that straytnes,   1950
Thou sall hym wytht gud relewe,
And in till state off honure prewe
That belyste is in [to] bownté.
And avynand is off honesté.
Off fayre affere and thewys gud,
Wertuws, and myld off mwde ;
Set that he want faculté,
Or kyn, and gud in till plente.
For the soyth, gywe yhe will say,
Welth and ryches wownt wes ay   1960
In wantones mare will to drawe
Than havyng fayr in mesure hawe.
And certys quha that habowndis
But ryches, in till gud thewys,
Lawte, wyte, and fayr hawyng,
He may noucht fale off owtward thyng.
For thai he may well set before
Sylvyr, gold, and all tresore,
And he may symply wyth that prys
Redeme, but mare, his landis wys,   1970
And fayre lordschip tyl hym wyn,
And grow in gentill kyth and kyn.

I meyne noucht his necessyte
That alway lywys in honeste,
Owtward hawand sufficians,
And inward wertuws habowndans;
He may be callyd a gentill-man
That wertu and fayr hawyng can
Off fre men ay the multitude
Sall set thame for till eyk the gude,   1980
Wyth honowre land and lordschype wyn
And helpe thare-self, thaire kyth, thare kyn;
Bot the threllys serwandys ay
Sall honesté at wndyr lay
And, but mercy, sall supprys
Quhen wantones mays thame to rys."

 The land off Cyzille in the Se
Wes that tyme off sic caytyfte,
Till nane honowre awenand,
Na till na statis sufficyand,   1990
Till tyrandys quhilum wndyrloute,
And quhill wytht serwandis in gret dowte,
And, wndyre gret exactyown,
Haldyn in till supprysiowne.

CHAP. XXII.

Quhen thai off Rome gert biggid be
Agayne off Cartage the cyté.

ANE hundyre and twenty yhere before
And ane to rekyn or God wes bore,
The Romanys in to that quhille
To Cartage send off thare famyle,

For till big wp agayne the towne,
And mak thare habitatyowne 2000
Thare, and hald it fra that day
Trybutare till Rome alway,
That twenty yhere and twa wes efft
That it wes brynt in colys left.

The hill off Ethna than off fyre
Brak out, and brynt in colys schyre,
[And] all the howsis off Catenes,
That in till Cyzille lyand wes;
And for that caus thai freyde were
Fra the trewage off ten yhere, 2010
Sa that thai mycht relewÿd be,
And byg agayne thare brynt cyté.

CHAP. XXIII.

*How many Romanis slayne wes,
And women rageand in wodnes.*

ANE hundyr wyntyr and ellewÿn,
Or Mary bare the Kyng off Hewÿn,
The Romanys wyth thare Consules
In were and batayle movyd wes
Agayne syndry regyownys,
Bath Duche and Frankys natyownys,
That set halyly thare intent,
Bwndyn apon ane assent, 2020
The Romanys till hawe wndone;
And thare apon thai semlyd sone
In fecht, quhar off the cytezanys,
Besid othire owte Romanys,

Foure score of thoussanddis wes slayne downe,
Besyd tha wytht-owte the towne,
Fourty thousand reknyd hale
Off Romanys slayne wythtin batalle.
Sex score off thousand in that fycht
Slayne to the dede wes dycht.   2030
That batell was off sic felny,
F. 67.   That bot ten men anerly
Off the Romanys fra that place
Etchapyd, for to tell the cas.
Than thai off Rome gret murnyng made,
And howerand in gret dowte abade,
Dredand sare that that menyhe
Suld wyn and tak wp thare cyté.
The Duche-men and thai [of] Cymbry
Togyddyr knyt in cumpany   2040
In Ytaly, as thai abade,
Thare sudjowrnyng for till have made,
Thame to refresche in wyntyr tyde,
And frostys fell for till ourbyde.
The Romanys wyth thare consules,
Or thai to fecht arayid wes,
Brak apon thame suddanly.
And slwe [thaim] downe dispytwysly,
Bot thai off Rome, in that dispyte,
Yhit wes noucht off all scathys qwyte,   2050
For off thaim mony slayne wes thare :
Thare inymyis yhit reknyd ware
Ane hundyr and sex[ty] thousand dede,
And presownerys tane in to that stede
Wes reknyd sevynty thousand gude,
Wytht-owte a gret multytude
Off wemen, rageand in wodenes,

And fallyn, for dule, in hewynes;
Quhill thai put thaim-self to dede,
And slwe thare barnys, but remede. 2060
　　In memor off that victory
The Romanys gert byg in hy
A tempill fayr, and that gert thai
Be Cymbry callid eftyr ay,
That syne wes haldyn in honore
Nere Saynct Mary the Majore.

CHAP. XXIV.

𝔗𝔥𝔢 𝔫𝔢𝔵𝔱 𝔣𝔬𝔩𝔬𝔴𝔞𝔫𝔡𝔢 𝔈𝔥𝔞𝔭𝔭𝔱𝔢𝔯𝔢
𝔗𝔢𝔩𝔩𝔦𝔰 𝔬𝔣𝔣 𝔣𝔢𝔩𝔩 𝔱𝔞𝔨𝔶𝔫𝔫𝔦𝔰 𝔰𝔢𝔯𝔢.

FOUR schore off wyntyr and sevyntene
Or lychtare wes the Madyne clene,
The state off Rome begouth to be
Stade in gret perplexyté, 2070
Amang thame-self dewysyd swa,
That thai ware lyk gret skath to ta,
Na ware the hape it sessyd sone,
Fra that thai to the dede wes done,
Throuch consalle off the Consules,
That the fyrst matyr off it wes;
Than throwcht fellowne taknys sere
The Romanys all [a]breyd were.
　　At Careptyne, as thai ware set,
Apon a day all at the mete, 2080
Apon the burde owte off thare breyde,
Thare brystyd owt the blud all rede;
Nere by [in] ane othire plas

F. 67. b.　　The erde clave and oppynnyd was,
And a low out off that ryfft
Strak wp evyn nere to the lyfft,
And alkyne best hamly thare
That amang men lyẅand ware,
Left thare stablys and thare fude,
And yhelland ran, as thai ware wude,　　2090
Tyll woddys and till wyldyrnes,
Leẅand thare auld hamlynes;
And hundys, that ay kyndly
Requirys mennys cumpany,
Ran wud as wolẅys to the wode,
Gowland in gret multytude.

　Fra thir taknys was all done
Othir casis hapnyd sone,
For Julyus Cesare, in Sampnyte,
Wes wytht his hale ost discumfyte,　　2100
That all his men bot he [al]ane
In to that land wes slayne or tane;
Pompeyus ẅencust wes alswa,
And in till othir landis ma
All the Romanys wes qwyte
In tyll thaire werys discumfyte.
Tharefor the senage a clethyng
Made thame, in takyn off murnyng;
And Julyus Cesare in that wede
Wes wytht thame clede, bot syne, but drede,　2110
Eftyre syndry juperdyis,
Quhare ẅencust wes his inymyis,
That garment he put fra hym sone,
And othire [weid] has on hym done.

　Pompeyus alsua, that Pretore
Discumfyte in tyll fecht before,

Wan and had great victoryis
In batayle, and in juperdyis:
Ascalon wytht his powere
He assegyde and wan off were; 2120
Auchtene thousand men wes tane,
Slayne, and dede, wyth thare chefftane.
The Were Civile was than sa fele,
Sa owtrageows, and sa cruel,
Sa ẅyolent, and than sa kene,
That sic befor wes nevyre sene;
For off the Romanys sere
Fechtand agane Silla were,
And off thame mony faucht alsua
Agaynis othir wytht Silla. 2130
Silla thane a Romane wes,
Ane chosyne off the Consules.
The Romanys in to tha dayis
Be thousandys, as Frer Martyn sayis,
Innowmerabill wytht-in that fycht,
Wytht dyntys downe to ded wes dycht.

 Quhill thai in were wes wedand thus,
A Roman than callyd Cantulus,
Till Silla sayde apon this wyis,
"In this were, and this juperdyis, 2140
We sla thaim all anarmyd downe,
That yhit releẅe wald oure renowne,
And nakyd we slay thame in pes,
That walde ws helpe to wyn prowes."
Than Silla made for that resowne
A tabyll off prescryptyowne,
Sa that fyrst proscryẅyd ware
Foure score off thousand men, and mare,
And fyẅe hundyr efftyr thai

F. 68.

Proscrywyd ware throucht this Silla. 2150
The Romanys swa was fra thare stede
Nere exylyde or slayne to dede.
This Were Civile ten yhere owte
Contynwyde wes wytht-owtyn dowte;
And off the Romanys slayne ware
Ane hundyr and fyfty thousand thare;
And endyng it begouth to ta
Eftyr that dede wes this Silla.
Pompeyus than the Oryente
Warrayd throuch fors and hardyment, 2160
And fawcht wyth twa and twenty sere
Kyngys off mycht and gret powere.

CHAP. XXV.

In till this next Chapitere,
Off Julius Cesare yhe sall here.

FOURE score off yhere, bot ane les,
Before that God off Mary wes
Borne, off Frans the regyownys
Tyll Cesare and sevyn legyownys
Gyvyn and delyveryd were,
To wyn off were wytht-in fyẅe yhere.
Off Trevyr syne, the gret cyté
He wan, and it dystroyid he. 2170
All Frans and Brettayne syne off were
To Rome he mad bath tributere;
And a bryg he gert mak syne
Atoure the gret ryẅere off Ryne.
All Duche-land syne he oure rade

And tributere to Rome it made.
　　Thire dedys quhen [that] he had done,
Till Rome he tuk his wayage sone.
Wytht mare honour than thoucht he,
For till have bene in that cyté　　　　　　2180
For his worschype gret resayvyde
Bot thare-off qwyte he was dyssaywyd
For thai off Rome fra Julius
Inclynyd till Pompeyus,
Quharfore thai wald noucht till hym do
Sik honowre as afferyde hym to,
Na wald noucht mak off thare tresore
Hys costys, as thai dyde before.
Agayne thare wyllys hale, for-thi
In till the towne wytht his maystry　　　2190
He mad entre, and wp brak
The tresoure hows, and syne cowth tak
Off thare tresowre a gret dele
Bath off mone and jowelle,
And furth in werys syne he past
Till he in Spayne come at the last;
Thare for till [telle] yhowe schortly
Ay all hym fell the wyctory.
In Ytaly syne turnyd he
Thare for to fycht wytht this Pompé;　　2200
And Pompeyus wyth stowtnes
To fecht wytht hym arayid wes.
Thare, efftyre lang and hard bataylle,
Pompeyus [ost] begouth to fayle,
And hym-self syne at the last
Turnyd the bak and fled rycht fast,
And past throuch Asy in till Tyre,
In Egypte syne, quhare lord and syre

That tyme wes Schir Tolomé,
That tuk and gert slay this Pompe; 2210
Syne off hys fyngyre he gert ta
Hys ryng, and his hewyd alsua
He gert stryk off, and thai he sent
Till Julyus Cesare in present,
That in tyll Alysandyr abade,
Fra he the chas off Pompe made;
Quhen he the hewyd saw and the ryng
Off Pompeyus, in gretyng
He fell, and menyd sare that he
On that manere suld endyde be. 2220
Julyus Cesare that tyme thare
Arrywyd in tyll the ile off Fare;
Off that ile all lord than wes
A man off gret mycht, Achilles,
Agayne Cesare he fell in fycht.
Quhare slayne wes mony a douchty knycht
Off Julyus Cesarys cumpany,
And than thai slayne war halyly
That before Pompeyus slwe.
Than Julyus til hys schippis drwe, 2230
And in that passage than he wes
Set in tyll sik thrang and pres,
That in tyll his bate, quhen he
Wes gane and in it made entre,
Throuche the charge at it bare,
In to the se it sank rycht thare;
Bot off that bate than in the se
He lape, and thare swymmand he
Held on till his schyppis fast,
Twa hundyre pasys swa he past, 2240
Haldand owthe the wattyre ay

Hys a hand as he swam that day,
And swa held all his lettrys dry,
In that hand closyd prewaly,
Till his galay qwyll that he
Come, and in it made entré.
Off Alysandyr the ost all hale
Off Se gawe hym than [harde] bataylle,
Thare bath thare nawyne and thare kyng
Takyn wes throuch hard fechtyng, 2250
Bot thare kyng off curtasy,
At thare askyng, [than] thraly
He lete pass, but rawnsone fre,
And playnly hym consalyd he
All his diligence to sete
Off the Romanys for to get

F. 69. Frendschype, tendyrnes, and luwe,
And nakyn were agayne them muwe.
  Bot that kyng, fra he wes fre
And all set in his awyn pousté, 2260
Left that counsalle, or all foryhette,
And for the were all halle hym sette,
But throuch this Julyus he wes qwyte
On Se thare-efftyre discumfyte,
And twenty thousand off his men
Wes slayne in to that jowrne then,
And twelf thousand men were thare
Slayne fra this Julyus [than] Cesare;
Thre scor and ten bargis lang
Was tynt and drownyd in that thrang 2270
And into this pres that kyng,
Awenand, honest, fayre, and yhing,
In to that bataylle wes sa mate,
That prewaly he gat a bate,

And to the land [than] walde haf past,
Bot Julyus oste on hym sa fast
Folowyd thare wytht sa gret pres
That slayne in to that fechtyne he wes.
And efftyre that apon that sand,
Quhare mony bodyis slayne thai fand 2280
And castyne wp, that kyng wytht crowne
Thai knewe welle be his habyrjowne
Wytht gylt mayle, for in that plas
Lyk till it nane fundyn was.
Till Alysandyr Julyus send
That hawbyrjowne, quhare thai it kend.
For dispayre the towne than wes
Yholdyn, and till Cleopatres
This Julyus Cesare gaw all hale
Off Egypt all the governale. 2290

Syne he passyd throuch Surry
And wan gret lordschyppis and syndry;
And efftyre that to Rome come he,
And [was] relewyd tyll heyere gre;
For Dytoure that tyme thai hym made,
And Consule als thare-efft, but bade;
Baythe Spayne and Affryk apon were
He made till Rome trybutere,
And efftyre that in Rome wes he
Ressaywyd wyth gret reawte. 2300

Than sevyn moneth and thre yhere,
Quhen all thare werys endyt were,
His stat he held as Empryowre,
And lywyd in wyrschype and honowre;
Bot wytht twa traytourys syn, Allas!
He falsly dyssaywyd was;
The tane off thai wes Cassius,

The tothir callyd wes than Brutus,
And yhit wes sayd that sexty may
In that consentyd to thai tway, 2310
Than in the [court] all suddanly
[Thai] stekyd hym rycht fellownly
Wytht scharpe pownsownys, and thai thare
Foure and twenty wowndys sare

F. 69. b. Gawe hym; and thus quhylle tha
Wes fellownly hym stekand swa,
And betwene thame thare bledand,
Stud ewyn wp wyth his rycht hand
[And] off hys gowne a lap tuk thare,
And cuveryd befor hys eyne bare, 2320
And wytht his left hand he held downe
The nethir lape thare off his gowne
Behynd lauch, that nane suld se
Spot, fylth, or wnhonesté
Behynd, in till his down fallyng.
This wes his last endyng
Eftyre that sax and twenty yhere
Off his eyld was passyd clere.
Hys body dede the pepyll syne
Brynt, and made off merbyll fyne 2330
A pyllare twenty fwte off hycht,
And it thai gert be set wp-rycht
In to the merket, thare gert thai
The powdyre and the banys lay.

Or Julyus deid, as I herd tell,
In Rome wncouth taknys felle;
Or he wes dede the hundryth day
Off fyrslaucht fell, brynt all away,
The fyrst lettyr off his state
That men apon his ymage wrate, 2340

Quhen that it wes fyrst wp set,
Ewyn in to the myd merkete.
C, that lettyre capytalle,
Is set in nowmerys wsualle
For ane hundyre, and for-thi
The Romanys had a fantasy
Fra C off Cesare wes away,
That abowte the hundyr day
Wouke, moneth, or moment,
Be [the] lest ay thare intent   2350
Be that nowmyre wes hoverand
And suddand casys abydand.

  Off the nycht neyst gane beforne
That Julyus slayne wes on the morne,
As he in tyll his chawmyr lay,
In tyll his bed lang forow day.
A suddane thude mad swylk a brus,
That all the wyndowys in a rus
Off his chawmyr quhare he lay
Brak wpe, and he than in affray   2360
Stert owte off his bed wytht that,
And lychtly on his solys gat,
For all the hows that tyme he wend
Off his lyff suld have made end.

  Quhen he was dede in till his hand
Thai priwe lettrys closyd fand,
That warnyd off his dede hade bene,
Gyff he before wald thame have sene.

  And all this tyme wytht-in Scotland
Ged oure the Peychtys was regnand.   2370

  The state off Rome fyrst gowernyd wes
Wytht Kyngis before Consules
Twa hundyr yhere, foure scor, and sevyn,

As Frere Martyne reknys eŵyn;
Foure hundyr wyntyr and twenty,
And foure to rekyn evynly,
Off Rome the gret stat governyd wes
Hale be chosyne Consules,
Quhill Julyus [Cesare] ras, and hale
Tuk till hym the governale. 2380

CHAP. XXVI.

**Off Octoviane yhe sall here
Next folowand in this Chapitere.**

TWA and fourty yhere beforne
Or Jhesu off Mary wes borne,
Octovyane, than neŵew
Till Julyus that [the] Romanys slwe,
Ras off Rome bathe lord and syre,
And governyd stoutly the empyre;
Fyŵe batayllis sere in his youthhede
He dyde, and proŵyd gret manhede.
The fyrst off tha fyŵe and the last,
That I haŵe lychtly [thus] owre past, 2390
He dyd stoutly wytht Marchus,
Be surname callyd Antonius.
Quhen fyftene yhere wes bygane
Fra fyrst begouth Octoŵyane,
For to regne in sic plente,
Off Rome the tresoure ekyd he,
The state [the] wyrschype and the fame
That thai than ekyd till his name
August, that in propyrte

Ay suld ckyng callid be, 2400
And sa the Romanys fra that day
Callyd hym Cesare August ay;
Fra thine he, and his successowrys
Succedand in till empryowrys,
For the tytill off thare state
All tyme Cesare August wrate,
And the empyre efftyre than
Wes all subjecte till a man,
And he fyrst as lord and syre
Off all the warld aucht the Empyre, 2410
And was callyd in Grew, for-thi,
Fra thine furth the Monarchy.
Syn this Octovyane
The land off Spayne wyth batell wan,
And mony othire landys sere,
Off were he wan wytht his powere.
 In thai dayis Pannony,
That marchand nere is Wngary,
Tyberyus, hys stepsone,
Wytht fellowne slauchtyr has wndone; 2420
And Duche-land syne als fast
Tyberyus oure rade and past.
This Duche-land cald Germany
Strekand lyis fra Pannony
To the gret rywere off Ryne,
As sayis Orosius and Solyne.
Thai sayis that rywerys thre
Off Germany suld callid be;
Alba, that throuch Boem rynnys,
And Adra, that nere it begynnys, 2430
And the Vyssill in Poleyn land
Begynnys, and throucht it is rennand.

F 70. b.
  Tyberyus wes warrayande
Thre yhere in this Duch-land,
Wytht legyownys tuelff off knychtys gud.
The were than als cruell stude
That nane wes till it off owtrage
To sauff the gret were of Cartage;
For off Rome than legyownys thré
Wes slayne and tane in that cuntré; 2440
Bot efftyre that till hys empyre
Octovyane, bathe lord and syre,
Wan all that land, and halyly
Off all the warld a Monarchy,
He had in quiete and in pes
And Empryowre thare-off he wes,
Regnand in gret reawté,
Honor, state, and majesté:
That all the men off his empyre,
Noucht anerly bathe lord and syre. 2450
Or empryowre thai wald hym calle,
Bot for hale counsall thai said alle,
For his prys and his waloure,
As God thai wald hym all honoure.
  All hys tyme in to unyté
The warld wes, and in cheryte,
And ilké man off ane accorde
Hym anerly kend for thare lorde;
He passyd noucht wytht-owtyn were
Off cyld ane and twenty yhere, 2460
Quhen he wes maid fyrst empryoure,
Bot it he led in gret honoure,
That for [his] prys and his gud fame,
August wes ckyd till his name.
  Off his name that moneth ay

Wes August callyd to this day,
Before than Sextile it wes cald:
Be that ensawmpyll yhit we hald
The monethys neyst it folowand,
The fyrst at Marche begynnand,　　　　　2470
Be the nowmyr thame to call,
As they are set per ordyre all,
Bot the Sextille turnyd the name
In August, for the realle fame
Off Octovyane, for that he
Wytht Anton mad rycht gret mellé;
Off that moneth the fyrst day,
For-thi thai callyd August ay.

　　In tyll the fywe and twentyd yhere
Off his empyre, for-owtyn were,　　　　　2480
Virgyle deyd in Brwndyis,
Bot in Naplis his body lyis:
And the fywe and threttyd yhere
Off his empyre, wytht-owtyn were,
The poet into Rome, Oras,
Deyd and entèryd was.
Thus in quiete quhill he wes
And stablyst all the warld in pes,
Regnand in tyll his majesté,
Honoure, state, and reawté,　　　　　　2490
Commendyt off gret douchtynes,
Off worschype, wyt, and worthynes,
Honest, habyll, and avenand,
At all poynt propyre and plesand,
Fayre off fassowne and off fas,
And large off lym and lyth he was,
Cunnand, curtas, and cumly,
Noucht lycht off latis bot luflly.

Thus he regnand lord and syre
Oure all the Warld in ane Empyre, 2500
He set hym haly for to wyt,
And to put in autentyk wryte
All kynrykys and all regyownys,
Cyteys, castellys, and all townys,
And quha that time wes lywand,
Tha landys than inhabytand;
And hale off all thai regyownys,
Kynrykys, cyteis, men and townys
He thoucht trewage for to tak,
And ger thame homage till hym mak. 2510
Apon that in hy he sent
Hys byddyng and his mawndement,
All kynrykys, and all regyownys,
All cyteis, and all othire townys,
And all the men that duelt thare-in,
Yhong and auld, batht mare and myn,
To wryt wp ilkane in tyll roll,
And regystere thaim be name and poll,
And efftyre that, but mare abade
Fra sowmownys had bene to thaim made, 2520
Ilké man to that cyté,
Quharoff beforne that borne wes he,
Or ellys to that ilké towne
That cheife ware off that regyown,
Suld cum, and thare, for his polle
[To] pay his trewage or his tolle
Off qwhyt sylver, a denere,
In nowmyre ten that sowndys here,
A denere comwnaly
Is in oure langage a penny, 2530
Bot that denere that thai suld pay

Suld have bene intyll walu ay
Ten pennys usualis than
That in to Rome for moné ran,
Havand the empryowrys crown,
Hys ymage, and his scriptyown;
That [thai] suld have bene in knawlage,
And taknyng hale off thare homage.
That thai suld aw to Rome, off det,
Sen thai ware made till it subjet,　　　　2540
And that sum callyd professyowne,
And sum it callid discriptyoune:
Professiowne in propyrté
Mouth grawntyng suld callyd be;
For quhen thai payid thare trewage,
Wyth mowth thai grawntyt thare homage,
And outh ilk[a] mannys polle
Hys name wes wryttyn and his toll:
Discriptyowne is wrytyng
In tyll owre propyr wndoyng,　　　　　2550
For all thare namys wryttyn ware
That payid toll, bayth les and mare,

F. 71. b.　And yhit ilke kynryk, land, and towne,
By tha layid thaire trewage downe;
In cyteys, mayre or aldyrman,
At thai bodyis fyrst began,
And ilké man cauld be hys crowne,
And gert hym lay his trewage downe;
Syne in the cyteis off the land
Wes certayne deputys resaywand　　　　2560
Off all the landys syne ilkane,
Wytht-in Rome wes the trewage tane.

　On this wyis batht land and towne
Tyll Rome made contributyoune,
And Cesare August, lord and syre,

Aucht all the warld in ane empyre:
Sa excellent off bewtó
Till ilke mannys sycht wes he,
That to [be]hald hym increly
Men had gret lykyn comownaly;   2570
Sa happy als he wes in deyd
That all thyng at his lykyng yheid,
And till his purpos and his thoucht
At ese hys wyll in all wes wroucht.
The senatowrys all hale, for-thi,
Gawe hym for counsall fermly,
Oure all the warld in hy that he
A God suld ger hym callyd be.
Bot he kest welle in tyll hys thoucht
A dedly man sen he was wroucht,   2580
Off hym he had a Creatoure
That aucht off resoune that honowre;
And till wsurpe till hym that name
It ware bot wane glore and deffame.

 Swa fra he herd thare intente
And efftyr thare awysment
Sybyll Tyburtyne in hy
He cald, and tald hyr halyly
Off the senatowrys the intent
And quhat was thare awysment.   2590
The space off thre days than in hy
Scho askyd to byd in hyr study,
And thai thre dayis in hard fastyng
Scho bade [and] in tyll thra praying,
And syne in tyll hyr prophecy
Scho made efftyre that study
Judicii Signum in to wers,
Bot thai ar lang now to rehers.

 The Empryoure syne till the hycht,

Scho gert behald, and swylk a lycht 2600
Hym wmbelappyd in that place
That gretly affrayid [than] he wes;
Syne he sawe a madyn fayre
Apone ane awtere in the ayre,
And a lytill barne allsua
Haldyn in hyr harmys twa.
And quhill he ferlyde off that sycht,
He herd a ẅoice that sayd [hym] rycht,
" Yhone thow wyt wyth-owtyne hune,
The awtere is off Goddis swne;" 2610
And to the erd rycht suddanly

F. 72.   He fell, and prayid devotly.
And syne the senatowrys gert he call,
And this sycht he tauld thaim all,
Quhar-off thai ferlyd gretly:
That chawmbyre syne he gert devotly,
In honowre off that madyn fre,
And off that barne als halowyd be;
For thare he saw that ẅysyowne
That raysid his deẅotyoune; 2620
Thare, in a kyrk off oure Lady,
Frere Mynowris now devotly
Wytht-in the Capytolle alway
Serẅys God, bathe nycht and day,
And that kyrk fowndyt in that place
Syne *Ara Cœli* callyd was.

Bot quhen the contributyowne
Wes payid, bathe off land and towne,
Off Nazareth and Galelé
Joseph, that tyme in Jwdé, 2630
Past to the cyté off Daẅy,
Wytht hys spowsyd myld Mary,
Bethleem callyd in that quhille,

For off that hous and that famylle
He wes off kyn and off renowne;
For-thi thare his professyowne
For tyll have made he sped hym yharne,
Wyth hys spows gret wame wytht barne;
Bot all the innys evryilkane,
Or thai come to the towne wes tane;   2640
And thare than wes sic a multitude,
Wytht-in the town off men and gud,
That tyll pure men it wes ill
For tyll get herbry to thare wyll;
Tharefor Joseph and Mary
Gat wyth-in hows na herbry.
Bot betwene howsis twa,
Quhare men gert a pentys ma,
Tyll hald confabilatyoune,
And have thaire recreatyowne   2650
In mete and drynk, and thare repayre,
As thare delyte wes till haẇe [thare];
Or for chapmen as buthys [makis]
Till oppyn and [to] schaw thare pakkys;
Joseph, wyth Mary his spous,
Hys innys tuk in swyk a hous;
And thare-in his bestys twa,
Ane ox and ane ass war thai,
Till a cryb that thare he made,
Or made perchawns he fwndyn hade,   2660
He band wp, and gaẇe thame hay,
And that ilk[a] nycht, or day,
That madyn Mary bare that byrth,
That caus wes off all oure myrth.

[Explicit Liber Quartus.]

THE FYFT BUKE

OF THE

ORYGYNALE CRONYKIL

OF SCOTLAND.

The Tytlis off the Fyft Buke.

  i. Off the byrth off Jhesu Cryst.
F. 72. b. ii. Off Tyberyus dayis.
  iii. Off Claudius and Gayus dayis.
  iiii. Off Nero and his dayis.
  v. Off Tytus and Ẅaspasiane.
  vi. Off Anaclete.
    Off Trajane.
  vii. Off Alexandyr and Adriane.
    Off the Pape Syxte.
    Off the Pape Thelesfore.
    Off Anton the Mylde.
    Off Pape Ingnyws.
    Off the Pape Pyus.
    Off Marcus Antonius Empryowre.
  viii. Quhen fyrst conẅertyd was Brettane.
    Off the Empyroure Comodus.
    Off the Pape Ẅyctore.
    Off the Pape Zepheryne.
    Off the Pape Poutyane.
  ix. Off the Empyrowre Philipe.
    Off the Pape Cornelle.
    Off the Pape Syxt.
    Off the Pape Dynys.
    Off the Pape Cayus.
    Off the Pape Marcellyne.
    Off the Pape Marcell.
    Off the Pape Ewsebyus.
  x. Off the Pape Sylvestere.

Off the Tyrand Maxentius.
Off Maximiane.
Quhen thai off Dace and Sythy arryẅyd in Brettane.
Quhen the Romanys gaẅe wp the suppowale off Brettan.
Off the Pape Marcus.
Off Constans and Constantyne Empyrouris.
Off Jwlyane the Apostata.
Off Felix and Damasus Papis.
Off the Pape Syrycius.
Off the Empryowris Galyone and Gracayne.

xi. Off Theodos and Saynt Ambros.
Off the Pape Anastacyus.
xii. Off the fyrst Pape Innocent.
Quhen Saynt Palady come in Scotland.
Off the fyrst Pape Benete.
xiiii. Off Saynt Gregore the gret Doctore.

THE FYFT BUKE

OF THE

ORYGYNALE CRONYKIL

OF SCOTLAND.

Next folowand yhe sall luk
The Proloug off the fyft Buke.

F. 73.
    Orosius apon syndry wys
Tyll Babylone Rome paryfyis:
Off Babylone the storys hale
Fra Nynus tais orygynale;
And off Rome the storys tays
Thare begynnyng fra Procays
The fadyr off Amylius,
And forfadyre tyll Romulus.
   Fra the fyrst yhere that Nynus Kyng
Had Babylon in governyng,   10
Tyll it wes stuffyd plentwsly,
And kyrnelyd abowt propyrly
Throucht Symyram[us] the Qweyne,
As yhe hawe herd me befor meyne,
Gane wes foure and sexty yhere.
Rycht swa in to the lyk manere
Fra the fyrst yhere at Procas
In Rome begowth and regnand was,

Or Romule made hade the Cyté
Thre scor and foure yhere gane wes fre.   20
Arbace als the Kyng off Mede,
Off qwham before yhe herd me rede,
Ryfflyd Babylon that yhere,
That Procas in Rome begouth to sterc.
Sa, as Oros[ius] signyfyis,
The West kynryk begouth to rys,
As the Est begouth to fayle
Be infortwne and hard batayle;
Quhare throuch the Warld is halyly
Now redact in a Monarchy,   30
And subject tyll ane empyre,
And a man off it lorde and syre.
 Swa now my purpos and my wille,
Gywe God wyll grawnt hys grace thare till,
Standys halyly for to schawe,
And clenly to ger yhow knawe
All the caus materyalle
Off the dowbyll governale,
Quhare wes wount to governyd be
Bathe the Warld and the Cyté.   40
Off this dowbyll governale
The grettast is the Spyrytuale;
The Temporalle is the les, but lete.
Thir are the twa gret lychtis set
In myddys off the firmament,
That oysis for to represent,
And to mynystyr thare serwys
Tyme be tyme, and thare offyis.
The grettare lycht is for the day,
And for the nycht the les alway.   50
Thir twa statis gret allsua

Sygnyfyis thai swerdys twa,
Quhareoff the specyall mentyowne
Wes sayd in Crystis Passyowne,
" Lord, lo! now twa swerdis here."
" Ynoch ar thai," wes his ansuere.
In to the Pape is the honowre,

F. 73. b. The state, the wyrschype, and the cure
Off the grettest governale;
And off the les state syne all hale   60
The soverane is the Empriowre
Be worschype, tytill, and honowre.
Swa now remanys for till telle,
How fyrst that thare begynnyng fell.

[𝔈xplicit 𝔓rologus.]

CHAP. I.

**Here next folowande yhe sall rede
Off Cristis byrth and his barnhede.**

A.D.
1.
Cesare August Octovyane,
Quhen that fourty yhere and ane
Off his empyre wes passyde clere,
Wytht-in the twa and fourtyd yhere
Apon the Sonondayis nycht
Mary myld, the madyn brycht,
But [threttyng], thrawyng, or dises,
Or ony smyt, delyveryd wes
Off hyr a Sown, [bath] God and Man;
That chyld wes tane and swelyd than,   10
And in a cryb syne layde he was
Quhar that ane ox stud and ane as,
And thai twa bestys devotly
On kneys, as wytnes the story,
Kend thare wes thaire creatoure,
Quhare-for thai dyd hym that honowre
That on kneys ay ware thai
Syttand, qwhill that he thare lay.
   The modyr held bed in gysyne,
But dowt yhit wes scho pure wyrgyne.   20
He name and circumsysown,
And scho puryficatyown,
Tuk, the tyme that ordanyd wes
Be the lauch statute off Moyses,
And the barne wes Jhesu cauld,
As the Angelle befor tauld;

Swa thai held and kepyd welle
All the lawys ilk[a] dele.
Oure Lord [Jhesu] thus wes borne
To sauff oure lyff that wes forlorne. 30
 Beyhond Tybere, as I herd telle,
Owte off the erd thare sprang a well
Off clere oylye, fayr and gud,
Quhare quhylum a famous tawerne stude;
And all that day in gret copy
That well ran owre habowndanly.
A cyrkyll abowte the Sone that day
Wes sene als, as I herd say,
That tyll ane arche off hewyn wes
Apperand lyk on lyklynes. 40
That ilk nycht, as I herd telle,
In Rome that gret Tempyll fell,
That quhen the Romanys twelff yhere
In pes and quyete lywand were,
In the honowre off Romule fre,
Off fyne entaylle gert fowndyd be,
And off this Romule a fygowre
Off hewys fyne and fayre payntoure,
F. 74. And othir symulacrys sere
Off ydolys that than honoryd were, 50
Thai set in to that Tempyll fayre,
Quhare thai mad access and repayre,
For to mak thare sacrifyis
To thai mawmentys on thare wyis,
Wyth dewote solempnyte
And wsuale festyvyte.
This Tempyle tytlyde wes off Pes,
For quhen fyrst it fowndyt wes,
Tyll Appollo, thair orysown

Thai made wyth gud dewotyown, 60
Certane knawlage for to get
How lang tyme that that Tempyll set
And fowndyd, in till [the] honowre
Off all thai mawmentys, suld endowre
And fermly stand in to that plas.
Off Appollyne the answere was,
That that Tempyll [sulde] endure
Ay quhill that a wyrgyne pure
Suld bere a barne off hyr body,
Thare-off the Romanys had ferly. 70
Noucht for-thi thai gert full tyte
Wytht gret lettrys brokyn wryte
Outh the dure at the entré,
Quhare thai mycht clerly red and se,
TEMPLUM PACIS ETERNUM; ay
Thir thre wordys ar to say,
The Tempill off Pes wyth-owtyn end.
Bot quhen Goddis Sone wes send
In tyll oure kyth, as yhe hard telle,
That Tempyll and thare fals goddys fell, 80
And thai symulacrys all
Ware fruschyd and brokyn in pecis small.

 Off the Oryent Kyngys thre,
Ilkane sere in thaire cuntré,
Be ane starne apperand newe,
Than borne the Kyng off Jowys knewe;
For that resowne thare wayage
Thai tuk in dewote pylgrimage,
Qwhill thai come till Jerusalem:
Fra thine thai passyd till Bethleem; 90
Thare, to the Sone off the wyrgyne,
Myr, and sens, and gold sa fyne,

In gret devotyoune offeryd thai,
Be-efft hys byrth the thretten day;
And quhen thai mad had thaire offerande
Hame agayne in to thare land,
By Jerusalem, passyd thai,
As thai war warnyd, ane othir way.
And how than Herrode had consaywyde
Throuch thaim that he wes dyssaywyde, 100
Quharfore the Innocentys he gert be
All slayne throuch his iniqwyté;
Haly Kyrk prechys clere
In to the wangyll ilk[a] yhere;
For that resowne now will I
Oure pas it here the mar lychtly.
    In Scotland that yhere Taram ras,
F. 74. b. And oure [the] Peychtis regnand was
A hundyr yhere as crownyd kyng.
And quhen his lyff had tane endyng, 110
Duchyl ras as kyng with crowne,
And regnand be successyowne.
Bot off thaire douchty dedis sere
I fynd noucht for to wryt in here.
    Kymbelyne of Tenwant
The sone and ayre was than regnant
As kyng wytht crowne off all Brettane.
Before that wytht Octovyane
He nwrysyd wes, till hys barnehede
Was passyd, and entryde in manhede, 120
And dyde gret prowes and bownté
In all kyn were or jowrné,
And tuk syne off that Empyrowre
The ordyr off knychthed wytht honowre :
To thame off Rome, for that resowne,

He stud in swylk effectyowne,
That in the tyme, quhen he wes kyng,
And Brettane had in governyng,
His barnage hale sayd, that he mycht
Wythhald the trewage wytht all rycht, 130
That Julyus Cesare before wan,
And payid was till Octovyan.
Agayne the wyll off his barnage
Till Rome he payid that trewage:
For that wyth his the were wes he
Comendyt in to all degre.

    And that ilké yhere alsua
Joseph passyd and Maria
In till Egypt; and sewyn yhere
Thare wytht the Barne thai duelland were. 140
Off his dedys in that quhylle
Fewe I find in the wangylle:
Bot quha that lykys for to rede
In tyll a Buk off his barnhede,
He sall fynd how be the way,
As wndyrneth a palme thai lay
At ese to slepe, or rest thaim thare
As pilgrymys that for-tyryd ware,
The mudyre makles off that chylde,
Mary brycht, the madyn myld, 150
Was in till scharpe hungyr set,
And had gret appetyt till ete
The crope thare off that palme tre,
That datys bare in gret plente;
Quhill scho was in [to] that thrawe
Wyth-all the buwys bowyd lawe,
Ewyn till hyr hand, swa at hyr wyll
Datys scho pullyd and ete hyr fyll;

Syne as wytht lewe, but brayd or bend,
Ewyn as before stud wp on end.   160
That tyme alsua Joseph thare
In tyll hard thryst was noyit sare,
Bot off [the] erd sone sprang a welle
Quhare-[of] Joseph, as I herd tell,
Drank his fyll off wattyr clere.

 Thare-efftyr, as thai herbryd were
In tyll a gret cove and a depe,

F. 75. Or thai begouth to fall on slepe,
Off that cove, all suddanly,
Twa gret dragownys and wgly   170
Ruschyd owte; thare Mary wes
And Joseph bathe in gret radness;
Bot thai twa wyld bestys kene,
Fra that thai the child had sene,
As thai had chastyid bene wyth awe,
Kest downe amang thare lymmys lawe
Thare hedys, and syne wyth gud speyd
Till wyldyrnes away thai yheyd.
Fra thine till Egipte in tyll hy,
As Joseph passyd and Mary,   180
A lyowne thaim kepyd be the way,
That serwysiabyll wes to thaim ay.
In tyll the land quhill thai ware fre,
And in it as thai mad entré,
Off Egypte hale the templis all
Fell and brak in pecis small,
[And] all the ydolys evryilkane,
That hale in to that land wes nane
Tempill standand off walu,
Na off nane ydole a statu.   190
Thir myrakyllis wryttyn yhe ma red

In till a buk off his barnehed.
　Fra thine Joseph and Mary
In Egypt duelt contynualy
Sevyn yhere, quhill the Angell brycht
Apperyd till Joseph on a nycht
In till his slepe, and bad hym ta
The Modyr, and the Barne alsua,
And pas in Israelle agayne,
" For thai," he sayd, " that wald have slayne　　200
The chyld, ar dede."　Than he, but hone,
All as the Angell bad has done;
Bot for caus, as the story sayis,
That Archelaus in thai dayis,
The quhilk brodyre that tyme wes
Till Herrode, full off wykytnes,
Off Jerusalem, as kyng
And lord, had all the governyng,
And dwelt in it contynualy;
For-thi, Joseph and Mary　　　　　　　　　210
Past wytht the barne by that cyté
Till Nazareth in Galelé;
In that cyté than fywe yhere
Wytht the Chyld thai duelland were,
That grew off wyt and wertu than,
And plesyd batht till God and man.
　Swa twelf yhere quhen he wes auld,
As Saynt Luke in his ewangyll tauld,
In Jerusalem, amang the gret
Mastrys off lawe, that held thare set　　　220
In to the Tempyll, for to schawe
The casys as thai stud in the lawe,
He sat, and wes rycht diligent
Till here, and mad sic argument

>
> That all that herd and stude hym by
> Off hys wyt had gret ferly.
>   And efftyr hys natyvyté,
> Quhen fourtene yhere wes passyd fre,
> Octovyane the empryowre
> Deyd in Rome wytht gret honoure,   230
> Quhen that sex and fyfty yhere
> Off his empyre were passyd clere;
> Ale the warld, as I sayd ere,
> He mayd to Rome tributere;
> In hys begynnyng the cité
> All abowte off Rome fand he
> Wytht dykys made off fayle or mude,
> Bot, or he deyd, off marbyr gude,
> Witht syment, lyme, or wytht hewyn stane,
> He made the wallis evryilkane;   240
> Off citesanys and burges fre,
> He left duelland in that cyté
> Fowr hundyr thousand nynty sys,
> And fourty thousand reknyd twys,
> As sayis Frere Martyne in his buke,
> Quha wyll his Cornyklys rede and luke:
> Yhit set he wes off this bownté,
> He wes noucht off all vycys fre,
> For he hade in usage offt
> Amang twelff maydynnys, yhong, and sofft   250
> Off hyd, and fayre off hew, to ly
> In lykyng, lust, and lychory.

F. 75. b.
A.D. 14.

CHAP. II.

The next Chapitere will tell
Qwhat in Tiberius dayis felle.

A.D. 15.

THE fyftende yhere efftyre that byrth,
That causyd all oure mekyll myrth,
Off Rome Tyberius empryoure,
Nest till Octovyane successoure,
His wyffis sone off lauchfull bede,
And had till wyff hys douchtyr lede;
For caus off that and hys bownté
Octovyane yharnyd hym to be 260
Hys ayre and his neyst successoure;
Swa fell that he wes emperyowre,
And ras off Rome bath lord and syre,
And stoutly governyd the empyre;
In deyd he doure wes and douchty,
And in till armys welle happy,
Kunnand, and off lettr[at]owre fyne,
Bot sle and dowtus off engyne.
Quhen men wald do be lyklynes
Hys wyll, or quhat his byddyng wes, 270
In frawde and swylk offt walde he say
That that hym lykyd be na way,
And ger the doarys punysyd be
Throuch wykytnes and crualte;
He wes rycht pert and eloqwent,
And full austere in jugement,
Curtays he wes in tyll his deyd;
In cornyklys sere off hym we reid

F. 76.
>That quhen hys procuratowrys ordanyd he
>In his nedis to passand be, 280
>Seldyn revocatyowne
>He mayd off that commyssyowne;
>He wald offt gere pyne and sla
>Thewys, and sakles men alsua;
>He tuk the trewage off Brettane
>That Julyus Cesare before wane;
>He regnyd twenty yhere and thre;
>In Chawmpayne syne quhen deide wes he
>Fele folk glad ware and [richt] joly,
>And few for that cas wes sary. 290

>Off Crystys dedis in that quhille
>Few I fynd in the Ewangylle,
>Tyll that tyme that he howyn wes,
>Bot as Josephus berys wytnes;
>He in tyll hys story sayis
>Thare wes a wysman in thai dayis,
>Gyff men mycht wyth resowne all
>In propyrté a man hym call,
>Off marwelus and gret dedys sere,
>He wes bathe doare and kennere, 300
>And mony off Jowys and Gentyl
>Till hym he drewe in till that quhille;
>Cryste that was, as Josephus
>Signyfyis in tyll hys buk till ws.

>The poete Ovyde in hys dayis
>Deyd exilyd, as the story sayis.
>Off hys empyre the fyftende yhere,

A.D. 80.
>And fra the byrth off oure Lorde dere
>The threttyd yhere, in wyldyrnes,
>Saynt Jhon the Baptyst prechand wes. 310
>Pylat off Powns procuryd to be

Chyfftane and prynce off all Jwde;
Off Powns he lord wes beforne,
Bot men sayd at he wes borne
Off Lyownys, in to Frans, sur Rone.
That yhere als off Baptyst Jhon
Jhesu Cryst, as sayde the Buke,
The baptysme in till Jordane tuke,
And the neyst yhere efftyr syne
He turnyd the wattyre clere in wyne.   320
Saynct Jhon the Baptyst als wes tane,
And efftyre that a yhere owre gane,
Throuch foly gret and crualté,
Herrode gert hym hevydyd be.
Than off Tyberius empryowre
Pylate wes made procuratoure
And specyall depute in Jwdé,
Sa fell that wndyre his powsté
Cryst tholyd thare [his] passiowne,
And mad his resurrectyowne,   330
Quhen that thretty yhere and thre
Were gane fra his natyvyte;
And in till August off that yhere
Saynct Stewyn was stanyde to dede, but were.
That ilké yhere alsua Saule
Convertyd, and was callyd Paule.
The empryoure Tyber eftyr that,
Quhen that he full wyttyng gat
That Jhesu Cryst to dede wes done,
He gert send efftyr [Pilate] sone,   340
And in hys presens hym gert he
Off jugement fals accusyde be,
Bot efftyre thai accusatyownys,
Ande his fals excusationis,

Tyll Vyen in tyll Burgoyne he
Hym send, and gert hym presownyt be;
Quhare lang he bad in pyne and care,
And slwe hym-self for sorow thare.
Herrode als that slwe that Jhone
Exylide he gert be onone   350
Tyll Vyen in till Burgoyne als,
Wytht his wyff, bayth fell and fals,
Herodyade, and thai twa
Wrachytly thare deyde alsua.
 Efftyr the Resurrectyowne
Off Cryst, and [his] Ascensyowne,
Saynt Petyr the appostylle fre,
Borne off the land off Galelé
In tyll the rew Bethsayda,
(He wes the sone off Jhon alsua,   360
And tyll Saynt Androw brodyr hale,)
Past in the landys Oryentale,
And in thai landys than held he
Foure yhere full the prestis sé,
And thare he sang the fyrst Mes
That in the warld evyre sungyn wes;
And in that Mes wes said na mare,
Bot the PATER NOSTER thare.
 Tyberius in that tyme wes dede,
And Gayus ras in till his stede,   370
This ilké Gayus wes alsua
Be surname callyd Gallicula.
Off the empyr lord wes he
Bot monethys ten, and yherys thre,
And awcht days, bot he wes
Ill wycyous, full off wykytnes,
Off gret lust and off lychory:

Hys awyn twa systyrys he lay by.
A dochtyr on ane off thai he gat,
And that he lay by efftyre that; 380
He nurré [was] and neŵew nere
Tyll the lord off Rome Tybere;
In crualte and avaryce
And mony odyr syndry ẘyce,
Sa lang he wedyde, quhill he was
Slayne wytht his men in his palas.
All thus quhen dede wes Gayus,
Till hym succedyd Claudyus,
That the empyre fourtene yhere
Governyd, and sevyn moneth clere, 390
And auchtene dayis fullyly.
    Saynt Petyr that tyme [coym] in hy
In Antyoche off the Oryent,
Thare sevyn yhere in gud entent
He bade, and helde the prestys sé;

F. 77.   Syne fra thine to Rome past he
As byschope thare and prest his lyŵe
Twenty yhere he led, and fyŵe,
And dayis awcht, till halde the date.
Twa pystyllys off canowne thare he wrate; 400
In Septembyre than ordanyd he
Ordyrys ilké yhere to be,
Thare byschypys sex, and prestys ten,
And deknys sevyn, he ordanyt then.

A.D. 40.   The fourtyde yhere efftyr that byrth
That made owre joy and all oure myrth,
The eẘangelyst Saynt Mathewe
Made and wrat hys ẘangelys newe;
And, efftyre that thre yhere alsua
Hys ẘangellys Mark begouth to ma, 410

And Saynt Petyr wrat thaim thare
For he before was his scolare.
In hungyr gret that ilk[a] yhere
The Romanys all anoyid were.
Appollynare Saynt Petyr then
Send to preche in tyll Rawen,
That wes a cyté gret and fayre,
Comowne, and off gret repayre,
In Ytaly pere till it wes nane,
To sawff off Rome the towne allane.   420

CHAP. III.

Off the Empryoure Clawdyus
Next successor till Schyr Gayus.

CLAWDYUS the empryoure,
That wes tyll Gayws successoure,
Off hys empyre the ferd yhere
In Brettayne come wytht hys powere,
Kymbolynys [son] than Widen kyng,
That Brettayne had in governyng,
Sone assemblyd ane ost in hy,
And wytht the Romanys stoutly
Faucht, and put thame to the flycht,
Quhare mony dowre to deyd wes dycht: 430
And quhill thai ware in to that cas,
A Romane, that amang thaim was
Hamo callyd, gat on that senyhé,
That Bretownys bare; syn can he fenyhe
Hym a Brettowne for to be,
For all thare langage welle kend he:

Quhen in tyll Rome ostagis sere
Of all landis duelland were,
And thai off Brettane ostage had,
He gret repayre amang thaim mad;   440
Be sic access he kend welle,
And leryd thare langage ilk[a] dele.
Sa in the thrang off that battaylle
He bare hym as a Brettane hale,
Quhyll that he come rycht till the kyng,
That off hym had na myslyẅyng:
That kyng off Brettayne thare he slwe,
And to the Romanys syne he drwe.

F. 77. b.   Arvyragus, that wes then
Brodyr to the kyng Wyden,   450
And saw this cas, and all this deyd,
Gat wpon hym ful gud spede
All hys brodyr armoure hale,
And held that ward in the batalle,
That [the] kyng hys brodyr had:
Thare fechtyng stowṭ and hard he made,
And lete hys ost wyt nakyn thyng
Off that cas fell to the kyng,
Quhill mony doure to dede wes dycht,
And all the Romanys tuk the flycht,   460
And Hamo slayne. In till that chas
The empryowre discumfyt was.

  Sa, to tell yhow schortly
The endyng off this juperdy,
Quhen Claudius the manhed kend
Off the Brettownys, he message send
Tyll Arẅyragus, than the kyng
That Brettayne had in governyng,
For till amese all were and stryffe,

And tak hys dochtyr till hys wyffe, 470
And to Rowme that tribwte pay
Wytht-owtyn drychyng or delay,
That the Romanys before wan
Fra hys eldrys off Brettan.
 Till this assented wes the kyng,
And sesyd were, and mad anyng:
For he thoucht, syne that generaly
All othir landys halyly
Bade wndyr the subjectyowne
Off Rome, he mycht wyth-owt chesowne 480
That trewage to the Romanys pay,
That thai had tane before his day.
Swa, now schortly to mak end,
Schyre Claudyus for his dochtyre send,
And Arẅyragus off Brettane
Weddyd that fayr lady than.
Betwene the Romanys and that kyng
All thus than fell the fyrst anyng.
 That ilke empyrowre off were
Past fra thine wytht hys powere 490
The Owte Ylys till assaylle,
And wyth hym in hys suppowaylle
That kyng passyd off Brettan,
And off fors the Owte Ylis wan,
And maid [thaim] to Rome subjet ay,
And gert thaim fra thine trybute pay.
 How that empyrowr thare-efft
That Kyng hys lutenand lefft
Off all the landys, that marchyd than
Nere wyth the kynryk off Brettan, 500
Hame tyll Rome quhen that he
Agayne passyd wytht hys reawte;

And how that kyng syne mad delay,
F. 78. And hale denyit for to pay
Till Rome the trewage off Brettane,
Quhyll Claudyus send Wespasyane
Wytht that kyng to fecht or trete,
Swa that for luwe, or than for threte,
Off fors he suld pay at he awcht;
And how the qweyne thare made thame saucht, 510
The Brute tellys it sa oppynly,
That I wyll lat it now ga by.

   This empryowre in all tyme wes
In all his dedys full rekles,
Na he couth hald in na memore
The thyngys that he dyd before.
It hapnyt in tyll suddane stryffe
That apon cas he slwe hys wyff;
At ewyn to bed syne quhen he past
Quhy sho come noucht, he askyt fast. 520
He thoucht till ordane and till ma,
Be statute, quhen men suld lat ga
Owte off thare bodyis ryfftys off wynd,
At mowth before, or than behynd;
For in to Rome off cas it fell
For schame a man, as he herd tell,
Forbare for tyll [lat] owt the wynd,
Wyth ryfft before, or blyst behynd,
Swa that he peryst in that thrawe;
Tharfor he thoucht, quhen men suld blawe, 530
Tyll ordane tyme be statute swa
That for that cas [men] suld dey na ma.
He wes the mast sobyr man
Off mete or drynk that lywyd than.
Massalyne wes callyd hys wyff,

Scho spendyt in swylk lust hyr lyff
That hyr oys was comownaly
In bordale nycht and day to ly,
Off that play [nevyr] yrk na sad
For all the copy at scho had, 540
And ladyis sere scho tretyd ay
In cumpany to pruve that play.
Yhit, be counsalle off this wyff,
That thus in lust led all hyr lyff,
Hys sone and hys ayre gert he
Off the empyre desheryd be,
And Nero, that had hys dochtyr weddyt,
And lauchfully wytht hyr had beddyt,
He ordanyd off the empyre
Bathe hys ayre, [and] lord and syre; 550
And that wes done agane the lawe
For luwe off woman, or for awe.

    Saynt Petyr, as the story says,
Fyrst come to Rome in till his dayis,
Thare ordanyt he befor Pas day
The Lentryne to be fastyt ay
Off fourty dayis, syne wox thre,
And the ferd part ordanyd he
All Crystyne man in fastyng hald,
That war full fourtene yhere alde, 560
Before the Natyvyté;
[That] the Adwent now call we.

CHAP. IV.

**Off Neroys tyme and Petryis dede,
Ande qwha next [ras] in to thare stede.**

NERO neyst wes successoure
Till Claudyus, and empryowre
[He wes] off gret Rome threttene yhere,
Aucht moneth, and a day, but were.
He prowyd welle off his manhede
Quhill he wes knycht in till yhouthede,
Bot fra he kend hym empryowre,
He excedyt all mesoure,   570
And worschype chawngyd in tyrandry,
Honowr in falshede and felny ;
He gert slay off the senatowrys,
That off det ware his counsalowrys,
A gret part, and alsua
His awyn brodyr he gert sla.
All Rome he set in tyll a fyre,
A low off that for to se schyre.
Hys modyr oysyd for to repruwe
And argwe hym wnkynd off luwe ;   580
Till hir that sufferyd thrystys sare,
And paynys hard quhen scho hym bare,
And wes in dowt off hyr lyff ay
Betwene hyr sydys quhill he lay,
But pety tharefor, or mercy,
He slwe hyr in hys tyrandry.
Syne he gert oppyn hyr and owte ta
Hyr bowellys, and sek in tha

And rype [thaim] all oure, theyk and thyne,
To sé the place that he lay in.   590
Off Rome syne the maystrys all
In till hys presence he gert call,
And bade wytht barne thai suld hym ma,
Or than thai suld thaire lyff for-ga.
Than efftyre thaire awysment
Thai gert [hym] apon ane assent
In tyll a drawcht off drynk swelly
A paddog yhong, lyand in fry;
Thai gert hym syne in mete and drynk
Sic mesoure oys as thai couth thynk,   600
Or [be] thare crafftys wndyrstude
Mycht have bene to that paddok fude.
Wytht that the tad begouth to wax,
And wyth-in hym rerde and rax,
Syne in hys body gnyp and gnaw,
And gert hym offt in thrichis thraw,
And in tyll perylle wes off dede;
Than off that dowt to get remede
He gert thai[m the] gret clerkys all
Agayne in tyll his presens call,   610
And bade that thai suld, apon payne
Off all thare cyne, or to be slayne,
Ger hym off hys barne be,
Bwt lang delay, delyveryd fre.
Than thai behuwyd for to fynd
All excusatyownys put behynd,
Sum crafft to lous hym off his payne,
Or all, but mercy, to be slayne;
Wytht a drynk than, at the last,
Owt at his mouth thai gert hym cast   620
That paddog wyth a blob off blude,

Wan made all but fassown gud.
He askyd than be quhat resown
Hys barne sa foule was off fassown,
And thare ansuere was that tyde,
For he couth noucht his [tyme] byde,
Na lang it mycht noucht lest in lywe,
For [causse] that it fell abortywe;
The paddoge dede thare-efft gert he
Wythin a towre enteryd be, 630
The quhilk wes made off lyme and stane
In to that rew callyd Laterane.

He wes in deid all fellowne,
And mad gret persecutyowne
Off Crystyn men, for thare fay
Abhomynabill he had alway.
Off Jacob rychtwys in his dayis,
The brothyr off God, as the Buk sayis,
Wyth a walkarys perk, but dowt,
The harnys all war strykyn owte. 640
He gert in tyll his felny sla
Hys awyn maystyr, Seneca,
That till Saynt Paule wrat letteris sere,
And wes tyll hym famwlere.
He leissit the trewage off Brettane,
That hys eldrys befor wan,
And othir allswa kynrykys sere,
That he fand till Rome tributere,
Ran in till prescriptyown
Off thare contributyown. 650
    For hys ecces [sa] owtragews
And his condytyown wycwys,
Saynt Petyr he gert crucify.
And off Saynt Paule, in his felowny,

He gert stryk off the hewyd, and swa
To dede he put thai posstyllys twa.
Quhen all the yherys ware cummyn and gane

F. 79. b. Off his empyre [for] to, sauff ane,
The Grekys than set thame thraly
Away till have tane prewaly   660
The bodys off thai postyllis twa;
That purpos qwhill thai ware on swa,
The dewyllys that in the ydolys ware
Off Goddys wyll and hys poware,
Cryit "Yhe Romanys succoure nowe,
For yhoure goddys are tane fra yhowe."
The Crystyn men, that than ware gud,
That off thai postyllys wndyrstude;
Bot the pagaynys thoucht allway
That off thare goddys that sayd thai.   670
Wyth that the Romanys halyly
Chasyd the Grekys dispytwosly;
Swa the Grekis at the last
Behuwyd on nede thai bodyis cast
In tyll a cysterne depe, quhare thai
Lay hyd, but wyttyng, mony day,
Quhill that the Pape Cornelius,
As the Cornykyll tellis ws,
Drew thame off that cysterne depe,
And honorably gert men thame kepe,   680
Quhill he had made his orysown
Till God, wyth gud devotyoune,
For tyll ken hym werraly
Quhilk wes off Petyr the body,
And quhilk off Saynt Paule mycht be
The body cald in propyrte.
Devotly sua quhill that he sat,

Inspyryd off God, ansuere he gat,
That the largyare body wes
Off the fyschare, and the les
Off the prechoure; syn wes sayde
Pape Silvestyr gert thame be layd
In till weyis; swa kend wes thare
Quhilk prechoure wes, and quhilk fyschare,
And off ilkane a kirk gert he
Honorably syne fowndyt be;
And off Saynt Petyr, wyth honoure,
The banys he put in sepultoure
In to that kyrk wes for hym made;
The banys off Saynt Paule he hade
In tyll hys kyrk, and thare gert he
Entyre thame wyth solempnyte.

 Off Nero yhit the empryoure,
That turnyd in till foule lust his honoure,
For na part off a man thoucht he
Mycht clene or luẅely callyd be,
All his men he luẅyd for-thi
In all tyme till oys rybaldry,
And all kyn ẅycys at thare wylle
He gaẅe consent and leẅe thare-tille.

F. 80. A robe he wald be nakyn wys
Put wpone his body twys,
Bot [in] a newe robe ilk[a] day
Hys usage wes hym till aray,
And till the hors that he on rade,
Off sylvyr schone he gert be made.
The byggyng mad off his palas
Large and welle anowrnyd was,
In all [the] pesys ovryilkane
Wytht sylvyr, gold, and precyows stane,

690

700

710

720

Evore syne, that na man mycht
Prys the cost, wyth all his slycht.
For the byrnnyng off the towne,
And dedys that he dyde felowne,
Hys barnage set thaim hym to ta
And pyne in presowne, or to sla.
For that caus, owt off his palas
He fled, and slwc hym-self off cas,
And outhe the erde, but sepulture,
As a dog, lay that empryoure,　　　　　　　730
Quhill all the flesche off his body
Wes ettyn wyth wolvys halyly.
Off Nero this wes the endyng,
That is ensawmpill and taknyng
Till thame that drawys thare delyte,
[Tyl] lust, and thare foule appetyte,
Throuch warldys welth and wantowne wylle.
Fra ẅertuose dede in vycys ille ;
But resowne, rageand in revery,
Confowndand peté wyth felny,　　　　　　　740
And wyll [noucht] thare hawtane haẅyng haw
Off God or man, but luve or lawe.

　　Galba off Rome the empryoure
Till Nero neyst wes successoure.
Off that state yhit, nevyrtheles,
Bot sevyn moneth lord he wes.
Quhen Nero herd off Surry tell
Agayne hym ras and wes rebelle,
Vespasyane he send off were
In Surry wyth a gret powere,　　　　　　　750
And in the kynryk off Judé
Lyand apon were wes he,
Fyrst quhen he herd Nero wes dede,

And Galba ras syne in till his stede,
Wytellus than in tyll Yrland,
And Oto in till Ducheland,
Held a yhere state as empryoure,
In Rome oysyd wyth honoure;
Syne ilkane slwe othir off cas,
Off thai twa swylk the endyng was. 760
  Syne Ytalyk off Tuskane
Borne, the sone off Esculane,
Ellewÿn yhere, and monethys thre,
And threttene dayis, held the se
Off Rome as Pape, and ordanyt than
That thare suld entyr na woman
In tyll the kyrk, as Petyr bade,
Bot gyff hyr hewÿd scho coveryd hade.
  Quhen that the Pape Lyne wes dede,
Cletus succedyt in his stede, 770
And held the sé ellewÿn yhere
Off Rome, as Pape; bot thai twa were,
As sum men sayis, in till thare lyve,
Nowthyr papys successywe,
Bot thai ware till Saynt Petyr ay
Helparys in hys latyr day,
Quhen he gave his vacatyon
All hale till hys devotyon,
Bathe Lyne and Clete thai papys twa
He despensyt wytht to ma, 780
And for to do the serwys all
That to the Pape off rycht suld fall;
In tyll the nowmyr tharfore thai
Ar reknyd off haly Papis ay.
Cletus comendyt gretly
All thai that oysid devotly

Haly pylgrymage to ta,
And mast ay [he] comendyt thai
That Saynt [Petyr] and Saynt Paule wald ẅysyt,
For that he callyd off mare [wyt and] meryt 790
Than for till fast twa yhere or thre;
All tha tharfore cursyd he
That lettyd thame off thare ẅayage
Till Petyre and Paule in pylgrymage.
  In to the Papys lettrys he
Gert fyrst *Salutem* wryttyn be
And *Apostolicam Benedictionem*, sua
Fra that he wes dede all tha
That succedyt to that state
Thai wordys in thare Bullys wrate. 800

CHAP. V.

Off Tytus ande Vespasiane, Saynt Clement and Domitiane.

A.D. 71.

EFTERE that borne wes God off Heẅyn
Thre score off yherys and elleẅyn
Vespasyane wan halyly
All the landys off Surry
To the empyre; and that day
Abowte Jerusalem he lay,
Wyth hys ost off gret powere
In tyll assege, as man off were,
Quhen be lettrys till hym send
He saw, and be thare tenore kend 810
That he wes chosyn empryowre.
That state tharfore wyth honowre

He ressaẅyd in Palestyne;
Titus his sone he callyd syne,
And till hym comendyt hale
Off his gret ost the governale.
Till Rome syne he passyd in hy,
Quhare he resayẅyd wes honorably,
And commendyt mekyll wes,
For hys gret worschype and prowes. 820
Syne in the flux hym hapnyd to de,
For thare is nane that cas may fle,
Bot in tyll his lattyre thrawe,
To dede quhen [he] begouth to drawe,
Evyn wp on his fete he stud,
And sayd, wyth hale ẅoice and gud,
" Ane Empryowre suld ay per-de
Than the erde fere hyere be."

In tyll that thrawe he tuk the dede,
Titus hys sone ras in his stede 830
Off Rome lord and empryoure,
And lede thre yhere wytht honoure.
He tuk and gert dystroyid be
Off Jerusalem the cyté,
And off the Tempill he tuk hale
Ornamentys, vestymentys, and ẅeschalle,
And till Rome all thai send he,
Syne brynt gert all the Tempill be,
And all the cytezanys slayne downe;
Thare was the mast confusioune 840
In ony tyme that yhe herd telle,
That evyr to the Jowys fell;
For off the Jowys slayne, the blude
Throuch all the towne in till a flude
On heẅyd wyth weltrand waẅys than,

As ryẅerys raysid wyth rayne ran :
Wyth suerd thare mony Jowys ware
Slayne, and [mony] deyd [war] thare
In hungyr, for the Romanys hale
Consumyt and held fra thame all ẅyttalle, 850
And off the Jowys at thame yhald
Till the Romanys, ay thai sauld
Thretty for a penny thare,
Yhit sellarys may than byarys ware;
For the Romanys alway thoucht
That the Jowys na thing doucht
To be haldyn in serẅyce,
That gert thame sel thame off sic prys.
In tyll Ẅespasyanys days,
And Titus, as the story says, 860
To Jerusalem this fell.
 But off Tytus mare to telle,
He wes off sa gret curtasy,
Pyté, gud wyll, and mercy,
That quhen agaynys his persowne
Men ware off conspiratyowne
Accusyd, and convic be the lawe,
Fra jugement he wald thame drawe,
And kys thame, and forgyff thame all
The danger that thai suld in fall, 870
And als hamelyly [withe] thame thare
Tak thame as befor thai ware.
He excedyt off largeas
All thai that before hym was,
Or in hys tyme, off ony gre;
For tyll hym tynt that day thoucht he
That na man come til ask hym oucht,
And quha that evyr tyll hym soucht,

He denyit nevyr that thyng
That wes resowne [of] hys askyng; 880
For it wes his oys to say
That nane suld sary pas away
Fra ony prynce, or lord, or kyng,
Quhen he schawyt his yharnyng.
He wes off wyrschype sa ẅertuus,
And off dedys sa mervalus,
That wyth all mankynd off his eyld,
He wes the joy callyd, and the beyld.
And efftyre that quhen ded wes he,
All thai that duelt in that cyté, 890
Gretand in tyll sobbyng sare,
Noucht les in all anoyit ware.
Na thoucht all thare kyn ilkane
War wndone, or wytht dede ourtane :
For his gret benygnyté,
Worschype, ẅertu, and bownte,
He past his fadyre in to fame
And callyd before hym is be name,
As in till all story ay
Rede and wrytyn fynd ye may. 900

 Quhen Petyr, Lyne, and Clete ware dede,
Saynt Clement sat in to thare stede
Nyne yhere Pape, and monethys twa,
And ten days full ekyd to tha.
Efftyr the baptysme ordanyt he
Crystyne-men to confermyt be,
But that, he sayd, na man mycht
Full Crystyn man be callyd rycht;
And syne to dede dispytwysly
He wes done throuch hard martyry, 910
And in the sé his body lay

Castyn thare efftyr mony day,
Quhille the Pape Cyryllus ras,
In tyll hys tyme it fundyn was;
And that the sé quhar lang he lay
Oysyd ilk yher tyll esche away
Fra that kyrk a gret space,
That off Saynt Clement fundyt was.
Fra are none off [the] evyn beforne
That hys fest fell on the morne, 920
Quhill the day [fere] efftyre nowne,
That Mes and offerand ware all downe.

    Than Domityane, the tothir
Wespasyianys sone and Titus brodyr,
Threttene yhere off the empyre,
And fyẅe moneth, wes lord and syre;
He wes in tyll his begynnyng
Off gret mesoure in all thyng,
Bot syne in tyll his state wes he
Sa vycyows in all degre, 930
That off [his] fadyre the gud name,
And off his brothyr the fayr fame,
Wes delete all halyly,
Throuch hys ẅyce and hys felny.

F. 82.   The nobylest off the senatowrys,
That wes the mast wys consalowrys,
He gert to fellowne dede be done.
Syne him-self he gert call sone,
Bothe lord and god off mekyll mycht,
Thare wes na fygure he gert dycht, 940
Or mak off hym-self to be,
Than it off sylvyr fyne made he,
Or than off gud gold and pure,
Welle fasownyt, off fayr portrature.

Fyrst to lordschype quhen he drewe
Hys systyr sonnys all he slwe,
Neyst efftyre Nero the fellowne,
He made fyrst persecutyown
Off Crystyn men, and thare fay
Supprysyd he held at wndyre ay;   950
And set that this Domityane
Wes sone to gude Wespasiane,
Yhit he wes off condytyowne
Mare lyk tyll Nero the fellowne,
Than till fadyr or brodyre he
Lyk wes [in] till ony gre.

 The ewangelyst Saynt Jhon,
That duelt than in till Epheson,
Hys ewangyle apertly
Prechand, passyd throuche Asy;   960
Tharefore this Domityane
Gert hym arestyd be and tane,
And send to presowne in the yle
Off Pathmos, swa, wyth-in that quhille,
Apocalipsis all he wrate;
Sa presownyd he bad in that state,
Quhyll that this Domityane
Throuch wnhape hys dede had tane.

 And in till this tyme Saynt Dynys
And hys falowys, in Parys,   970
Off dede tholyd [the] passyown.
The tempill than als off Pantcown
Quhare syne was Mary the Rotound,
Agrippa Marcus than gert fownd,
And than that tempyll, as men sayis,
All thus was fowndyt in thai dayis.

 Quhen the senatowrys herd tell

That the Perseys ras rebell,
Agayne [the] state off Rome, than hale
Thai ordanyt, apon set counsalle,   980
To send furtht Marcus Agrippa,
On the Perseys were to ma,
For he wes prowest off the towne,
Commendyt welle off gret renowne;
To this thai thoucht hym for to threte,
Bot, or thai hys will mycht gette,
To delyvere hys entent,
He askyt thre dayis awysment.

Swa in hys slepe, apon a nycht,
A yhong lady, fayre [and] brycht,   990
Aperyt tyll hym quhare he lay
In tyll hys bed, lang forow day,
And callyt hyr nam Dame Cibeles,
That modyr off all goddys wes;
Scho sayd, Gyff [he] thare, Agrippa,
Lelyly wald hecht to ma,
In honowre off hyr, as scho
Couthe and walde kene hym to do,
A tempyll fayre, the Perseys qwyt
He suld in batell discumfyte.   1000
To that sone he gawe assent,
And avowyd, wytht lele intent,
For to fulfyll, in tyll all thyng,
Off that fayre lady the yharnyng.
And one the morne, qwhen day wes lycht,
All, as he saw this on the nycht,
To the senage he tald hale;
And syne gert ordane his batele
Wyth a gret navyn apon sé,
And knychtys wycht off gret bownté   1010

In legyownys fyẅe; and wyth tha quyte
The Perseys hale he discumfyte,
And agayne that tribwte wan,
That thai payid till Octovyan.
Syne for that caus he mad onone
The tempyll that thai callyd Pantheon,
In honowre off Dame Cybeles,
That modyre off all thare goddys wes.
 And in that tyme Domytyane
Throuche wnhape hys dede has tane,   1020
And thare him fell a foule endyng
For hys fals and yẅyll lyvyng,
Wyth hys awyne men slayne he was,
Off suddane chawns in his palas.
And Nerva, quhen that he wes dede,
Ras Empryowre in tyll his stede.
Hys empyre stude bot a yhere,
And foure moneth to reknyn clere;
He wndyde and dampnyd hale,
As [wes] gevyn hym be counsale,   1030
All the dedys evryilkane
Before done throucht Domytyane:
For thai ware fundyn all off ylle
Done by the lauche for-owtyn skylle.
Swa by that ordynans Saynt Jhone
The eẅangelyst till Epheson
Passyt agayne, off presown fre
Lowsyd; thare welle resaẅyde wes he.

CHAP. VI.

Off Anaclete, and als Trajane,
And Evariste, contemporane.

A.D.
102.

A<small>NE</small> hundyr yhere and twa gane,
Fra God off Mary flesche had tane,   1040
Anaclete, off natyowne
A Grek, borne off the regyowne
Off Athenys, nyne yhere,
Twa moneth, and ten dayis clere,

F. 83.

Wes Pape off Rome, and held that sé,
And off Saynt Petyr than made he
A memore, and till othir ma
Byschapys in hys tyme allswa
Steddys fayr, off gret honowre,
He ordanyd for thare sepultoure.   1050
Tyll all Crystynmen he prechyd,
And thraly wytht hys lettrys techyd,
That befor all othir thai
Suld prestys hald in honour ay;
For he sayd, syne thai specyaly
Oysyd till God to sacrify,
Thai suld nevyr supprysid be,
Bot relevyt in all degre,
And honoryd wyth ilka man.
This Anaclete gert ordan than   1060
That quhen thai yhed to sacrify,
Or do thare serẅyce devotely
To God, thai suld wyth thame tak
Wytnes, that suld knawlage mak

That thai sacrifyid welle,
And dyd thare devore ilka dele,
He ordanyd clerkys, wytht honowre,
To schawe thare berde and were tonsoure.
    And efftyre hym, quhen he wes dede,
Evaryst sat in hys stede   1070
Ten yhere and monethys sevyn,
And twa dayis to rekyn evyn.

To thir twa Papys Schyr Trajane
Wes Empryoure contemporane,
And nyntene yhere off the empyre
Stude lord, empryoure, and syre:
All Asy, Babylon, and Pers,
And hale Ynde, as I herd rehers,
He throwche rade and wan off were,
And made thame till Rome tributere.   1080
He gert wythin the Rede Se
A gret navyne gaddryde be
Off Ynde the marchys till distroy,
And hale that land for till anoy.
Off the empyre the bowndys brade,
Swa, in hys tyme, he gert be made,
That all the Oryent mad homage
Till Rome, and payid thare trewage.
Men oysyd for his wyrschype ay
In till comowne prowerbe say,   1090
Quha happyare than Octovyane,
Or quha evyre bettyre than Trajane?
He wes als sa liberale,
Sa luwand, and sa specyalle,
Till [all] abowt hym, fere and neyre,

Quhethyr evyr hale or seyke thai were,
That in propyr persowne he
Walde pas, and thare necessyte
Walde he wysyte and amend,

F. 83. b. And thare-wpon his gud dispende. 1100
 Be thra counsale and felown
He made gret persecutyown.
Off Crystyn-men, bot yhit he wes
Comendyt off gret rychtwysnes.
The story sayis, evyn in that tyde
That till hys werys for tyl ryde
Hys fute he hade in sterape set
On hors to lepe, but ony lete;
Be the fute a wyff hym gat
And benely carpyt efftyre that, 1110
"Now," scho sayd, "Schyr empryrowre,
Thow lywys in ryches and honoure,
Weldand warldys welth at wyll,
And I, anoyit in angris yl,
My lyff ledys, but help off thé,
That dettyde is to succoure me.
The comfort off my care, my sone,
Agayne the lauche to dede is done:
For the beld off thine honowre.
Thow do me lauch, Schir empryoure, 1120
Off thaim that that innocent
Has done to dede but jugement."
To that he ansuerd and sayd, "Dame,
Alssone agayne as I cum hame,
For thi sone I sall ger do
That laucht wald war done thare-to."
"Schyr empryoure," than sayd the wyff,
"Off thi gayne-come wytht thi lyff

Art thow sekyre, or quhilk is he
That thi bowrche wyll thare-off be." 1130
" Dame," than sayd the empryoure,
" Sek than till my successoure
For thi sone, I trowe he wyll
Off hys dett the laucht fullfill."
" Off thi successoure the deyd
May nothire payre na mend thi meyd,"
The wyff sayd, " Schyre empryoure,
Thow art off laucht to me dettoure,
And, gyff thi successoure wyll
His awyn det, in his tyme, fulfill, 1140
On na wys can thowe sykyre be
Quhy thow suld set hym than to me,
And his awyn det to qwyt
May noucht mend thi mede a myt."
Owt off his sterape he wyth that
Drw his fute, and down he sat,
And dyd full lauche and jugement
Off thame that slwe that innocent.
Quhen that wytht the lauch his sone,
For a trespas that he had done, 1150
Suld have lesyd [his] eyn twa,
Ane he gert be tane off tha

F. 84. Fyrst owt off hys awyn hevyde
That ane mycht till hys sone be lewÿde,
And ane lefft tyll hym-self alsua;
Swa tynt and haldyn war eyne twa,
And the lawys ilk[a] delle
Kepyd ware and haldyn welle.

In tyll this tyme Schyr Placydas,
That callyd wes effytr Saynt Eustas, 1160
Off hys knychtys evryilkane,

For worschype prynce wes, and chyftane.
The clerk Plynyus in his dais,
Wrate tyll hym, as the story sayis,
That Crystyn-men, one nakyn wys,
He suld dysses, or yhit supprys,
For in thame, sayd he, wes nane yll,
Bot, nevyr that he cowth fynd, thare wyll
Wes nevyr for to mak sacrifys,
Na do thare honowre, na thare serwys,   1170
Till mawmentys; bot thare oys wes ay
Lang to rys wp befor day,
And than thare Cryst devotly
Honowre, and till hym sacrify.
Fra thine he cessyd for to wede
Agayne the Crystyne-men in dede;
Bot, throuch his persecutyown,
Mony sufferyd the passyowne
And payne off ded, throuch martyry,
Off fell counsale and tyrandry,   1180
Before that Plynyus till hym wrate,
Commendand Crystynmenis state.

  This emprioure Schyr Trajane
Tuk the trewage off Brettane.
And in hys tyme Duchill ras,
And atoure the Peychtis was
Wyth-in the kynryk off Scotland
Twenty yhere kyng regnand.

  And quhen this Empryoure wes dede
Schyre Adriane ras in his stede,   1190
Bot Trajane sa douchty wes,
And be way off his rychtwysnes,
Saynt Gregore, with devotyown,
Made specyall and thra orysown

That God wald grawnt his saule to be
Owt off hel delyverit fre;
And full wyttyng tharoff he gat
Off the angell efftyre that
That God had herd his orysown,
And at his petityowne   1200
Trajanys saule wes owt off hell,
Quhare it condamnyd wes to duell.
 Bot fra thine Saynt Gregor ay
In till lestand langure lay,
And [in] paynys till his endyng,
For hys wantown thra askyng.
[For quhy, the Angell bad hym cheis
Owthire Trajanys saule to leys,
Or ellis to tak hym a seiknes,
Sen his askyn unskylfull wes;   1210
And the feveris tyll hym tuk he,
And sa he broucht the saule to gle;
And this was eftyre fyve hundyre yeire
That Schir Trajane was broucht on beire.
And the cause of this peté was
For he hard of his rychtuusnes,
And of hys lyf, and his gude deid,
And for he thret was, as we reid,
Be cruel consaill and fellone,
To mak sic persecutione   1220
Off Crystyn men, and noucht of will,
This gart Sanct Gregor tak hym tyll
That seiknes, and broucht hys saule to blys,
Quhare now baith he and he ay is.]

CHAP. VII.

Off Alysawndyr and Adryane
Syxt, Thelefor, and mylde Antane.

F. 84. b.
A.D.
122.

Ane hundyr and twa and twenty yhere
Efftyr the [byrthe] off oure Lorde dere
Alysandyr the Pape off Rome,
And kepare off all Crystyndome,
Fywe moneth and aucht yhere
And twa dayis full to rekyn clere,　　　　1230
In tyll the Papys sege sat;
Bot syne it wakyt efftyre that
Fully fywe [yere] and thretty dayis.
　　He ordanyd, as Frere Martyne sayis,
Watyr and salt tyll halowyt be;
Haly watyr swa fyrst made he,
Wytht effectuus orysownys,
Agayne all yl temptatyownys.
Syne he bad that men suld fast
That watyr in thare howsys cast,　　　　1240
And that Haly Wattyr ay
Suld be made on the Sownday.
In to the Mes he ordanyd syne
The watyre to be put in wyne;
The bred als that the oyst suld be
Rownd, [and] off lytill qwantyté,
Bot off floure and watyre clere,
And, but ony othyr matere,
He ordanyd, and efftyr his day
The Kyrk has oysyd that manere ay.　　　　1250

Syne in till the Canowne he
Made off the Mes, *Qui Pridie*,
That is oysyd to be sayd
Quhen yhe se the chesybyll layde,
And the preyste makys hym bown
To mak the levatyowne.
  The empryoure Schyre Adriane
Gert Alysandyr this Pape be tane,
And presownyd hym in to gret pyne;
Throuch martyry he slwe hym syne.   1260
  Thus quhen Alysandyr wes dede,
The Pape Syxt sat in his stede
Ten yhere and monethys thre,
And ane and twenty dayis fre.
Bot or that Alysandyr wes Pape,
Or off Rome wes maid byschape,
The empryoure Schyre Adriane
Off the empyre all state had tane,
And lyvyd, in wyrschype and honowre,
Twenty and a yhere empryoure.   1270
Jerusalem, in his tyme, he
Gert agayne welle byggyt be,
Bot the Jowys he held ay
Wndyr yhok till his end-day.
He wes awenand and abylle,
And in all dedys honorabyll,
And made lawys imperialle,
And wes rycht wis in governalle.
And a pillare he gert be made
In till Rome, that his name had.   1280
  This Empryoure Schyre Adryane
Wes nere newew till Trajane,
Bot at hys state he hade inwy

That wes luẅyde sa specyaly.
For that inẅy gret landys sere,
That to the empyre wonnyn were,
Hale Babylon and Armeny,
And all the landys off Surry,
Throuch wyt and ẅertu off Trajane;
This empryoure Schyre Adryane   1290
Leẅyd, and swa set hym sone,
Off all Denmarke tyll have done;
Na ware hys counsalle made hym lete
And hym on othyr purpos set.
All the tyme off hys empyre,
That he off Rome wes lord and syre,
He lyẅyt in qwyete and [in] pes,
And a welle lettryd man he wes,
Bathe off Latyne and off Grew,
He wes welle facund in Hebrewe,   1300
He mony rychtwys lawys made,
And in Athenys he ordanyd hade
Off fayre werk a gret Lybrare;
And bade that nane sa hardy ware
Crystyn men, on ony wys,
For ony cryme for to supprys,
Bot gyff lele pruff agayne thame made,
And the lauch conẅyct thame hade.
The Kyrk, in hys tyme, Oryentale
The oys off service changyt hale   1310
In to langage all off Grewe,
Owt off the langage off Hebrewe:
He ekyd gretly the tresoure,
And held his knychtys in honoure:
Off Jerusalem, quhen he
Had all up byggyt the cyté,

He gert wall in all that stede
Quhare Cryste the passyowne tholyd off dede;
And Crystyn-men ay lewyt he
Wyth-in the towne to mak entre;   1320
Bot he wald grawnt off nakyn wys
To the Jowys that franchyse.

Quhen that his barnage come hym tille
And sayd hym, at it ware thaire wylle,
And full counsale, thai gave alle,
Cesare August his sone to calle;
He said, it suld suffice that he
Agayne hys wyll stud in that gre,
And, but dyssert, regnyt empryowre,
Thoucht that stat and that honowre   1330
War noucht spylt in swylk ane-othyr,
Quhethir ewyre he ware sone or brodyre,
Thare sulde na state succede be blude,
Bot thare ware undyre wertu gude;
A lorde borne wyth-owte meryte
Is noucht worth, he sayd, a myte;
A kyng off byrthe and wnworthy
Regnys, he sayd, unhappyly;

F. 58. b.   The fadyr, he sayd, he couth welle prove
Dysspoyleyhyt the sone off fadyr love   1340
Mare chargis on hys bak to lay,
Than he mycht lychtly bere away;
For swa he settys hys besynes
Till smore hys sone be lyklynes,
And wyndyr byrthe hym to supprys
But helpe off hym wytht it to rys;
For-thi, suld men in thare yhowthede
Be techyd well, swa prove in dede,
And the effect oys off thare lare

Quharin before thai oysyd ware,　　　1350
Gyff that thai grewe swa off ẅalu
Throuch wyt, wyrschype, and ẅertu,
That thai ware lyk thame till excede
That thai in honoure walde procede,
Than thai suld clyme as thai ware calde,
And stedfastly thare steppys hald
In to that hycht quhill thai ware set
That thai thame pressyt before to get,
Than regne and reule thaire reawté,
Wytht luffe, and lauche, and leawté.　　1360

 Quhen Schyre Adriane regnyde thus,
The phylosophyre Secundus
Wes in hys flourys and his state,
Bot hys sentens all he wrate,
For strayte sylence he held ay,
The cas thare-off I wyll noucht say,
For yhe may find it in his buke,
Gyẅe yhe wyll all hys tretys luke.

F. 86. b. In tyll hys tyme, as I herd tell,
Oure the Peychtis Wordegell　　　1370
Rase, and kyng was in Scotland
Twenty wyntyr hale regnand.

IN till this Adryanys dayis,
Syxt, as the Cornykyll sayis,
Wes Pape off Rome, and ordanyt ay
Sanctus [thryse] at the Mess to say,
Neyst efftyre the prefatyown,
Befor the levatyown.
He ordanyt als the Corporalle
Off clene lynt to be made hale,　　　1380

Fayre and quhyt, but ony lyt;
And als that nane suld handyll it,
Na nakyn thyng that halowyit ware,
Chalyce, towale, or awtare,
Bot thai that mynystryd in thare gré,
And ordanyt ware, and had powsté.

AND eftyre hym quhen he was dede
Thelefore sat in his stede
Thre monethis, and ellewyn yhere,
And twa and twenty dayis clere.   1390
He ordanyt men for to fast ay
Sevyn owkys hale befor Pays day,
And *Gloria in Excelsis* he
Ordanyt at the Mes to be
Sayd, and on the Yhule day
He bad thre Messys be sayd ay:
At the cokcrawe the fyrst Mes,
For Cryst that in that tyme borne wes;
The tothire syne ordanyt he
In the dawyng to swngyn be,   1400
For that tyme Cryst in clathis clene
Wes swelyt, and wytht the hyrdys sene,
And anowrnyt devotly,
As Luk berys wytnes werraly;
Syne the thryd Mes off that day
Efftyre Ters he ordanyt ay
To be sayd, quhen that the lycht
Offe oure redemptyowne [schynyt] brycht.

AND efftyre that Schyre Adriane

Fayr deyt in tyll Champane, 1410
Antone the mylde off the empire
Stud Empryoure, bathe lord and sire,
Thretty yhere and monethis thre,
In to Rome that state held he.
Mawche he was tyll Adriane,
And till all Crystyn men, ilkane,
He wes rycht meyke and off gude wyll;
For-thi, that name wes gevyn hym tille
That myld Antone thai oysyd alle,
And thare fadyre hym to calle. 1420
And als in hys tyme landys sere,
That oblyst tyll gret dettys were,
Off thare dett he made thaim fre,
Bot yhit thaire homage ay held he.
The medycynare, Galyene off name,
Wes in hys tyme off gret fame,
And Tholomé, in astronomy,
Wes than commendyt grettumly.
And that tyme als Pompeyus,
That callyd be name wes Trogus, 1430
A Spaynayle kynd off natyowne,
Commendyt wes off grete renowne,
Off all the warlde the storys
Fra Nynus kyng begouth to rys
Till that tyme that Octovyane
The warld all to the Empyre wan,
This Pompeyus in Latyne
Cornykyld and dyvysyt syne
Tha in fourty bukys and foure,
Thare-eft Justyne that red thaim oure 1440
Abbregyde all tha gret storys
In smallere and in les tretys.

F. 86. b.

This myld Antone oysyd to say
That fere leware he had alway
A man off his to sauff wnslayne
Than off hys fays to sla agayne,
For [that] a man a thowsand hale,
How evyre the werd yhed off batalle.

Antone the Myld this Empryoure
Alway to gud men dyd honoure,   1450
He hade a dochtyr callyd Fawstyne,
Off face fayre, and off fassown fyne,
In tyll hyr solace, as scho past,
Scho saw quhare men ware fechtande fast,
On ane off thai scho set hyr luẅe,
For manhed that scho saw hym pruẅe,
And brynt in lust sa stratly,
That bathe scho sek was and sary,
And all lyk for to be dede,
Bot gyff scho sonnare gat remede.   1460
Hyr husband, thare-fore, off Caldé
Gert medicynarys sone fetchyde be,
To se and ken quhat malady
Traẅalyd hys wyff sa grettumly.
Quhen thai come and had sene hyr welle,
And scho had tauld thame ilk[a] delle
The matere off hyr malady,
Thai [gaf] for counsale halyly
The man that swa hys manhed pruẅyde,
And at scho sa stratly luẅyde,   1470
To be slayne, and syne his blude
In tyll a ẅeschall tycht and gude
Sulde be put; syne hastyly
Thai suld wesche oure hyr body
Wyth that blud quhill it war hate.

All thus thai dyd wyth-owt debate,
And [qwhen] this counsall wes all done
Hyr temptatyown cessyt sone,
And coveryt welle off hyr malady,
And lefft hyr folys fantasy. 1480
 All this tyme in tyll Scotland
The Peychtis duelt, and ware regnand,
And Dekothet than off thame kyng
Had fourty yhere thaire governyng.
 In till this tyme Thelesforus
The Pape deyt, and Ignius
Foure yhere and monethis thre,
Quhen he wes dede, that state held he.
He made and ordanyt the clergy
Dystynct be greis propyrly. 1490
The god-fadyre he bad alsua,
Or the god-mudyre, the barnys ta
Off the fownt quhen howyn thai ware.
He ordanyt alsua that manare
Quhen barnys suld confermyt be.
Syne in a generalle lettyre he
Off God and Mannys unyown,
And Crystys Incarnatyown,
He wrate to be haldyn ay,
But ony dowte, off Crystyn fay. 1500

T<small>YLL</small> the Pape Ignyus
Neyst succedyt Schyre Pius,
Ellewyn yhere and monethis foure,
And ane and twenty days oure,
Pape off Rome he werray was,
In hys lettrys he said Hermes,

A doctor gret off Crystyne fay,
That welle wes lettryd in hys day,
Sayd, that ane angell, brycht and quhyte,
In tyll ane hyrdys pure habyt,   1510
Apperyt, and gawe bydding ay.
Pasce to mak apon Sownday;
For-thi, off oure autoryté,
We appruwe that solempnyte
Ilka yhere to be done ay,
As cours rynnys on the Sownday.

M ARCUS than Antonius,
And hys brodyr Aurelius,
Off the empyre nyntene yeire
Empryowrys and lordys were;   1520
And off Rome the empyre swa
Than wes dyvysyt betwene thame twa,
Bot quhen Aurelius the dede had tane,
Mark Antonius hym allane
Held and governyd the empyre.
All Asy throuch fra Tars to Tyre,
Ynde, and all the Oryent,
And gret part off the Occident,
He gert pay contributyowne.
Bot mony tholyde the passyown   1530
Off martyry for Crystyne fay
Wndyr hym; yhit wes he ay
Off gret wyt and off stabylnes,
For nane mycht ken that evyr he wes,
For ony word, off cas hapnand,
Changyt in hys assembeland.
Wyth mesure and benygnyté

All his landys tretyde he,
And all tyme [he] commendyt wes
Off worschype, honoure, and larges. 1540
Hys tresoure quhen he dispendyt hade,
Hys weschale, that off fyne gold wes made,
And all hys wywys hed-gere hale,
Wyth mony othire fayre jowale,
He gave his knychtis in thare fé,
For he defawte had off mone ;
Na he his comownys on na wys
Wyth imposityownys wald supprys
But mare hys wyll stude to relewe
Than wndyr hym ony man till aggrewe. 1550
Bot off landys syne syndry
Quhare that he wan the wyctory,
He recoweryt wondyr welle
Hys distres all ilk[a] delle ;
F. 87. b. And mony landys that than ware
Subject to Rome and tributare,
He releschyde thare trewage,
Reserwand tyll hym thare homage.

Combust, as oure story sayis,
Oure the Peychtis in hys dayis 1560
Wes twenty wyntyr kyng regnand
Wyth-in the kynryk off Scotland.

In hys tyme Pius the Pape wes dede,
And Anyclet rase in hys sted,
Nyne yhere and monethys thre
And foure dayis full he held that se.

Sothere syne hys successoure
Nyne yhere and thre moneth oure
And ane and twenty dayis fre
Sat in to the Papys se. 1570

He bade the nunnys on na wys
Suld cens the kyrk in thare serẅys,
Nowthir chalice na corporalle,
Awtare halowyt, na towale,
Thai suld handyll be na way,
And he gave byddyng to thaim ay,
That thare ẇale ware na tyme leẅyde,
Than than suld were it on thare heẅyde.

CHAP. VIII.

*Qwha Pape and Emprioure was than,
Quhen fyrst convertit wes Bryttan.*

A.D. 185.

ANE hundyr and fourscore off yhere
And fyve full, or thare by nere   1580
Quhen that Sothere the Pape wes dede,
Elewtherius tuk hys stede,
And sat in till it fyftene yhere
Sex moneth and fyẅe dayis clere.
　The Kyng off Brettane Lucyus
Wrat to this Elewtherius,
And made hym instans specyally
In till Brettane to send in hy
Off hys clerkis, for to preche
The Crystyne trewth, and syne to teche   1590
The Brettownys baptysme for to ta;
And he to be the fyrst off tha
He made full professiowne,
And hecht wyth gud devotyown.
　This Pape than Elewtherius
At the instans off Schyr Lucyus

Send twa religious men,
Fugane callyt and Damyen,
In tyll Brettane for to preche
The Crystyne trewth, and men to teche   1600
Baptysme to tak; for na man may
But it be sauff on ony way.
  Than at the fyrst off that cas
The Kyng off Brettane howyn was;
And all the barnage off his land
Than baptyst wes, and welle trowand,
And stedfast stud in to that fay
Till Dioclityanys day:

F. 88. That is, gyff the soume be sene,
Ane hundyr wyntyr and sextene,   1610
Or nere thare-by, as sum men wrate,
And variis as thai set thare date.
  Aucht and twenty byschappys than
Wes off ydolys in Brettane,
And thre archebyschoppys als
Ware that tyme thare off ydolis fals;
The byschappys thai callyt thane Flamynes,
The archebyschopys callyt than wes
Archeflamynes: syne thare-efft
In to stede off thame wes lefft   1620
Byschopys, quhare was Flamynes,
And archebyschapys quhare grettyr wes.
Off that Papys autoryté
He gert Schyre Lucius howyn be.
This Pape als Elewtherius.
That Brettane to the trewth wan this
Ordanyd that na man suld be
But chalange put owte off his gre,
For Cryst, he sayd, wyst welle [that] Judas

Bathe a theffe and a traytoure was, 1630
Bot for he wes noucht off swylk thyng
Wytht the lauch accusyd off tholynge,
He wes noucht put off his offyce,
Bot bade and dyde furth his service.
Amange the Appostyllys, and quhat that he
Dyde wyth thame for thare dignyte
Ferme and stabyll it wes lefft
And approwyd welle thare-efft.

Iɴ till Rome Schyre Comodus,
The sone off Mark Antonyus, 1640
That tyme wes made empryoure,
And threttene yhere in that honoure
He stude, and wes in dedys fell,
Owtrageows, and rycht cruelle;
Off Duche-land yhit halyly
He wan and had the wyctory,
And held it subject all his days.
  In Egypt syne, the story sayis,
He send off Rome a douchty man,
That callyt be name wes Phylype than, 1650
Chefftane wndyr hym to be,
Off Alysandyr, the gret cyté.
This Philipe had a douchtyr fayre,
That suld off lauch have bene hys ayre,
Bot, for [luf] off [the] Crystyne fay,
Scho fra hyr fadyr stall away
In mannys wede, all prewaly,
And tuk wyth hyr in cumpany
Twa geldyt men and off gud fame,
That Prot and Jacmit had to name. 1660

Scho baptisme tuk in prewaté,
And held hyr madynhed ay secré
And Ewgenyus callyt be name,
F. 88. b. Comendyt off rycht honeste fame,
And lete ay that scho wes a man.
Scho, and hyr twa geldyngys than,
That conversyt togyddyr ay,
Had acces gret tyll ane Abbay,
And thaire, off thare devotyownc,
Tuk habyte off relygiowne,   1670
And lyvyt thare religyowsly,
And dyde thare office perfytely.
Sa sone the abbot of the plas
Deyt, and entèryd was,
And this Ewgenyus, in his stede,
Wes chosyn quhen that he wes dede.

A woman than off pollute fame,
That callyt Melancia wes be name,
Wes nere duelland that abbay,
And [gret] repayre had tyll it ay;   1680
Off that repayre swa that scho hade,
And sawe this Abbot [was] new maid,
For luve scho yharnyt inkrely
Till have hade off hym copy.
Quhen scho mycht noucht get assent
Off that Abbot till hyr intent,
Scho defamyt that abbot hale,
And till the mwnkys tald a tale,
That he wald have lyin hyr by
And [had] supprysid hyr vyleusly,   1690
Na ware the pyth scho put agayne.
And helpyt hyr wyth mycht and mayne.
Quhen this qwene had carpyt thus,

This abbot syne Ewgenyus,
That hard this accusatyowne,
Before the prowest off the towne
Wes tyt and tane be howe and hare,
Quhill all hyr clathys ryvyn ware;
Swa in that toyle quhill scho wes tyt,
It wes persayvyt, throuch a slyt,   1700
That scho wes woman propyrly.
Than the prowest werraly
That beheld and saw this cas,
And kend at scho his douchtyre was,
Lowyt God, syne howyn wes he,
Wyth all hys court and his menyhe,
And the wykkyt quene Melans,
Throuch subitane and fell wengeans,
Off fyrflaucht fers in to that stede
Peryst, but ony kyn remede.   1710

QWHEN Elewtherius the pape wes dede,
Victor sat in tyll hys stede
Twa moneth and ten yhere,
And twelff dayis passyd clere.
A gret Consalle he gert be
Haldyn wyth solempnyte;
Thare stablyst wes that Pasce suld ay
Be done apone [the] Sownday;
For mony byschapys off Asy,
And all the Oryent halyly,   1720
Oysyd ilke yhere to do thare Pasce,
As than the Jowys maner was.
Gyff ony man in dowte ware stade,
And nede off helpe or mystyr had,

And yharnyt in that poynt to be
Crystyne man; than ordanyde he
That man to be howyn thare,
In quhat kyn [ply] that ewyre he ware.
    Quhen that Victor pape was thus,
The empryoure ras, Elyus,   1730
Till ilke man in his degré
Myld and cumpynabill wes he.
Bot wyth-in the fyrst yhere
Off hys empyre, for-owtyn were,
He wes slayne off cas, and dede.
    Than ras Severus in hys stede,
And sevyn yhere off the empyre
He empryoure, bath lord and syre,
Stude, and prowyt gret douchtynes,
And a welle lettryd man he wes: 1740
He wes cruelle, and fellowne,
And made gret persecutyowne
Off Crystyn men, that mony were
Dede throuch hym in paynys sere.
    He faucht wyth syndry natyownys,
And wan, and made thare regyownys
Till Rome subject; and Brettane
Off thai the last wes that he wan.
And thare he mad wyth-in that Ile
A wall lang off a hundyr myle   1750
Wytht thretty myle thare-till and thre,
Strekand ewyn fra se to se,
In the takyn that he wan
Off were the kyurike off Brettane.
    In till Yhork syne he wes dede.
Caracalla in tyll hys stede
Sewyn yhere wes empryoure;

Bot lust supprisyt hys honoure :
Severyus sone he wes but dowte,
Bot he wes were than he all owte.　　　1760
In all poynt off lychery
He lywyt at lykyn fullyly.
Hys awyn step-modyr tyll wyffe
He tuk, and led wyth hyr hys lyffe.

S̃YNE Zepheryne the Pape off Rome,
And kepare off all Crystyndome,
Neyst succedyt till Wyctor,
Qwham off yhe herd me rede before,
And that sege held monethys sewyn,
Wyth twa dayis full and yheris ellewyn.　　　1770
He ordanyd than that ilke yhere
Thai that off eyld passyd were
Twelff yhere suld [be] clenly
Schrewyn, and tak syne devotly
The Ewcaryst on the Pasche day,
That Goddys body is werray.
　　Qwhen this Zepheryne wes dede,
Calixt the Pape sat in his stede
Fyve yhere, and monethis twa,
And ten dayis wyth-outyn ma.　　　1780
The Pape Calixt in thai dayis
Ordanyt, as the story sayis,
The Catyrtens in dere fastyng.
　　Syne quhen his lyffe had tane endyng,
His successoure wes callyt Urbane,
That was off natyoune a Romane.
Thretten wyntere, and ellewyne
Monethys, and twelff dayis ewyn,

In Rome he held the Papys sé;
Waleriane convertyde he, 1790
That spowsyd wes wytht Saynct Cecyle;
And wndyr hym, in to that quhille,
The kyrk ras till possessiownys
Off rentys, and gret regyownys,
That befor hys tyme alway
Lywyd off tendys or monay
That wes gywyn in offerande,
Be oys or statute off the lande.

 Till the Pape Calixt and Wrbane
Thre Empryowrys contemporane, 1800
Ware in thare tyme successywe,
And ilkane fellowne in thare lywe.
Off thai the fyrst wes callyt Martyne,
He lywyd bot a yhere; neyst hyme syne
Antonyws wes empryoure,
And thre yhere stud in that honoure;
Hys body brynt swa in delyte,
And off foule lust in appetyte,
That alkyn kynd off lychory
He oysyd als commownaly, 1810
As he a best, but wyt, had bene.

 Neyst efftyre hym, wyth-outyn wene,
Alysandyr his successoure
Was threttene wynter empryoure:
And that tyme Orygenes
The Doctor in hys flowris wes:
And Caramacert in Scotland
Twenty wyntyr Kyng regnand
Wes oure the Peychtis in thai dayis,
As owre Scottis storys sayis. 1820

THIS tyme alway till Urbane
The Pape succedyt Pontayne,
That twa moneth, and fyẅe yhere,
And twa [dayis] full for-owtyn were
In Rome held the Papys se.
In Sardyny syne dede wes he,
And Cyryak, hys successoure,
Held bot a yhere that honowre.
Bot cesyd off devotyown,
Ancheses than, off natyown 1830
A Grek, he ordanyd in his se:
In cumpany syne past he
Wytht the elleẅyn thousand madynnys clene
That before than hoẅyn had bene,
Tyll Coloyne fra the court off Rome,
And wyth thame tholyd martyrdome.
Bot, for caus that his clergy,
Wend for lust off his body,
He had wyth thai madynnys gane,
Reknyt he wes noucht as ane 1840
Off the Papys, quhare thai ar set.
Ancheses efftyre him, but lete,
Ordanyd byschapys for to be
Transferyd, for caus, fra se to se.

To thire Papys, contemporane
Thre yhere fyrst Maximiane
Stud Empryoure; quhen he wes dede,
Gordyane ras in tyll his stede
And sex yhere in the empyre
Stud off Rome bathe lord and syre. 1850
Quhen Fabyane wes Pape off Rome,
And kepare of all Crystyndome,

Neyst till Ancheses successoure,
And thretten yher in that honoure
He sat, and ordanyt the Creme ay
To be made on the Skyre Thurisday.
Quhen the congregatyowne
Sat in thaire electyowne,
And Fabyane amang thame thare,
A quhyte dow on hys heẅyde bare   1860
Lychtyde, and said he sulde be Pape
And off the warld the mast byschape ;
Throuch that electiowne in that plas,
Pape off Rome he chosyn was.

CHAP. IX.

*In this next plas yhe sal se
Qwhat Empriowre fyrst [tuk] Crystyanté.*

A.D.
246.

TWA hundyre wyntyr and fourty
And sex oure-passyd fullyly,
Efftyre the Incarnatyown
That mad oure salvatyowne,
The Empryoure Gordiane dede,
Philipe ras in till his stede   1870
Off Rome lord and empryoure.
And quhille he was in that honoure
He made hys sone partynere
Off the empyre, and sevyn yhere
Tha twa governyd halyly
Off the empyre the senyhowry,
And bath Phylipe thai ware cald ;
Bot, as I fynd, Phylipe the alde

Wes the empryoure that tuke
Fyrst Crystyndome, as sayis oure buke; 1880
And how that fyrst fell yhe sall here,
As I fynd wryttyn, the manere.
 In Rome quhilum a senatoure,
Marcus callyt, in till honoure

F. 90. b. Lyẅyd, and weddyt a lady,
That be name wes callyd July;
Togyddyr lang thai led thare lyff
In rest and ese wytht-owtyn stryff
And luẅyde rychtwysnes alway,
Bathe trewe and stedfast in thare fay. 1890
Sa betwen thame twa, off cas,
Grete wame wytht barne his lady was,
And, as hyr tyme wes cummand nere,
Scho oysyd fastyng and prayere;
As wemen in sic perylle stade
Offtsys for thare lyff sa rade,
Hechtys and aẅowys mare,
Than efft to qwyt off wyll thai are.
 This lady ẅowyt gret pilgrymage,
And tuk furth thare-on hyr ẅayage, 1900
And ẅysytyd hyr goddys, ane and ane,
And soucht the tempyllys evryilkane.
Sa in the tempyll off Jupytere,
As scho was makand hyr prayere,
The preyst revestyd on hys wys,
For to resaẅe hyr sacrifys,
Fra that he sene had this lady,
[He] chawngyd hewys rycht suddanly,
And worthyd owt off his wyt sa wode,
That thai ferlyd that by him stode; 1910
He tuggyd wyth hys teth in taggys,

Hys ẅestyment ryẅand all in raggys.
Wyth that thai that stud hym by
Tuk and held hym stalwartly,
And syne hys bak layd at the erd.
Bot ay wytht rarys reche he berde,
Wedand, but wyt, as a wod-man,
And his comowne word was than,
Amang thame [al] in to that stryffe,
" Owte ! owt ! oute apon yhone wyff ! 1920
Hyr byrth sall brew ws mekyll bale
That howre fell in the dysemale
Quhen scho consayẅyd," he sayd, " off man
That wes betwene hyr sydys than :
For, as I wate welle, I yhoue warne,
In till hyr wame now is a barne,
That sal gere our goddis alle
Be brokyn in to pecis smalle,
And owre templys cast[yn] downe,
And wndowne oure relygyowne ; 1930
Off oure goddis mekyll off mycht
In me," he sayd, " the spyryte rycht
Gerrys me spek this in prophecy,
That yhe sall fynd full certanly."
This was noucht that spyryt brycht,
In twngys off fyre wyth lemeand lycht,
But brynnyng, that on Wytsownday
Illumynyd the Appostillys, swa that thai
Oppynly spak in all langage,
Quhare throuch all natyownys had knawlage 1940
Off haly wryt, quhen that thai
F. 91. Prechyd haly kyrkys fay.
This spyryte that spak in to the brest,
As yhe haẅe herd, off this wode preste,

Wes off the de[wi]le that, but drede,
Throuch mycht off God behowyd on nede,
But certane wyt, that thyng to tell,
As in to deyd thar efftyre fell.
God has till hym reservyd all
The wyt off that that is to fall; 1950
Sa it is Goddys propyrté,
To ken the thyngys or thai be.
Off all hys creaturys thare is nane
That tell can thare-off the certane;
Bot [qwhen] the ill spyryte is swa
Trawalyd that he man ansuere ma,
Hys ansuere alwayis is dowtows,
And the conclusyowne perylows.
The prest thus beryd lang and fast,
Swa the lady, at the last, 1960
That beheld and saw this cas,
Affrayid owte off mesure was.
Wpe sho ras, and full gud spede
Owte off the tempyll gretand yhede,
And entryd in a hows nere by
The tempyll, dulefull and sary;
Thare quhylle scho swonyd, and quhill scho swete,
Quhill wepyt, quhill scho wongys wete,
Quhill wyth hard and hewy stanys
Bryzyd bathe brest and bak at anys; 1970
And ay scho sayd, Allace! allas!
That evyr scho borne, or gottyn was,
That byrth to bere, that suld gere all
Thaire templys on thare goddys fall;
And lete gyff scho had hade a knyff
For tyll hawe slayne hyr barne, hyr lyff
Scho wald have put in awenture,

Had noucht bene the senature,
Marcus, hyr lord, that saw hyr swa,
Bathe hewy in till hys hart and wa, 1980
Quhile he hyr chastyd wyth manas,
And quhill hyr comfortyd wyth solas.
For all the murnyng that scho made,
Hyr kyndly tyme off nede scho bade,
And than was lychtare off a sone,
The quhilk to dede scho wald have done,
Had noucht the fadyre nere bene by
That snybbyt hyr rycht grewowsly,
And bad hyr off hyr birth forbere
To byd, gyff thaire god Jupytere 1990
Wald reweng hym at hys wylle,
Syne large off mycht he wes thare-tille.
The barne, he sayd, thai suld noucht sla
Gyff he wald wengeans off hym ta.
The chyld than gert thai tendyrly
Be nursyt, quhill thare wes gane by
Oure hys eyld full sewyn yhere;
Fra thine on buk thai gert hym lere
Hys primytyvys, quhill he couth welle,
And all hys grammayre ilka delle; 2000
Bot hys fadyr gert hym ay
Draw fra Crystyn men away,
In[til] intent that destyné
Off thare goddys suld brokyn be.
Apon a day, yhit nevertheles,
As to the scule he gangand wes,
By a chapell he come nere,
Qwhare Crystyn men than syngand were,
And the Psalme, as I hard telle,
Wes *In Exitu Israëlle;* 2010

And, [as] Vincent mad rehers,
Thai ware syngand than this wers,
> *Deus autem noster in cœlo: omnia quecunque*
> *voluit fecit: Simulacra gentium argentum et*
> *aurum, opera manuum hominum.*

This is, in oure twng, to say,
" God, forsuth, in hevyn is ay,
And all thyng that he wald has wroucht;
Thir mawmentys off the folk ar noucht
Bot gold and sylvyr made throuch man."
Off this grete thoucht the barne had than,
And quhen he herd thaim [syng] thir wers,
Ay off thame he made rehers.   2020
In to the chapell syne in hy
He yheid, and drewe in cumpany
Till Crystyn men that thai wers sang,
And sa conversyt thame amang,
That off the Pape Pontyane
Haly baptysme he had tane,
And callyd be name wes Pontius.
  Swa quhen he wes hovyn thus,
And hys devor all wes done,
At certane tyme he sped hym sone,   2030
[And] off hys chang glayd and fayne,
Till his fadyr hame agayne;
And sone efftyre that thai met samyn,
And melyd togyddyr off thare gammyn,
The fadyr speryt at the sone
In to the scule howe he had done,
Syne the tyme before than last,
That he had fra his fadyr past,
And made [hym] examynatiowne
Off his lare and his lessowne.   2040

The chyld than ansuered hys fadyr dere,
"Syn that tyme that I last wes here,
A bettyre lessown newyre wes red
Than I herd in a priwa sted."
The fadyre speryt than how it was,
And the chyld tauld all the cas;
Syne throucht hys wys argument,
Hys fadrys hart and hys intent
Wes hale inclynyd baptysme to ta.
Than togyddyre bathe thai twa   2050
F. 92. Passyd in hy till Pontyane,
That werray Pape off Rome wes than;
There wes he baptyst, and, that done
In hy, wytht Pontyus his sone,
This Marchus in thare tempyll past,
And brak downe off thare mawmentys fast,
And kennyd Cryst for thare Creatoure,
And dyd hym serwyce and honowre.
  Sa fell, efftyr mony day,
Quhen this Marcus wes dede away,   2060
This chyld wes takyn apon threte,
For honoure off his lynage grete,
And present to the Empryoure,
That held hym in till gret honoure
Off gre, and state, and senyhowry,
As till hym fell off awncestry.
Sa quhen the empryoure herd telle
That Frans agayne Rome wese rebelle,
Owt off hys cowrt he send a knycht,
That Decyus to name had rycht,   2070
Wytht a gret ost, as man off were,
Frans to dawnte wyth that powere.
And quhen this Decyus past in Frans,

For till amese thare this distans,
Rynnand wes the thousand yhere,
As reknyt wes and countyt clere,
Fra Romulus gert wallyt be
Off Rome, as yhe herd, the cyté;
And, for that caus, the Romanys hale
All that yhere held festywalle,　　　　　　　2080
In turnamentys and justyng,
Menstralcyis, and gret dansyng;
And ilk[a] day apon thare wys,
Dyd till thare goddys thaire scrẅys,
And held thare solace and thare play.

　The Empryoure swa, on a day,
Ordanyd hym, on hys best wys,
To pas and mak hys sacrifice
Till his god Jovys, devotly;
Swa tuk [he] in hys cumpany　　　　　　　　2090
This chyld Pontyus, that was
Gruchand in that way to pas;
Bot, in the way, swa quhen he
Saw his oportunyté,
He sayd, " Me thynk, Schyr Empryoure,
This serẅyce till yhoure Creatoure,
Wyth gud wyll yhe sulde dispend
That has till yhowe that honowre send."
" Sone," he sayd, "tharefore I ga
Now to the tempill, for to ma　　　　　　　2100
Till Jupityr my sacrifyis,
As is my det, on my best wys;
For he is that God off mycht
That has me hevyd to this hycht."
The chyld sayd, " Schyre Empryoure,
Yhe ar imployd in gret erroure,

Yhoure mychty Makar to forsake,
And tyll a dewyll yhoure serẅys mak.
Yhon similakare callyt Jupityr
Can nowthire spek, luk, na here, 2110
Set he haẅe mouth and erys twa,
Handys, nes, and eyne alswa;
For it is bot a lumpe, but lyve
It has nane off the wyttys fyve,
Bot is bath dum, and deffe, and daft,
Off metall made wyth mannys crafft."
"Swylk, sone," sayd the Empryoure,
"Suld I than call my Creatoure?"
"Schyr," sayd the chylde, "He that yhow wroucht,
And all that is has made off noucht; 2120
That borne wes off the madyn chast,
Consayvyd throuch the Haly Gast,
And syne mad oure redemptyowne,
Throwch ẅertu off his passyowne."
Throuch thir wordys, and othir ma,
The Empryoure, and his sone alsua,
Past to the Pape, Saynt Fabyane,
And off hym baptysme sone has tane,
And Phylip cal[ly]d ware thai twa,
The fadyre, and the sone alsua, 2130
In hy togyddyre als[ua] fast
To the tempill sone thai past,
And thare thaire symilacrys all
Thai tuk, and brak in pesys smalle;
And swa the destyné wes welle
Fulfillyd and haldyn, ilké delle,
That the wod prest off fors said,
Quhen he wes brankand in hys brayd.
    Swa stedfast syne in Crystyne fay

Thai ware, that on the Pasce day 2140
The fadyre, and the sone alsua,
To the kyrk past, for to ta
Thaire housyll amang Crystyn men,
And the Pape, than Fabyen,
That herd thare confessyowne,
Gert thame, wyth contrityowne,
Thare pennance do wyth-owt the qwere,
Quhare the comownys standand were,
Quhill bathe the Serẅyce and the Mes
Wes done, as than the manere wes, 2150
And syne on kneys devotly thai
Goddys body tuk ẅerray.
Thus Philip, empryoure off Rome,
The fyrst wes that tuk Crystynedome.

Decyus this tyme in till Frans
Was, and amesyd gret distans,
And wan thaire subjectioune,
And tuk thare contributyoune,
And ressayvyde thare homage,
And off the grettast tuk hostage, 2160
And gert thame sele thare ragman welle
Off all thare poyntys ilké delle.
F. 93. In all that deyde he was sa wys,
That worschype gret he wan, and prys,
And pompus hawtane in hys fere
He past all mesure and manere,
Swa [that], wyth gret bost and deraye,
Off Frans to Rome he tuk the way,
And Phylip, than the Empryoure,
For till have ekyd hys honowre, 2170
Hys state, hys wyrschype, and his gré,
Arayid hym wyth great reawté,

And all hys barnage halyly,
For till hawe met hym realy.
Quhen he herd that Decyus come,
He tuk hys wayage owt off Rome,
And on that purpos come onone
Nere till a cyté cald Werron,
And quhen he herd thare that hys knycht,
This Decius had, for that a nycht   2180
Wyth-in that cyté tan herbry,
For dowt off ryot or rywery;
And that thare metyng fyrst suld be
Sene wytht all the comunaté,
In tyll a-pert wyth swylk honowre,
As ordanyt wes the Empryoure
In till a lawnd wytht-owte the towne,
Gert disscend hys pavylowne,
And all the lordys that than thare
Come, and off hys duellyng ware,   2190
As thai off state ware and off gre,
Nere hym he gert herbryde be,
And gat hym wyttalle off the land,
The towne for to leve abowndand,
That till hys knycht na thyng mycht fayhle,
That for hym tane had that travayhle.

  This Decyus that ilké nycht,
Well anarmyt at all rycht,
Prewaly out off the towne
Past on to the pavylowne   2200
Quhare that the Empryoure than lay,
And slwe hym thare lang befor day;
Syne to the pawylownys, ilkane,
He past, and tuk wpe ane and ane
Off the lordys thare, as thai

Slepand in thare beddis lay,
And sum wytht trettys, and sum wyth awe,
He gert all till hys serẅyce drawe.
To Rome he passyt syne in hy,
Wyth all thai in his cumpany. 2210
 Quhen the Romanys than herd tell
How that that cas hapnyd sa felle,
[Thai] begouth, on thare best wys,
Agayne this Decyus for to rys.
That fellowne slawchtyr he aẅowyd,
And sayd, he suld be welle alowyde
And commendyt wyth thaim, na thai
Suld it murthyre call na way,

F. 93. b.   For tyll wndo thare goddys fa,
How lychtlyast thai mycht hym sla; 2220
Syne he wes the fyrst off Rome
Empryoure that tuk Crystyndome,
Ensawmpyll and juge agayne thare fay,
But sulde the blythare be alway,
That he to dede ware put sa sone,
Or that thare trowth war all wndone.
Be swylk slycht, and swylk qweyntys,
The Romanys forebare to rys
Agayne hym, as thai fyrst thoucht:
Hys purpos syne till end he broucht, 2230
Swa that he wes Empryoure,
And twa yhere full in that honowre
He stud, cruell and fellowne,
And made gret persecutyowne
Agayne Crystyn men alway,
And at wndyr held thare fay,
And ay martyrys off thame he made,
Quhill that he lyff in lestyng hade.

He slwe the Pape Fabyane,
And othir martyrys mony ane 2240
He made wndyr [that] culoure
That Phylipe he slwe, the Empryoure.
 Quhen Philip yhong herd be tauld
That his fadyr, Philipe the awld,
Wes slayne and dede, away he stall
And hys tresoure levyt all
Till Saynt Sixt, that than byschape
Wes,˙and off Rome efftyre Pape.
This Phylip yhong ay was sa lowryde,
That men mycht newẏre, for play na bowryd, 2250
In na sted, na in na quhylle,
Ger hym blenk, na lauch, na smyle.
This Saynt Sixt, I spak off are,
Till auld Phylype wes tresorare;
Yhong Phylipe his sone, for-thi,
Quhen he away stall prewaly,
Lefft wyth that Sixt that tresore,
As I haẅe made rehers before,
And, in till Sixtys passyowne,
Saynt Laurens has mad mentyowne 2260
Off that tresore, as is kend
And wrytyn welle in his legend.

Qwhen Fabyane the Pape wes dede,
Cornelius sat in till his stede
Thre yhere and monethys twa,
And full elleẅyn dayis to tha,
Syne wes he slayne wyth Decyus.
Till hym succeedyd Lucyus,
That twa yhere, and monethis thre,

And twa dayis, helde the Papys sé. 2270
Than Gallus and Velusiane
War Empryourys contemporane
Twa yhere and monethis foure,
Quhen [Decyus] dayis war all done oure.
   Quhen Lucyus his dede had tane,
Stewyn, off natyowne a Romane,
Pape off Rome wes yheris foure,
Twa moneth, and twa dayis oure.
Prestys and deknys he bad that thai
Suld noucht in comowne oys alway 2280
The halowyt vestyment on thame bere,
As claythys that thai oysyd to were,
But quhen thai ware in thaire office,
In kyrkys doand thare service :
Off almows mony dedys sere,
He dyd, that I will noucht tell here :
Throw martyry syne he wes
Done to dede, syngand his Mes.
   Waleryane than and Galiene
In to the empyre stud fyftene 2290
Yherys, and dawntyd halyly
All Grece, Gotland, and Asy.
Wyth Sapor syne, the kyng off Pers,
Thai faucht, and, as I herd rehers,
Thai empryourys wyth thaire ost, qwyte
Ware in that batalle discumfyt,
And thare than wes Waleryane
Yholdyn and as presownere tane,
And set that he wes empryoure,
Ay schame he tuk and dyshonoure ; 2300
For alway quhen the kyng off Pers
Wes for till ryd, I herd rehers,

That empryowr behoẅyd off fors
To ly eẅyn down besyd hys hors,
Lauch on erd, quhill that that kyng
Wald clyme on hym at hys lykyng,
And on hys crag, or on hys face,
As the wyll off that kyng was,
Ay hys a fute he walde set,
Quhill he mycht the tothire get   2310
Essyly in hys sterype,
Apon his hors quhen he wald leipe.
Gernard-Bolg nyne yhere than
In till Scotland wes oure-man.

 Neyst hym syne Wypopenct
In Scotland held the kyngis set
Oure the Peychtis thretty yhere;
Till all the tymys passyd were
Off thire Papys successyẅe,
That yhe herd me last dyscryẅe,   2320
And sex Empryourys than
To thai Papys contemporan.

E̲FFTYRE the dede off Pape Stevyn,
Saynt Sixt that só held thre yhere eẅyn
Elleẅyn moneth and sex dayis.
Befor that, as the story sayis,
He in Spayne as Legat past,
Thare Crystyne throwth he prechyd fast,
And twa fayre yhong men thare he fand,
Honest, habyll, and aẅenand,   2330
The tane be name was callyd Lawrens,
And the tothire wes callyd Vyncens;
Thir twa luẅyt Sixt specyaly,

And wyth hym wes contenualy
Quhill he wes in Spayne prechand.
Syne, quhen he turnyd off the land,
For luwe, tha twa folowyd fast,
And furth to Rome ewyn wytht hym past,
And wyth hym in thare serwyce bade,
Pape off Rome quhile he wes made, 2340
And efftyre that tyme als[sa] fast
In Spayne Saynct Vincent agayne past.
Bot in till Rome Saynct Laurens bade,
And wyth that Pape hys duellyng made ;
And he than made hym hale kepare,
And, at hys lykyng, delyverare
Off all the gud and the tresoure
That Phylip the Empryoure before
Had delyveryd hym quhen he past
Owt off the land, and fled rycht fast 2350
Fra Decius, that wes [sa] fell
Till Crystyn men, as yhe herd tell.
Quhen this Sext wes [Pape] off Rome
And kepare off the Crystyndome,
[He] ordanyd prestys for to say
Thare Mes on halowyd awterys ay,
That ware perfytly mad off stane,
Quhar befor hys tym wes nane
That swa oysyd to say the Mes.
Throuch martyry syne slayne he wes 2360
Wndyr Decius yhong, that syre
And lord than wes off the empyre.

    Efftyre that Waleriane
And Galiane the dede had tane
This Decyus yhong wes rycht fellowne,
And made gret persecutiowne

Apon Crystyn men alway,
And mekyll at wndyr held thare fay,
And mony martyrys he gert may;
This ilké Sixt wes ane off thai 2370
That wndyr hym deyd throuch martyry.
 Saynct Laurens than, that nere wes by
And sawe this persecutyowne,
And Sixte lede till hys [passiowne],
Sayd than, "Fadyr, quhethir nowe
Wytht-owt mynystyr passys thowe,

F. 95. Quhethire art thow hast wyth sa gret hy,
But ony serẅand swa anyrly,
Thow wes wownt on nakyn wys
To do but dekyn thi serẅys? 2380
Leẅe me noucht, my fadyr dere,
Swa anyrly behynd thé here,
For the tresore now, but dowt,
All hale I have dyspendyt owte."
 Quhen Cesare yhong, this Decius,
Herd hym spek off tresore thus,
He bad that he suld tyll hym bryng
That tresoure all, but delaying,
And Laurens than off dayis thre
Askyd delay, swa that he 2390
Mycht it all in a sowme get;
That grawntyd wes till hym, but let,
For Decyus yhong, the empryoure,
Thoucht till have gottyn that tresoure;
The delay thare-fore wes
Grawntyd wytht the mare blythnes.
And in this mene tyme Saynct Laurens
Gadryd, wytht rycht gret diligens,
Off pure folk a gret menyhé,

Off eyld, and off debilyté, 2400
That in tyll gret ned war stad,
And mystyr off thare fyndyng had,
And closyd thame all prewaly
In tyll ane hous, and syne in hy
He yheyd to the empryoure,
And bad hym cum, and hys tresoure
Se and ressawe, gyff hym thoucht
That it war worth, or gaynande oucht.
Wyth that Decyus past in hy,
Wyth Saynct Laurens rycht blythly, 2410
For till hawe gottyn than, thoucht he,
Off gold and sylvyr gret plenté.
Saynct Laurens than wndyde the dure,
And sayd, "Lo here, Schyre Empryowre,
Off the kyrk the gret tresore,
Quhare-off I mad the hecht before;
That mekyll may to thi saule awayle,
And newyre mare is lyk to fayle,
Gyff that thow may ware welle this
The growyng sall be hewynnys blys." 2420
Thare than quhen Schyre Decyus
Saw he wes begylyt thus,
In malancolyne, tene and ire,
Kyndyll he gert [be] a gret fyre,
And thare-on rostyd Saynct Laurens;
Throw swilk torment and pennens,
To Jhesu Cryst the saule he send
In joy to duell wyth-owtyn end.
 This Decyus yhong, I spak off are,
Was noucht callyt August, bot Cesare, 2430
And fra gud Octovyane
All the empryowrys [evry]ilkane

To tytyll Cesare August hade
Befor this Decyus had mad
Off Pers hys awne intrusyowne,
For-thi, the les wes his renowne.
For nowthir be rycht off lynage,
Na be laucht off herytage,
Off Rome he wes Empryoure;
Tharfor his state and his honoure   2440
Wes the les, bath in his fame
[And] in the titill off hys nam.

DYNYS till Syxt neyst successoure,
Twa wyntyr sat in that honoure,
Aucht monethys and dayis thre:
Fyrst kyrk-yhardys ordanyd he,
And till the kyrkys parochys;
And ilk prest, off his offys,
He ordanyd to kepe the parochy
Till hym assygnyd, distinctly,   2450
And hald hym off his part content,
Usurpand noucht oure his extent.
   Felix neyst hym sat twa yhere,
And thre monethe passyd clere.
And efftyr hym Euticiane,
That wes off natyowne [a] Tuskane,
Wes Pape ten moneth and aucht yhere,
And dyd gret almows dedys sere.
   Claudyus and Auriliane
Wer empryour[is] contemporane,   2460
Quhen Dynys and Felix successywe
War ilkane Papys in thaire lywe.
This Aurilyane in till Frans

Gret werys amesyd, and distans,
And syne, apon the wattyr off Layre
He fowndyd a cyté, gret and fayre,
And the name off that cyté
Orlyens, efftyr hym, callyt he,
And sua is yhit callyt to this day.
Syne, quhen he wes dede alway,   2470
Tatikus wes Empryowre,
And Probus his neyst successure,
Floryane, and syne Clarus:
Thire empryowris sex successywe thus
Regnyd thre and thretty yhere.
   And Fawchna-Qwhyt than ras off stere,
And twenty yher was regnand
Oure the Peychtis in Scotland.

F. 96.   GAYUS syne wes the Pape off Rome,
And kepare off all Crystyndome,   2480
He ordanyd hym that prest[ys] suld be
For till be ordanyd, gré be gré,
Crownebenet fyrst, accolyte neyst,
Subdekyn, dekyn, and syne preyst.
He ordanyd als that na paganc
Or herytik, a Crystyn man
Chalange suld on ony way,
Or ony sclandyr on hym say.
He bad als that nane suld drawe
Clerkys, for till suffyre lawe   2490
Befor [ony] Juges Seculare;
And, gyff ony dowtys ware,
Or gryt questyownys off swylk were,
That ware deficyle to declere,

Thai suld at the Pap[ys] sé
Referryd and decleryd be.
  All this tyme Dyoclytyane
And [his] falow Maximiane
Off the empyre thretty yhere
Wes ane wyth othir parsenere.   2500
Il and fellowne all were thai
And held at wndyr Crystyne fay.
Thai gert bryn wp in tyll a fyre
Off dry schydys, brynnand schyre,
All the bukys off Crystyne lawe,
That nane throwch thame the treuth suld knawe.
This Dyoclytyane past off were
Owt off Rome, wyth hys powere,
In to the Oryent; thare landys sere
To Rome he mad tributere,   2510
And all that trowit in Crystyne fay
To dede war done wyth-owt delay.
  Maximiane his falow than
In Ewrope mony landys wan.
All Frans [at] that tyme wes cruell
Stowt agayne Rome, and rebell;
Wytht hys ost he throwch [it] rad,
And to Rome it subject mad.
Syne all Ducheland, and Spayne,
Norway, Denmark, and Brettayne   2520
This Maximiane wan off were,
And dawntyd hale wyth his powere.
  And Ingland than, as sayis the buk,
Thare Crystyndome all hayle forsuk
Throwch the persecutiowne,
That wes austere and fellowne,
Done throuch Dyoclytiane

And his falow Maximiane;
Swa that wythin thretty dayis,
As Vincent, and Frere Martyne sayis, 2530
Twa and twenty thowsand were
Martyrys mad in landys sere.
Saynt Jorge and Saynt Anastas,
Saint An, Lucy, and Agas,
And othir mony martyrys sere,
That may noucht all be reknyd here,
Off dede tholyt the passyowne,
Throuch thaire persecutyowne.

THE Pape Gayus than martyrdome
Tuk, and neyst hym Pape off Rome 2540
Marcellyne sat sevyn yhere,
And twa moneth passyd clere,
Twenty dayis thare-till and fywe:
For dowte off tynsall off hys lyve,
He mad on the Paganys wys
Till ydolys fals hys sacryfyis.
Bot a Senyhe solempne syn he
Gert in Chawmpayne gadryde be,
Ane hundyr byschopys and four score,
Welle rewestyd hym before; 2550
Wyth opyn and playne confessyowne,
And wyth werray contrityowne,
He jugyd hym-self for to be
Deprywyd off his dignyté,
And curssyd all thai that wyth honowre
Suld put hys cors to sepultoure;
For he sayd, at cowatys
Off gold gert hym mak sacrifyis

Till fals mawmentys, and for-thi
He wes till presthad wnworthy.   2560
Till Dyoclytyane syne he past,
And confessyd before hym fast
That he wes lele Crystyn-man;
The emprioure gert sla hym than,
And efftyr that mony [a] day
Wngrawyn outht the erde he lay,
Quhill Marcellus the byschape,
That efftyr hym wes chosyn Pape.
Saynct Petyr, the appostill brycht,
Apperyd till hym apon a nycht,   2570
In wysyowne, lang before day,
Quhare slepand in hys bed he lay,
And cald hym be hys name, " Marcell,
Gyff thow be slepand, now me tell."
" Lord," he ansuered, " quhat ar yhe
In till this tyme [that] callys on me?"
" Off the appostillis prynce am I,
Petyr," he sayd, " and askis quhy
" My cors thow thoyls wngrawyn be
Lyand outht the erd?" Than he   2580
Ansuerd and sayd, that he herd tell,
[His] predecessor, the Pape Cornell,
At the reqwest off Saynct Lucyne,

F. 97.   In tyll a towmbe off marbyr fyne,
Gert hys body beryd be,
Wytht festywalle solempnyte.
" Nay," sayd Saynct Petyr, " Marcellyne,
That has mync successoure bene syne,
And my falow in all degré,
Wngrawyn lyis, as thow may se: 2590
Gywe thow likys," he sayd, "till luke,

Thow sall fynd wryttyn in the Buke,
Quha that wyll draw hym on hycht,
Lawch downe behoŵys hym for to lycht;
And quha that haldys hym in the lawe,
Till hycht hys meiknes will hym drawe.
He has denyd, and saw dide I,
In that oure partys fell eŵynly,
And syne, efftyr [his] contrityowne,
Off gud wyll tuk the passyowne   2600
Off dede, for Jhesu Cryst, hys lard,
That heŵyn has gyvyn hym for rewarde.
He hym meikyd in mekyll thyng
That hym forjugyd fra graŵyng;
Tharefore," he sayd, " I byd thé
And nere me ger hym dolŵyn be;
For honoure suld noucht be denyid
Tyll hym that grace has justyfyid."
Marcellus than, his successoure,
Apon the morne, wytht gret honoure,   2610
Entèryd hym nere by that place
Quhare that Saynct Petyr lyand was.

Qwhen Marcellyne all thus was dede,
The Pape Marcellus in his stede
Sat fyŵe yhere and twenty days.
Maximiane, as the story sayis,
For caus he wald noucht sacrify
Till fals mawmentys deŵotely,
Gaŵe hym byddyng for to kepe,
As herdys dois, nowyt and schepe;   2620
Syne in thare stabill gert hym be
Closyt, quhill thare-in dede wes he.

Waleryus, Constans, and Lacyne
Governyd all the empyre syne.
  This Constans wes a dowchty knycht,
And in all werys wys and wycht:
Quhen he to Rome had wonnyn Spayne,
He past off counsalle in Brettane,
For to wyn till hym that land,
And till hald it in hys hand   2630
He come to Brettayne. Bot Coel,
That herd weill off hys commyng tell,
Send messyngerys till hym to say,
That he off Rome wald [al] his day
Hald; wyth thi he payid na mare,
Than hys eldaris [had] payid are.
Constantyus grantyd thare-till,
And tuk hostage it to fulfill.
  Coel deyd in a moneth syne;
And lefft a dochtyr a ẅyrgyne,   2640
That excedyt off bewté
All the ladys off that cuntré,
That nane in Brettayne wes sa fare:
And, for he saw scho wes hys ayre,
He leryd hyr off mynystralsy,
And off all clerenes off clergy:
Scho hat Elane, that syne fand
The Cors in to the Haly Land.
Constans tuk hyr till hys wyẅe,
And mad hym kyng efftyr belyve;   2650
And apon hyr gat Constantyne,
That Empryowre off Rome wes syne.
Thare-efft, or past wes nyne yhere,
This Constans wes broucht on bere;
And till hys sone the land lefft he,

That worthyt off sa gret bownté,
And off sa stowt and sturdy dede,
That he come man in his yhowthede.

T YLL Marcell Pape than successoure
Ewsebyus wes, and that honoure 2660
He held twa moneth and twa yhere
And fyẅe and twenty dayis clere.
Hys successoure Mylchiades
Syne Pape off Rome twa wyntyr wes :
He bad that men be na way
Sulde fast apon the Sonownday.
 Than Canatulmel sex yhere wes ;
Neyst hym Devortenauch-Notales
Wes bot a yhere in Scotland
Oure the Peychtys kyng regnand. 2670
Feredauch-Fyngell neyst to tha
Wes kyng regnand yheris twa.

CHAP. X.

Off Silvester the Pope syne,
And off the Emprioure Constantyne.

A.D. 312.

E FFTYR the byrth off oure Lord dere
Thre hundyr wyntyr and twelff yhere
Gud Constantyn, that Elane
The kyngis dowchtyr off Brettayne
Borne off hyr body, wes Empriowre ;
And thretty yhere in that honoure
He stude, and Haly Kyrkis fay

He supprysyd mony [a] day. 2680
In hys tyme till Melchiades
Silvestyr succedand wes
Pape off Rome, and twenty yhere
And thre to thai to rekyn clere,
F. 98.   Ten moneth, as oure story sayis,
He sat, and ellewyn days.
In Nycia, that cyté,
A solempne Senyhe held he;
Thre hundyr byschopys and auchtene
Thare revestyt well ware sene, 2690
And clerly expowndyt thai
In that Senyhe Haly Kyrkys fay.
   This Sylvestyr thare-efftyr flede
Fra Constantyne, for he hym drede,
For he was austere and cruelle
Ay till he in lypyre felle,
Brokyn owt in foule myselry,
Quhare-for till medicynarys in hy
For to recowyre hys hele he soucht,
Bot all thare crafft awaylyhit noucht, 2700
Quhill the bischapys off the land,
That in the templys wer serwand
Till the mawmentys, sayd that he
Behuwyd off nede bathyd be
In till innocentys blud all hat,
Gywe he recowyr suld hys stat.
Of this counsall als[sa] fast
The sarjandys apon byddyng past
And tuk wp barnys here and thare,
Quhare-evyr that thai waverand ware, 2710
In hous, or gat, as thai thaim fand,
To the sowme off thre thousand,

And put thame in gret sykyrnes
Till the tyme that ordanyt wes
And set, quhen he suld bathyd be.
And that ilk[a] day as he
In tyll hys chare fra hys palas
In hys way past to the plas
That ordanyd wes for his bathyng,
Wyth dulefull chere and sare murnyng, 2720
The modrys off the barnys thare
Gretand, fra thare heẅyd the hare
Tyte and raẅe as thai war wude,
And in that rage on thai yhud
Till thai met wyth the emprioure ;
Befor hym than, in that doloure,
They fell on kneys and cryid sa fast
That thai hym devyd at the last.
And quhen he herd that stedfastly
The caus that made thame sa sary, 2730
He stud eẅyn wpe in till his chare,
And, till al that abowt hym ware,
He sayd, "Ilkane in yhoure degre,

F. 98. b. I praye [yow], gyff yhoure wyllys be,
Nere togyddyre nowe yhe drawe,
And gyffys audyence to my sawe.
Off the empyre, the reawté
The state, the worschype, and the gre,
As all [your] phylosophyrys syngys,
Owte off the well off pyté spryngys ; 2740
Na thare sall na state endure,
In caysere, kyng, na empriowre,
Quhare that mercy tays na stede,
Bot all wyth awe and greẅ is lede.
For-thi, gud empriowrys beforne,

That had this state or I wes borne,
As Tytus and Wespasiane,
Alysawndyr and Adryane,
Trajane," he sayd, " and othir sere,
That in thare dedys dowchty were,　　　2750
Quhen in batalle thai displayt
Thare banerys, and thare fays assait,
Thai gave in byddyng rycht stratly,
And gert all oure thare ostys cry,
That nane suld barne or women sla,
Na clathys off thare bodiis ta,
On payne off all that thai mycht tyne,
And to be hangyt and drawyn syne:
Now sen sa gud before oure dayis
Thus led thame, as oure story says,　　　2760
Bettyr me ware wnborne to be,
Na now fall in that cruawé
All yhone innocentys to sla,
For ony helpe at thai mycht ma
To the hele of my body,
That to recowyr fullyly
Be na way can I certane be;
And set thai mycht recowyr me,
Yhit it ware oure cruelle thyng,
Off sa mony barnys yhyng　　　2770
Off oure awyne natyowne
For to mak sic distructyowne.
Quhy suld we slay," he said, " our awyne,
And thai forber that are wnknawyne,
It is no speyd for to supprys
Wyth fecht or were oure innymys,
Gyffe we wyth mare cruawté
Amang oure-self discumfyt be;

F. 99.

Men off armys wyth thare mycht
Thare fays ourcummys in to fycht, 2780
Bot wyce, or syne, for to supprys
It is off wertu a qwyntys;
In swylk pres it hapnys ay
That we ar starkare fere than thai,
Bot in to this, but dowt, we ar
Starkare than oure-selff befare.
Quha-evyr may happyn for to be
In to that fecht discumfyte, he
Wynnys hale the wyctory,
And the victor certanly 2790
Efftyre hend his gré is qwyte
In till hys jurnay discumfyt,
Quhare that mercy and pyté
Discumfyt lyis throuch cruawté.
For-thi," he sayd, "in to this fycht
Pety owre wyll sall have the mycht,
For bettyr," he sayd, "oure innymys
In all kyn pres we may supprys,
Gyff it may happnyn gywe we be
Wytht mercy wencust and pyté. 2800
He may be cald," he sayd, "a larde
That mercy haldys in to warde;
Bettyr it is me to be dede
Than to recovyr," he sayde, "remede
Off my langwre, wyth the blude
And slauchtyr off sic a multitude
Off barnys, yhong and awenand,
Off oure awyne natyowne now growand."
Wyth that till thaire modrys he
Gert delyvyr the barnys fre, 2810
And gawe thaime gyfftys gret allsua,

And hame syne frely lete thame ga.
   That ilk[a] nycht, lang befor day,
As slepand in hys bed he lay,
The honorabyll appostylis twa,
Saynct Petyre and Saynct Paule alsua,
Apperyd to this empriowre
That gretly menyd hys languore,
And sayd, " Jhesu Cryst, our lard,
That has all gud [thyng] in hys warde,   2820
Has send ws for to comfort thé,
And byddys at thow sykyre be
Thi hele for till recowyre welle
Off all thi seiknes ilk[a] delle;
For thow lefft to spylle sakles blud
Off swa gret a multitwde
Off innocentys for thi body;
It is oure counsalle hale, for-thi,

F. 99. b.   To the byschope Sylvestyr,
That prewaly is bydand nere,   2830
Thow send, and he sall informe thé
Quhare-in that thow may bathyde be,
And off thi lepyr swa thow sall
The hele rycht wele recovyr all;
And syne to Cryst, thi werray lard,
Thow sall mak sa gud rewarde,
That off fals ydolys thow sall gere cast
Downe the templys als[sa] fast,
And haly kyrk thow sall restore
In bettyre state than it before   2840
Thow fand, and syne honoure ay
God, and hald wele Crystyne fay."
   Quhen thus our-drywyn wes the nycht,
And on the morne the day wes lycht,

The Empryowre gert knychtis pas
To sek quhare Saynct Sylvestyr was;
And quhen he saw thai knychtys nere,
He wend that thai cummyn were
Hym to draw in thare felny
For till have tholyt martyry.   2850
Bot fra thai had melyd sammyn
All togyddyr off thare gammyn,
Thai past to the Empryowre,
And he resaywyd wyth honoure
Saynct Sylvestyr, and syne ononc
Per ordyr al hys wysione
He tauld, and askyd hym alsua
Gywe Petyre and Paule war goddys twa.
The byschop Silvestyr maid answere
And [said] thai Goddys Apostylis were;   2860
Syne schawyd he to the Empriowre
Off Saynct Petyr the fygure,
And ane ymage off [Sanct] Paule alsua;
And quhen the Empryoure saw thai twa,
He affirmyt that thai war thai
That apperyd quhare he lay
Till hym in his wysione.
The Pape Sylvestyr syne ononc
Baptyst this Constantyne,
And injwnyd till hym syne   2870
In fastyng all a w[ou]ke to be,
And all in presowne to be fre
Lowsyd qwyte off thare pennans.
This Constantyne syne ordynans
In fredome mad off Crystyne fay,
That he devotly tuk that day.
For statute lawch fyrst ordanyd he

That Cryst a god suld honoryd be;
Neyst that wes hys ordynans
That he suld tholle and bare pennans, 2880
Quha-ewyr wyth heresy wald blame
Cryst, or set on hym defame:
Gyff ony syne wyth-in the land,
Agayne the lauch, wald tak on hand
A Crystyne man for to supprys,
Or for to wrang hym ony wys,
The tane half off hys gudis all
Till the empryoure suld fall
In till eschete, wyth-owt remede,
Or ony instans in till plede. 2890
He ordanyd alsua that the Pape,
That off the warld is mast byschape,
Suld be owre byschapys in honoure,
As is owre kyngys the emprioure.
Alsua quha that to the kyrk wald fle,
Thare gyrth he suld have and saufftè.
Als that nane ware sa hardy
Wyth-in ony parochy
Kyrk to byg, or oratore,
Wyth-owtyn lewe gottyn before 2900
Off byschape, or off [the] patrowne
Off that parochy, or off the towne
Quhare that byggyng mad suld be.
And efftyre that neyst ordanyd he
That the teyndys off all feys,
Landys, and regalyteis,
And off alkyn possessyown,
Suld, to the sustentatyown
Off Haly Kyrk, be payit ay.
 And efftyre than, the auchtand day 2910

Till Saynct Petrys kyrk in hy
He come bare fute devotly,
And mad hys confessiown,
Wyth gret and sare contrityown,
Off all the synnys that he had done.
A mattok syne he tuk, but hone,
And wyth that rypyd to the grownd
Quhare that he thoucht a kyrk to fownde,
And on hys schuldrys thare, but dowt,
Off erd twelff bakkatys he bare owt. 2920
 Quhen Constantyn wpon this wys
Was howyn, as I yhow dewys,
And off the Romanys a gret delle
Baptysyd ware, and trowyt welle,
Be the ensawmpill off Constantyne,
And off Saynct Sylvestyr the prechyne,
A gret part off the cytezanys,
And mony off [the] suburbanys,
Senatowrys, and othir [ma] sere,
That noucht baptysyd na trowand were, 2930
Assemblyd befor the Emprioure
And sayd at thai wald thaire murmwre
Rewelle till hym, gyff that he
Wald noucht at thame displesyd be.
And quhen he gawe thame lewe to say
All that in thaire gule lay,
Ane for all than spak in hy,
And sayd that, "Throwch the novelry
That is oysyd in till Rome
Syne that yhe tuk the Crystyndome, 2940
And oure falowys has lefft the fay
That oure eldrys held alway,
Ilké day is oure cyté

Stade in hard perplexyte;
For, as yhe wate, and has hard telle,
Nere here by a dragowne fell
Wndyr erd in a cowe lyis,
And to the towne reparys offtsys,
And as he rewmys and he berys,
All the towne in stynk he sterys,   2950
Quhill sex thousand on a day
Throwch pestilens qwyt dede away
Now comownaly may fundyn be
Off yhowng and auld in oure cyté.
The madynnys," thai said, " off oure land,
Yhoung damysellys and awenand,
Bath ryche and pure in thare degré,
Off the land and the cyté,
Ilké yhere on thare best wys
Oysyd to mak thare sacrifys   2960
Till Dame Westa dewotly,
That wes bath goddes and lady,
Thaire hope, thaire heille, and [thar] awowé
Off thaire myrth and thare jolyte;
Than thare almws halyly
And the releyff off thare mawngery,
Thai oysyd to cast to that dragowne
That now is on ws rycht fellowne.
Swa throwch mycht off that lady,
And releyff off that mawngery,   2970
Ay still in till hys den lay hé,
And noucht anoyid the cyté;
Bot sync yhe and thai off Rome
Off newe now has tayne Crystyndome,
And has lefft oure eldrys fay,
We are anoyid ilk[a] day

Throwe owtrage and throw ẅyolens
Off yhon best in this pestilens.
For-thi, Lord, we ask yhowe, hale,
Off this," thai said, " now yhoure consalle   2980
And yhowre helpe, at oure cyté
And we may sauff wnperyst be."
 Wyth that Sylvestyr that wes by
The Empriowre, and mast redy
F. 101. Off answere, bad that thai suld tell
Hym quhare that dragown lay sa fell.
And quhen thai sayd hym that thai walde
Ken hym to that bestys halde,
Till his orator he past,
And hym revestyd als[sa] fast,   2990
And wyth hys clerkys syne in hy,
And thai Romanys in cumpany,
Till the cove off that dragowne
He yheid in till processyowne,
And the cros on his body
He mad offtsys devotly,
And in the cove syne he
Wnabasydly mad entre,
A hwndyr greys eẅyn dippand down
Wndyr [the] erd to that dragown;   3000
And throwch hys devote prayare
That felowne beste sone brystyd thare;
And wpe agayne syne as he past
Wytht yhettys off bras he closyt fast
Off that deipe den the entré,
That nevyr mare sall opnyd be
Befor the mekill day off dome.
Than als[sa] fast [al] thai off Rome
That befor that had noucht tane

Crystyndome, than trowyd ilkane 3010
In Jhesu Cryst, and baptisme tuk,
And fals mawmentys qwyte forsuke.
   Thus Constantyne wes off Rome
The fyrst, that tuk Crystyndome
Neyst Philipe, that Decyus fell
Slwe, as yhe before herd tell,
And to the Kyrk gawe all the land,
That Papys sene syne had in thare hand;
And fefte the Kyrk on mony wys
Wytht gret and fayre and fre franchys. 3020
On hys modyr halff, a Brettowne
He wes be kynd off natyowne,
For he wes son off Saynct Elane;
And off hys fadyr half, a Romane;
And wes in hys begynnyng
Bot anerly off Brettane kyng.

In Rome that tyme a tyrande
Cruell and austere wes regnand,
That had to name Maxentius:
He had all tyme a comowne ws 3030
Till dysheryd the nobill-men,
That in Rome war duelland then,
And demanyd the empyre
Wytht tyrandyis, and werth, and ire.
He put to ded Saynct Katerine,
That gloryws and that pure virgyne;
And thai that chast war off thaire land,
Come till Constantyn till warand,
And tauld hym off hys tyrandyis,
F. 101. b. And maid hym prayere mony wys 3040

To cum wytht thaime, and wyn thare land,
And hald the empyr in his hand.
He went with ane oste gret and stowte
Till Rome, and maid it wndyr-lowte,
And syne he had the Monarchy
Off all the gret Warld halily.
 Constantyne apon this wys
Tyll Rome come, as I yhow deẅys,
And thare in to the lepyr felle,
And helyd wes, as yhe herd me telle.   3050
Dame Elane and hyr emys thre
Wytht hym till Rome that tyme had he:
And deputys behynd hym he lefft
To keipe Brettayne tyll hym thare-efft.
 Bot Octaveus a gret man syne,
That cummyn wes off kyngys lyne,
Ras, and thai deputys has slayne,
And held the kynrik in demayne.
He maid hym kyng, and off the land
He chasyd hys fays wyth stalwart hand.   3060
 Quhen this tyll Constantyne was tauld,
Thre legyownys gret off knychtis bauld
Wyth Dame Elanys eme Traen
In tyll Brettayne send he then,
That aryvyd wytht mekyll mawcht,
And Octaveus thare he fawcht,
And ẅencust hym and all hys mycht.
Bot he etchapyt fra the fycht,
And went till mychty men thare-by
To sek helpe: bot specyaly   3070
He prayid his men, thai suld thame ma
Wytht sum slycht Traen to sla:
And an erle off hys cumpany

Watyde Traen sa bysily,
That wytht ane buschement he had slayne
Traen. Octaveus than agayne
Come in to Brettayne, and tuk the lande
All hale agayne in till his hand.
He chasyd the Romaynys al away,
And wes kyng till hys enday.   3080
    All this tyme off the empyre
Constantyne wes lord and syre,
And Sylvestyr Pape off Rome,
And kepare off all Crystyndome.
He maid wyth gret dewotyowne
Solempne dedicatiowne
Off the kyrk in till hys dayis ;
To that ensawmpyll yhit alwayis
That [is] oysyd ilk[a] yhere,
As the tyme fallys [annywersere].   3090
And quhen that he awterys off stane
In ilké kyrke gert fyrst ordane,
In till Saynct Savioris kyrk he
The fyrst awtere, made off tre,
He gert hald wp, for Petyr ay
On it oysyd hys Mes to say ;
And all othir in thare lywe
Efftyr hym Papys successywe,
Quhill this Sylvestyr rysyn was,
On it oysyd to say thare Mes.   3100
For the persecutyowne,
That ay wes dowtows and fellowne,
There wes na place off stedfastnes
Quhar-in prestys mycht syng thare Mes ;
Bot in tyll honest howsys sere,
Quhare men off gud fame duelland were,

Or wndyr erd in cawys depe,
That men oysyd fra fylthe to kepe,
Or betwene howsys and pentys
That ordanyd were off sere qwentys, 3110
Prestys foure oysyde to bere
To swylk stedys that awtere,
That wytht four nwkys holl wes mad,
In ilké nwke a ryng it had,
And prestys foure oysyde to bere
Wyth thai foure ryngys that awtere.

 The Comete, as the story sayis,
Fyrst apperyd in thai dayis;
That is a starne wyth blesys schyre,
Brycht as is the lowe off fyre, 3120
And ay betakynnys pestilens;
Quhen that it makys apperens.
Dede off lordys, or hungyr sare,
And ay the beme it strekys thare
Quhare that infortune sall rys;
That the Comete signyfyis.

 Constantyne the Empriowre
Hys lyff than endyt wyth honoure.
In Rome than ras dyssentyowne
Abowte the successyowne 3130
To the empyre; for Maximiane
And the fell Dyoclytyane,
Off quham before yhe herd me tell,
Fra thare state of the empyre fell:
Off cownsalle and [of] ane assent,
And wndelyveryde awysement,
To thaire state thai ranownsyde hale
For thai sustene wald na trawale,
And thocht tyll lywe off thare tresore

That thai had gadryd lang before 3140
In ese and qwyete, but trawale,
And thole thaim [to] tak the governale
That suld succede be lynage
To the empyre off herytage.

F. 102. b. This consent wes done in-dede
And let the ayrys be laucht succede.

Efftyr all this Maximiane
Agayne the Empyre wald have tane;
And for that caus in tyll gret stryffe
He [lede] a lauge tyme off hys lyffe 3150
Wyth Constantynys sonnys thre,
That anelyd to that ryawté.

Octaveus in to thai dayis,
As off the Brute the story sayis,
Off [al] Brettayne hale wes kyng,
And had that land in governyng.

He had a douchtyr yhong and fayre,
That off laucht than wes hys ayre;
Hys counsale mast part thowcht, that he
Suld ger that douchtyr maryd be 3160
Wyth sum ryche man for hys ryches:
And Conane-Meryaduk, that wes
Hys nevew, neyst [hym] suld be kyng,
For he wes neyst off thare offspryng.
Bot Baradok Duke off Cornwayle
Thoucht, it suld welle mayr awayle
To feche at Rome Maximiane,
That off the empriowrys wes ane.
Swa it fell hym syne, that he
In Brettayne come wyth gret menyhe, 3170
And that lady to wyff has tane.
Sa wrathe at that than wes Conane,

That he assemblyd all hys mycht,
And mellayd welle offt into fycht,
And owrcome quhylle [he, qwhile] he,
Qwhyll at the last the hale barné
Off Brettayne knyt thame in sawchtnyng,
Bot Maximiane be lefft kyng.

Q WHEN that fywe yhere ware efftyre gane,
Swa prydyt hym Maximiane 3180
For hys gret sylvyr and ryches,
That hym thowcht Brettayne lytyll wes
For to mayntene hys ryawté
Bot he wald ga wyn Frawns all fre.
Tharfore all the chewalry,
That wes in Brettayne, halyly
He wytht hym to the Se has tane,
And alsua Myreadok-Conane.
And Armaryk fyrst conqwest he,
That Lytill Brettayne now cal we; 3190
And all that gave he to Conane:
And syne off Brettayne gert be tane
Off hwsbandys a hundyre thowsand,
Till inhabyt and hald that land;
And fyftene thowsand armyt men
Wyth hym als he lewyt then;
And Lytill Brettayne gert it call.

F. 103. This Conane and hys ofspryng all
Governyd it sa wyttyly ay,
That it hate Brettayne to this day. 3200
Quhen Maximiane wonnyn had
All Frawns, and till him subjecte mad
Treverys, [he] to Rome went syne,

Quhare he slayne wes be cuvyne
Off the Empriowre Gratyane.
All thus endyt Maximiane,
And [the] Brettownys, that wyth hym ware,
Ware slayne, and chasyd here and thare:
And the Quhene, that etchapyd than,
In Brettayne passyd till Conan.   3210

Qwhen thai off Dacy and Sythy
Saw, quhow Brettayne wes wtraly
Lewyd all woyd off armyt men,
In Brettane thai arywyd then,
And townys and castellys wp has tane:
For wyth hym had Maximiane
All the gud fechtarys off the land;
Nane lefft, that evyr wytht strenthe off hand
Mycht warand the small folk fra the fycht,
Na for [to] stynt thare fayis mycht.   3220
    Bot fra Rome come twa legyownys
Till help and succoure the Brettownys;
Munyceps Gratyane than was
Thare chyftane, that the sé can pass.
Wytht thare fayis he met in fycht,
And wencust thame wyth mekyll mycht,
And chasyd thame till Yrland.
    Syne off Gret Brettane all the land
He tuk till hym, and mad hym kyng.
Bot he wes in sum kyn thyng   3230
Tyrand, that [the] comownys halyly
Ras, and slw hym dyspytwsly.
    Quhen he was dede, thai that fled ware
Tyll Yrland, agayn cummyn are

In Brettayne, and it wastyd more,
Than evyr thai had done before.
   The Brettownys than that wyst na rede
Till help thame-selẅyn fra the dede,
Send word [to Rome] thare help to craẅe,
And sayd, thai wald thaim al tyme haẅe   3240
To thaire lordys, gyff that thai
Wald put thare fays wytht fecht away.
Than thai off Rome a legyowne sent,
That hastyly to Brettan went,
And put tha alyenis away.
   A Wall thare-efftyr ordanyt thai
For to be made betwene Scotland
And thame, swa that it mycht wythstand
Thare fays, that thame swa skayth[it] hade;
And it off comon cost thai maid;   3250
And yhit men callys it Th[r]yl Wal.
   Quhen this was done that I say all,
The Romanys to Rome has tane thare way.
Bot, or thai went, thai can thaim say,
That thai wald cum na mare agayne:
For, or thai suffere wald swylk a payne,
And for thame offt be traẅalit swa,
Thaire tribwte leẅyre thai wald forga.

Q WHEN that the Romanys passyt ware,
The alienis, that [war] chasyd are,   3260
Repayryd, and nere all the land
Dystroyit wyth fyre and fellown hand.
The Walle bot litill helpe thame made;
For thai, that it in kepyng hade,
Ware drawyn wytht crukys oure the wall,

Quhill thai fled, and lewyt [it] all.
Than thaire fayis, that laysere had,
Sloppys in syndry placis mad.
　The Bretownys wyst na counsell than;
Bot a byschope, a worthy man,　　　　　　3270
In Litill Brettayne till Audroen
Thai send, that thare wes regnand then,
To byd hym cum, and be thare kyng;
For he wes off the ofspryng
Off Brwtus, that all Brettane wan,
And in the ferd gre fra Conane.
　He wald nawys thare-till assent;
Bot [his] brudyre wytht hym [he] sent,
Constantyus, and twa thowsand
Off men armyt bathe fute and hand.　　　　3280
　Thai arrywyt, and syne fawcht,
And thare fayis wyth mekyll mawcht
Wencust, and chasyd off the land.
Than the barnage tuk on hand
To mak thare kyng this Constantyne,
That the land welle governyd syne.
　Now I suspend here off Brettayne
The storys, quhill I have ouretane
Off the Romanys the storys
A part, as yhe herd me dywys.　　　　　　3290

EFFTYRE the dede off Sylvestyr
Mark succedyt, [and] twa yhere
Aucht moneth and twenty dayis
He Pape was, and the story sayis,
At solempne Mess[is] he
Ordanyd that the Creyd suld be

Sayd or songyn, as the Mes
Done wyth note or prywe wes.
    Quhen this Mark [the] dede had tane
Julyus succedyt, a Romane,   3300

F. 104.   And Pape off Rome wes ellewyn yhere
Twa moneth and aucht dayis clere.
A gret Senyhe gaderyt he
In tyll Nyce[a] that cyté,
Thre hundyre byschopys and auchtene
In to that Senyhe solempne ware sene.
Saynct Hylare and Saynct Nicholas
That tyme in thare statys was,
And mony odyr byschopys ma.
Anastas that tyme allsua   3310
Mad *Quicunque wult* in dede,
Quhare all the artyclys off the Crede
Ar dystynyt halyly;
Quha trowys noucht in thame stedfastly,
Lyppyn he nevyr sauff to be
Fra the pyne off hell all fre.
That Senyhe condamnyt halyly
Off Arryus the heresy:
He [helde] that Goddys Sone wes les
In Godheide than the Fadyr wes;   3320
Off the Fadyr and the Son sua he
Denyid the equalyté.
The Senyhe made condamnatyowne
Off that fals oppynnyowne.

A.D. 345.   T̲H̲R̲E̲ hundyr fywe and fourty yhere
Efftyr the byrth off oure Lord dere,
Off Constantyne the sonnys thre

That wyth [his] body gottyn had he,
In [t]hys tyme to the empyre ras ;
Constantyne the eldast was, 3330
Neyst Constans, syne Constantyus,
Thir thre bredyre callyd war thus.
Amang thame-selff gret were thai mad,
And thai off Rome gret scathys had
Throwch thare were and thare fechtyng,
That enduryt and had lestyng
Fully foure and twenty yhere,
The Romanys all anoyit were.
Bot the eldest Constantyne
Wan fra hys twa bredyre syne 3340
Hale the empyre, and was than
Empriowre and gud Crystyn man.
The yhongest off the bredyre thre,
That Constantyus ere callyd we,
Had wyth hym men off cownsall fell
That ware in dedys rycht cruell ;
Tha the eldare bruthir slwe.

F. 104. b.   Constantyus to the empyre drwe,
And governyd it wyth gret stowtnes,
Bot a foule herytyk he wes, 3350
And lywyt all in to that fay
That Arryus held in tyll hys day ;
For hym [and his] oppynnyown
He made ay gret defensyown.
Off Constantynopill quhare than he had
Hys duellyng and hys prechyng mad,
For hys oppynnyown the clergy
Gert hym be sowmownd rycht stratly,
To here the condamnatyowne
Off his fals oppynyowne. 3360

Swa on that certane set day,
That for that caus assygnyd thai,
As this Arryws hym sped
Till that assignyd certane sted,
Off nede, swa he oure-takyn wes
That hym behowyd to do hys es :
Wyth hast thare-fore he tuk hys sete
[Opyn and] playne in the markete,
Thare thrawand thrystys hard hym thrystyt
Quhill hys bowalys wyth-in hym brystyt,   3370
Hys guttys rawe, bath gret and small,
And [his] kwnditys opynnyd all ;
For the stynk off his foule gare
Mony that abowte hym ware
To ded brystyd ; and all thus
The end fell off foule Arryus.
   Donate than wes in his state,
And in that tyme hys libell wrate,
That now barnys oysys to lere
At thaire begynnyng off gramere :   3380
And Saynct Jerome in thai yheris
The best wes callyd off his scoleris.
   Off Saynct Andrew the body was
That tyme translatyd fra Patras
Till Constantynopill : and [of] Saynct Luke
The body als, as sayis the buke,
Translatyd wes that tyme alsua.
   Julyane the Apostata
In ane Abay mwnk hym made,
For off Constantyus dowte he had   3390
That he wald hym to dede hawe done,
Bot yhit he changyd purpos sone,
For all tyme fra land to land

In habit off mwnk he wes vagand.
For he wes to gud Constantyne
Brodyre sone and nere cusyne,
F. 105.   He yharnyt tyll have bene emprioure,
And ay anelyd to that honowre,
And for-thi quhare[evyr] he past,
At wychys and at spaymen fast   3400
He thraly speryt gyve that he
Mycht ewyre opteyne and wyn that gre.
In lyklyness off a spayman,
Off cas the dewyll spak wyth hym than,
And sayd he suld be empriowre;
Swa fell he sone in swilk erroure,
That he away kest fra hym qwyte
The mwnkys rewle and the habyte,
And throch that dewillys suggestyowne
He made renuncyatyowne   3410
Off baptysme and off Crystyne fay,
And lywyd furth in paganys lay.

THAN ras he Empryowre in the sted
Off Constantyus quhen he wes dede.
For leth and felny that he had
Till Crystyne men, gret lawys he mad
Agayne thare Crystyndome; sa mony
Wndyr hym deyd throwch martyry;
Paule and Jhone thare passyowne
Tholyt wndyr hys persecutyowne.   3420
   Off Mede the kynryk, and off Pers,
And Asy, as I herd rehers,
He wan till hys subjectiowne,
And tuk thare contributyowne.

Throwch Capades syne as he past
Saynct Basyle he anoyit fast,
That byschope wes off that cyté than,
And wes off lyff a haly man:
This Julyane made in to that qwhille
Gret manans tyll [this] Saynct Basille   3430
And till othir Crystyne men
That wndyr hys powsté lyẅyd then.
Than this Saynct Basyle specyaly
Hys prayer mad till oure Lady,
Wyth thra and gret devotyowne,
In fastyng and in urysowne,
That scho wald sum ẅengeance ta
Off Julyane that Apostata.
Swa slepand on a nycht hym thoucht
All sudanly that he wes browcht   3440
In till a kyrk off oure Lady,
Quhare men and woman war mony;
Sum on kneyis in urysown,
And sum in contemplatyown,
That thoucht off halynes suld be
Callyd and haldyn in propyrte;

F. 105. b.   For wys men suld on na kyn ẅys
Oys ony othir merchandys,
In chapel, kyrk, or orator,
Bot that that thai ar ordanyd for;   3450
That is contemplatyown
Or prayer wyth devotyon.
This haly byschope Saynct Basyle
Slepand saw, in to that quhille,
The ymage off oure Lady brycht
Downe [out] off ane tabernakyll lycht,
That outhe [the] autere standand was,

And tuk hyr rayk wyth mov[and] pas
But in the kyrk, wyth-owtyn bade,
Quhare that a grawe off new wes made, 3460
And layd in till it a dede knycht,
That Mercurius callyd wes rycht.
Than Basyle herd that ymage say
To the body that thare lay,
"Rys, Mercurius, rys and sla
Julyane the Apostata,
And wyth wengeans sa thow qwyte
The defoule and the dyspyte
That that herytyk has done
To me," scho sayd, "and to my Sone." 3470
Wyth that the ymage als[sa] fast
Off oure Ladye agayne past,
And in the tabernakyll yhede;
The dede body ras, gud spede,
And tuk a spere in till hys hand,
That in the kyrk he saw lyand,
And raykyt off the kyrk hys way.
The byschape Basyle quhare he lay
Than waknyt and oure-drawe that nycht
Quhill on the morne that day wes lycht; 3480
Than herd he tell that Julyane
Ourtakyn wes wyth dede subytane;
Then past he to the kyrk in hy,
And thare the spere he fand bludy.

Than wes Saynct Martyne in hys flowris,
And othir syndry confessowris
Till hym ware contemporane.
In Scotland than Saynct Nynyane
In tyll the tyme that Martyne wes,
Led hys lyff in halynes. 3490

And be oure Cornykyll off Scotland
Garnat-Rych was than regnand
Kyng oure [the] Pechtis fourty yhere.
Syne quhen hys dayis endyt were,
[Talarge] wes kyng, and led hys lyve
In Scotland twenty yhere and fyẅe,
Till all the yheris war oure-gayne
Off Constantyne and Julyane,
And all the empryowrys be dene,
That betwene thame twa had bene.   3500

F. 106.   LIBER, Felix and Damasus,
Efftyre the dede off Julyus,
Off Rome ware papys in thare lyẅe
Ilkane till othir successyẅe.
This Damasus I herd rehers
Couth mak rycht well in metyre ẅers,
Saynct Jerome wrate till hym, but were,
Amang othire haly wryttys sere,
Gloria Patri in [till] twa ẅers;
And bade that he suld ay rehers   3510
Efftyre ilk Psalme tha twa;
All haly kyrk yhit oysys swa.
   Quhen Damasus wes pape off Rome,
The gloryus doctor Saynct Jerome
Wes hys luẅyd famyliare,
And translatyd the psaltare
At hys request and his instans.
This Damasus made ordynans
That prestys and clerkys in to the qwere
Suld stand, as now is the manere,   3520
On ilk[a] syd ordenaly,

And off the Psalmys dystynctly
The ta part suld the fyrst wers say,
The tothir syd the neyst wers ay
Suld begyn, and ilk[a] syd
Suld wayte thare tymys and abyde,
And wers sa efftyr wers suld say
Quhill endyt all the Psalme had thai,
And *Gloria Patri* at the fyne,
Wyth *Sicut erat* efftyre syne :   3530
All Haly kyrk efftyre thai dayis
Syn syne has haldyn this oys always.

   Efftyr the dede off Julyane
Jovyne and Valentynyane
Empreowris war successywe ;
Bot Valentyne in to the lywe
Off the Apostata Julyane
Off all hys knychtys wes chyfftane,
And than, as hym behowyd on nede
Tyll lewe Crystyndome, or knychthede,   3540
He lefft hys knychtys off gud wyll,
And Crystyne trowth he chesyd hym till :
Bot syne efftyr that Julyane
Wes endyt wyth dede subytane,
To that fell persecutoure
He hapnyt to be successoure.

   The Saxonys that ware wycht,
And agayne Rome mekyll off mycht ;
Wyth hys nawyne apon the sé
And wytht hys ost abawndonde he.   3550

F. 106. b.   Fayre off fassowne and off face,
And sutyle off ingyne he was ;
Pert off wult, and eloquent,
And cwynlyk in till jugement ;

Off wordis few, and myld off mwde,
And in all thyng off hawyng gude.
　Hys brodyre Walens held that fay,
That Arryus held in till hys day:
All Crystyne men he thoucht for-thi
Tyll have dysesyt grettumly;　　　　　　　3560
Bot Walentyne this empreowre
Resystyd ay till hys erroure.
　Durst-Hyrbsone in Scotland
Wes oure the Pechtis kyng regnand,
And held that state a hundyre yhere,
And dyd a hundyr batalys sere.

EFFTYRE the dede off Damasus,
The Pape off Rome, Syrycius,
Ellewyn moneth, and xv yhere,
And fywe and twenty dayis clere,　　　　3570
The Se he held as pape off Rome.
The clerk in hys tyme Saynct Jerome
Translated the Bybill off Hebrwe,
The Testymentys bath Auld and Newe
He translatyd in Latyne.
In tyll his tyme Saynt Austyne
Ressawyd off newe Crystyndome
Quhill this Syryce wes pape off Rome,
Saynt Ambros in the Anfeuere
Antemys mad, and Respondys sere,　　　3580
And in it wersyklys als can wryte,
Syne ymnys he made in till fayre dyte,
And [the] antemys ordanyd he
Amang the Psalmys sayd to be
At Matynys and at Ewynsang.

At Prime and Howris thare-amang:
Fyrst on this wys and in this manere
Begouth oure serẅyce in the qwere.

 And in this tyme yhe herd me telle
In Emaws quhar wes a castell,   3590
A barne thar wes that tyme borne,
That few off swylk wes sene beforne,
For at the naẅyll it was a mas,
And outhe and neuthe dyvysyd it was,
Wytht foure eyne and heẅydys twa,
Foure eyrys, and foure browys alsua,
Twa mowthys dowbill-tuthyd wyth-in,
Neyssys twa, wyth doubill chyn,
And foure handys it hade yhete,
With twenty fyngrys and foure fete,   3600
Twenty tays it had rycht swa,
Betwene the theys yherdys twa;
And dowbyll wyt be lyklynes,
In to that barne apperand wes,
For quhen the ta heẅyd oysyd to slepe
The tothir than wald waik or wepe,
And quhen the tane wald tak the mete
Than wald the tothir nevyr ete.
The barne wes lyẅand twa yhere
On this wys and this manere,   3610
And quhen the ta parte wes dede away
The tothir lyẅyd quhill the thryd day.

 Than wes Orosius in his state,
And hys buk till Saynct Austyne wrate.

G{ALYEUS} syne, and Gratyane,
And yhong Valentynyane,

Off the Empyre the reawté
Foure yhere held amang thame thre.
Syne ras the secund Gratyane,
And hys brodyr Valentynyane,   3620
And Theodosius, all thre,
Sex yhere held that ryawté.
This Gratyane thare-efftyre syne
Come off were till Argentyne,
And thretty thowsand in [till] fycht
Thare off his fayis to dede he dycht,
Throw wertu off the Crystyne fay
That stedfastly he held alway;
For in hys tyme all Ytaly
Off Arrius held the heresy,   3630
Bot in till hys dayis he
Gert it all conwertyd be.
He wes off gret literature,
In mete and drynk off gret mesure,
All lust off body he ourcome,
And endyd syne in Crystyndome.

CHAP. XI.

*Off the empryoure Theodose
And the byschope Saynct Ambrose.*

A.D.
387.

THRE hundyre yhere, foure score and sewyn
Efftyre the byrth off God off Hewyn,
Teodosius past in were
In to Grece, wytht gret powere,   3640
And wan the towne off Tessaly,
Ane gret [cyté] and a mychty,

That had conspyryde in gret ire
Agayne the state off the empyre.
Hys lutenandys thai slwe thare,
And offycerys that off hym bare
Cure or state, thai slw all downe
In to that wpset rycht fellowne;
This Teodosius, for-thi,
Gert sla all downe wyth-owt mercy, 3650
Wyth thai mysdoarys saclas blude,
That sowmyt wes in multitude
Fywe thowsand men, bathe barne and wyffe,
And wele ma thare lefft the lyff;
And efftyre that destructyowne
Owt off that land he mad hym bowne,
And come in Lumbardy agayne
Ewyne to the cyté off Mylayne.

 Saynct Ambroys the haly man,
That byschape off that towne wes than, 3660
And herd how that saclas blude
Wes spylt in tyll sic multitude.
As Teodosius on a day
Fra hys palace tuk hys way
Towarte the kyrk: in to that quhille
This Saynt Ambros wyth-owte the style
Hym met, and sayd, " Quhare art thow bowne?
I mak thé inhybytyowne
In Goddys kyrk to mak entre,
Quhill thi trespas amendyd be. 3670
Thow kennys thé as empryowre,
And noucht thi dedys off horroure,
Can thow noucht ken the fellown
Charge off thi presumptyowne,
Becaus off thi gret wodnes

Quhare slayne mony ware sacles,
Bot the welth that thow art in
Gerris thé perchans mysknawe thi syne;
Tharefore it worthys that resowne
Wnrewlyd statys inbawdowne.   3680
Oure nature, certys, ay suld be
Knawyn, and owre mortalyte,
And off oure tyme the lettyre day;
The powdyr off oure eldrys ay
That lywyd in thare tyme before
Ay suld we draw till oure memore,
And off quhat thyng that we ar wrocht;
And till quhat end we mon be browcht.
Nowthir in pyth off oure yhowthed,
Na in fresch coloure off oure fayrhed, 3690
Na in [to] robys off purpure,
Is off oure stays the honowre,
That felys the infyrmyté
Off brukyll fleysch, bot yhit ar we
Ay lyk till men in oure nature
For all the hycht off oure honure.
Thow art bot serwand yhit, I wys,
Off swylk serwandys as thow is;
A lord is God, at we [on] call,
Kyng and makare off ws all,   3700
How dare thow wyth thi cyne se
The tempil off the Trynyté,
How may it cum in thine intent
To stampe on halowyd pathement
Wyth thai fete that sa fast yhude
For till spyll the sacles blude;
How may thow hewe thai handys in hycht
Tyll Hewyn, or till God off mycht,

Quhare-off sacles blud drepand
Yhit wanhewys bath slew and hand ;   3710
How may it fall in thine intent
Tyll ask the haly sacrament?
Pas hame agayne, and pres thé noucht
To that fyrst syn that thow has wroucht,
For till eyke ma quhill thow that mend,
And that quhat God will on thé send.
Perchans it may be medycyne
The cumbyre that thow art fallyn in."
Thir wordys all the empryowre,
As cunnand man off literatoure,   3720
Herd, and consayvyd welle
Quhat fell to presthad ilké dele,
[And] past hame agayne wyth sare sychyng,
Menand hys state in gret murnyng,
Till aucht moneth nere ware past,
And Yhule thareefft wes cumand fast,
The tyme that Jhesu Cryst wes borne,
To sauffe oure lyff that wes forlorne.
Than Rwyffyne hys famylyere
That in all tyme wes till hym dere,   3730
Speryt the caus off his laugure ;
Than sayd till hym the empryowre,
Menand gretly hys trespas,
" Allace! allas! that I borne was
Matere, or any caus to ma,
The kyrk to be remowyde fra,
That comowne is to knawe and knycht,
And all that Crystyne man is rycht,
Tyll fre-man, gentyll, and to thrall,
The kyrk is oppyn, and kepys all   3740
That cummys wyth dewotyowne

Till God to mak thare orysowne;
Is stekyd for my mysdede me fra,
And heẅyn is closyt fra me alsua."
Than sayd Ruffyne, " I will ga trete,
But ony worde off awe or threte,
Wyth the byschope, to chawng or thrawe
Hys decrete in myldare lawe."
Till that than answeryd Teodos,
" Pas on, bot I trow that Ambros 3750
Sall neẅyre decerne bot that is rycht,
And that decrete, be nakyn mycht
Off knycht, or kyng, or empryowre,
Or clergy, may be made erroure,
Na nevyr sall reẅokyd be

F. 108. b. For all thaire mycht or thare powsté;
For I ken hym sa eẅyn a man,
That all thare wyt hym mend na kan."
Efftyr that thus spak Teodos,
Ruffyne past on tyll Ambros, 3760
And as he pwt furth hys treté,
Ambros sayd, " Ruffyne, me thynk yhe,
Lyk a kene dog that ay bayis,
As thow me in this thyng assayis,
Berkand agayne the majesté.
Off mychty God, be thi tretté,
Set, as thow sayis, the empryowre
Mak hym to cum, for his terroure
I sall wyth-stand, and let that he
Wyth-in the kyrk sall mak entre. 3770
Suppos the state off hys empyre
In tyrandry he change and ire,
The dede I sall thole wylfully,
Or he me wyn wyth hys maystry."

Rwffyne than, hys medyatowre,
Agayne past to the Empryowre,
And all the wordis of Ambrose,
He referryt till Teodos,
That answeryd and sayd mekly,
" To the byschope bodyly, 3780
I wyll pas, and here quhat he
Off my defawte wyll say to me."
All thus he dyd, bot noucht for-thi,
For all hys gret senyhowry,
Wyth-in the kyrk he durst noucht ga,
Bot wyth-oute hys bad to ma
He set hym, and for to se
The byschopys oportwnyte.
Syne quhen the byschope bodyly
He saw, and haylyssyd hym mekly 3790
That he wald lows hym off hys syne
And bandys that he was cumbryd in,
He made hym stedfast prayere.
The byschope than on this manere
Sayd, " Thi presens certanly
Is all lyk till tyrandry:
Thow mays thé agayne God to wede,
And to supprys hys law in dede."
" Nay," he sayis, " on na kyn wys
Thynk I agayne that law to rys, 3800
Na I thynk nevyr for to wyrk
Agayne the state off Haly Kyrk;
Na yhit in it to mak entré,
Quhill yhe Fadyr assolyhe me,
And lows me off this band off syne,
And cumbyr that I am fallyn in,
And let noucht stek agayne me

The yhete off Hewyn, that ay suld be
Oppyn till all man penytent,
And mercys askys wyth gud intent;   3810
For God hym-selff is tyll mercy
Than till wengeans mare redy.
This is the sowme off my prayere,
As I am mekly cummyn here."
The byschape sayd, "Than quhat pennans
Has thow yhit done, or repentans,
For thi gret fell inyqwyté;
Quhat medycyne can thow lat se
Till hele or till ras thame agayne,
That in [thi] brethe thow gert be slayne?"   3820
Mekly than the Empryowre
Sayd, wytht rewerence and honowre,
"Yhoure part is, Fadyre, till injwne
The pennans that yhe wald war dwne,
And teche the rycht way to ga:
Tempyre yhoure medycyne rycht swa,
I oblys me for to fullfill
All yhoure byddyng wyth gud wyll."
The byschopys hart in mare meknes
At thir wordys turnyd wes,   3830
And sayd, "Syn resowne thine entent
Rewlyd noucht in all jugement,
Bot rageand reche in [till] wodnes
Held noucht ordyr off rychtwysnes,
For lauch I will now thow ger dyte
And wyth hast in lettrys wryte
The sentens off ewyne rychtwysnes,
Fordo[is] decretys off wodnes,
Wryte als and for lauch alwayis
Hald that full thretty dayis,   3840

Sentens off dede or banysyng
Be haldyn in wryte, but publyssyng,
To byde jugement off resowne
Wyth rype examinatyowne,
Than ire may be seysd welle.
Ourepassyd thai dayis ilk[a] dele,
And be lele lauch and lawtè;
All thyng may welle dysponyd be.
Swa sentens gyẅyn lauchfully
Sall hald and bynd all sykyrly,　　　　　3850
And sentens gyẅyn but fowrme off lawe
The juge may wyth swylk cownsall hawe,
That nowthir sall folow syn na schayme
Na till hys state sall fall defayme,
Na be oure hasty jugement
Sall be supprysyd the innocent."

　　The Empryowre consayẅyd welle
All thir wordys ilk[a] delle,
And oblysyd hym to fullfill
All thir statutis wyth gud wyll,　　　　　3860
And made welle hys confessyowne,
And tuk thare absolutyowne.

F. 109. b.　And in the kyrk wyth gude entent
He entryd and kyssyde the pathement,
And bade standand wytht-owte the qwere,
Quhare all the comownys standand were,
Herand the Mes thare all that qwhille,
Quhill done and red wes the Eẅangylle,
And kepyd the tyme off Offerand;
On kneys than to the prestys hand　　　　3870
He mad, and stude styll in the qwere,
Off the Mes the lave tyll here.
The byschape than wyth movyd wyll

Askyd quhy he bad thar sa styll,
Haldand wyth-in the qwere that plas,
That newyr to that state ordanyd was.
The Empryowre sayd mekly,
" For nakyn hycht off senyhowry
I byd here, bot in gud entente
For to ressayve my sacrament." 3880
The byschope chargyd till hym than
The archedene, a cwnnand man,
That sayd till hym, " Schyre Empryoure,
To leve the qwere is yhoure honoure;
For the qwere all halyly
For prestys is ordanyt specyally,
And to clerkys on thare wys
To syng or say thare thaire serẅys,
Set yhoure aray off ryche purpwre,
Schawe yhowe now here Empryowre, 3890
Yhoure purpure may noucht preystys ma,
Owt off the qwere I rede yhe ga
A[nd] bwte, amang the comwnawté,
Byd [thar] youre oportunyté
Than to tak yhoure sacrament."
Than bwt he passyd wyth gud entent
And sayd wyth-owt rebellatyowne
In till hys excusatyowne;
" I wend that cwstume here had bene,
In Constantynopyll that I have sene, 3900
That in the qwere off honowre
Is a sted for the Empryowre.
Bot leve [God]," he sayd syne,
" This is bot halesum medycyne
For the [wodnes] off my syne
That I have lyine stynkand in.

And in this mene tyme yhe herd me tell,
Hys wyff, that was callyd Dame Placell,
A fayre lady and a plesand,
Honest, abyll, and aẅenand, 3910
Haly and relygyows,
Dyd mony dedys off almows.
Scho oysyd to ẅysyt bodyly
All powr [folk] that wes nere hyr by,
In mete, or drynk, or clethyng,
And in all odyr nedfull thyng;
Scho sparyd noucht thare fete to weysche,
Na yhit to sete thame fysche or fleysche;
Bathe to powre, seke and sare,
Hyr besynes scho wald noucht spare, 3920
Bot serẅyt thame wyth hyr awyne handys,
Lypnand noucht till hyr serẅandys.
Quhen scho [wes] arguyd that that mycht be
Ondone welle for hyr honesté,
Bot for [to] gyẅe thame in payment
Swm thyng off moné wytht gud entent;
Scho sayd swylk dedys off honoure
Fell tyll hyr lord the empryowre,
Bot to sympyll all wes scho,
Swylk dedys as scho dyde to do. 3930
Scho sayd alsua tell hyr lord,
"Yhe suld wyth yhoure-selff record
Quhat yhe have bene and is to be,
Thare-till alsua thynk suld yhe
To be kynd till yhoure creature
That has yhow put in that honure,
And hald the law; swa sall yhe welle
Yhoure empyre goẅerne ilk[a] delle."
    Betwene thys byschope Ambros

And the empryowre Teodos 3940
Wes made be mediatyowne
Gud reconsylyatiowne,
And be thame bath landys sere
Wes efftyre done off ẅertu clere.
 The dedys off this empryowre
Sulde be, lordys, yhoure merowre,
To forbere inyqwyté,
And deme wyth lauch and lawté,
Off haly kyrk bath lare and lawe
To bere and luve, and hald wyth awe, 3950
Wyth nane oure hasty jugyment
Set to supprys the innocent.
Till byschope all tyme bowsum be
And prestys luẅe in cheryté,
Pay that yhe awe thame blythly,
Tak na thyng fra thame wrangwysly.
It is a wnhonest tohyle
To se the qwyk the dede dyspoyle,
Quhen he is wondyn in hys schet,
The lyk it is I tell yowe yete, 3960
Or than till it it is the neyst,
A gentill-man to reẅe a preyst.
Off preystys, at yhoure begynyng,
And all yhoure tyme till yhoure endyng,
And efftyre that yhe have mystyr ay;
Tharefore wyth reverens gret suld thai
Be tretyd and led honesty,
And forborne rycht gretumly.
 Efftyr all this, this Empryowre
Furthyryd hys lyff in gret honoure, 3970
Bathe pure and rych in thare degre
He luẅyd and led in honeste;

Tyrandryis and mawmentryis,
Herrysys and Lollardyis,
He fordyd, and kest all downe
The tempill off thare devotyowne.
He hade gret fame off gret powes,
Off wertu he comendyt wes,
In Melane syne he tuk hys dede;
Tyll Constantynopyll fra that stede   3980
He wes translatyd, and thare he lyis,
Hys sawle in joy off paradys.

To the Pape Syrycius
Succedyt Anastasius,
And held [the] Papys sé thre yhere
And sex and twenty dayis clere.
This Pape ordanyd in that quhille
The prestys or deknys, the Wangylle
At the Mes war hard redand,
Suld be bare-hewyd, on fut standand.   3990
He ordanyd in hys tyme alsua
Thet na clerk suld ordyr ta,
Off hys lymmys bot gyff he
Ware hale wyth-owte deformyté.
  Than till this Teodosius,
Archad, and Honoryus
Tuk till thame the senyhowry
Of [al] the empyr halyly,
And threttene yhere thai held that state.
  A byschope that tyme callyd Donate   4000
Tuk a dragowne, that fellowne was,
And spyttyt ewyn in till hys face;

Wytht that he slw that fell dragowne,
Ane wgly best and a fellowne.
   And oure the Peychtis in that quhylle
Regnyd Golarge-Makamyle.
Ten yhere than Nectane-Kellamot.
Thretty yhere Drwst-Gortynot.
Galam neyst thame was regnand
Fyftene wyntyr in Scotland.   4010
Drwst-Gygnowre wes fywë yhere kyng.
And aucht yhere syne Drust-Hoddrylyng.
Syne the fyrst Drwst yheris foure.
Sex yhere Garnat-Gygnowre.
Hys brodyre efftyr Kylturnane,
Regnyd kyng fywë yhere and ane.
[Talarg] syne Makmordely,
Drwst neyst hym Makmonethy,
And Gagalad, fyftene yhere
Thai thre in Scotland kyngys were.   4020

www.ingramcontent.com/pod-product-compliance
Lightning Source LLC
Chambersburg PA
CBHW021233300426
44111CB00007B/527